STATA SURVEY DATA REFERENCE MANUAL

RELEASE 11

A Stata Press Publication
StataCorp LP
College Station, Texas

The suggested citation for this software is

StataCorp. 2009. *Stata: Release 11*. Statistical Software. College Station, TX: StataCorp LP.

Table of contents

Cross-referencing the documentation

When reading this manual, you will find references to other Stata manuals. For example,

[U] **26 Overview of Stata estimation commands**

[R] **regress**

[D] **reshape**

The first example is a reference to chapter 26, *Overview of Stata estimation commands*, in the *User's Guide*; the second is a reference to the `regress` entry in the *Base Reference Manual*; and the third is a reference to the `reshape` entry in the *Data-Management Reference Manual*.

All the manuals in the Stata Documentation have a shorthand notation:

[GSM]	*Getting Started with Stata for Mac*
[GSU]	*Getting Started with Stata for Unix*
[GSW]	*Getting Started with Stata for Windows*
[U]	*Stata User's Guide*
[R]	*Stata Base Reference Manual*
[D]	*Stata Data-Management Reference Manual*
[G]	*Stata Graphics Reference Manual*
[XT]	*Stata Longitudinal-Data/Panel-Data Reference Manual*
[MI]	*Stata Multiple-Imputation Reference Manual*
[MV]	*Stata Multivariate Statistics Reference Manual*
[P]	*Stata Programming Reference Manual*
[SVY]	*Stata Survey Data Reference Manual*
[ST]	*Stata Survival Analysis and Epidemiological Tables Reference Manual*
[TS]	*Stata Time-Series Reference Manual*
[I]	*Stata Quick Reference and Index*
[M]	*Mata Reference Manual*

Detailed information about each of these manuals may be found online at

http://www.stata-press.com/manuals/

Title

intro — Introduction to survey data manual

Description

This entry describes this manual and what has changed since Stata 10. See the next entry, [SVY] **survey**, for an introduction to Stata's survey commands.

Remarks

This manual documents the survey data commands and is referred to as [SVY] in references.

After this entry, [SVY] **survey** provides an overview of the survey commands. This manual is arranged alphabetically. If you are new to Stata's survey data commands, we recommend that you read the following sections first:

[SVY] **survey**	Introduction to survey commands
[SVY] **svyset**	Declare survey design for dataset
[SVY] **svydescribe**	Describe survey data
[SVY] **svy estimation**	Estimation commands for survey data
[SVY] **svy postestimation**	Postestimation tools for svy

Stata is continually being updated, and Stata users are continually writing new commands. To find out about the latest survey data features, type `search survey` after installing the latest official updates; see [R] **update**.

What's new

This section is intended for previous Stata users. If you are new to Stata, you may as well skip it.

1. New command `margins`, for use after all estimation whether survey or not, should be of special interest to those doing survey estimation. One aspect of `margins`—predictive margins—was developed by survey statisticians for reporting survey results.

   `margins` lets you explore the response surface of a fitted model in any metric of interest—means, linear predictions, probabilities, marginal effects, risk differences, and so on. `margins` can evaluate responses for fixed values of the covariates or for observations in a sample or subsample. Average responses can be obtained, not just responses that are conditional on fixed values of the covariates. Survey-adjusted standard errors and confidence intervals are reported based on a linearized variance estimator of the response that accounts for the sampling distribution of the covariates. Thus inferences can be made about the population. See [R] **margins**.

2. Survey estimators may be used with Stata's new multiple-imputation features. Either `svyset` your data before you `mi set` your data or use `mi svyset` afterward. See [MI] **mi**.

3. Survey commands now report population and subpopulation sizes with a larger number of digits, reserving scientific notation only for sizes greater than 99 trillion.

4. Survey estimation commands may now be used with factor variables; see [U] **11.4.3 Factor variables**.

1

5. New reporting options `baselevels` and `allbaselevels` control how base levels of factor variables are displayed in output tables. New reporting option `noemptycells` controls whether missing cells in interactions are displayed. These new options are supported by existing prefix command `svy` and existing postestimation commands `estat effects` and `estat vce`. See [R] **estimation options**.

6. New reporting option `noomitted` controls whether covariates that are dropped because of collinearity are reported in output tables. By default, Stata now includes a line in estimation and related output tables for collinear covariates and marks those covariates as "(omitted)". `noomitted` suppresses those lines.

   `noomitted` is supported by prefix command `svy` and postestimation commands `estat effects` and `estat vce`. See [R] **estimation options**.

7. New option `vsquish` eliminates blank lines in estimation and related tables. Many output tables now set off factor variables and time-series–operated variables with a blank line. `vsquish` removes these lines.

   `vsquish` is supported by prefix command `svy` and postestimation command `estat effects`.

8. Prefix command `svy` now supports new option `coeflegend` to display the coefficients' legend rather than the coefficient table. The legend shows how you would type a coefficient in an expression, in a test command, or in a constraint definition. See [R] **estimation options**.

9. Prefix command `svy` now supports new option `nocnsreport` to suppress reporting constraints; see [R] **estimation options**.

For a list of all the new features in Stata 11, see [U] **1.3 What's new**.

Also see

[U] **1.3 What's new**

[R] **intro** — Introduction to base reference manual

Title

> **survey** — Introduction to survey commands

Description

The *Survey Data Reference Manual* is organized alphabetically, making it easy to find an individual entry if you know the name of a command. This overview organizes and presents the commands conceptually, that is, according to the similarities in the functions they perform.

Survey design tools

svyset	Declare survey design for dataset
svydescribe	Describe survey data

Survey data analysis tools

svy	The survey prefix command
svy estimation	Estimation commands for survey data
svy: tabulate oneway	One-way tables for survey data
svy: tabulate twoway	Two-way tables for survey data
svy postestimation	Postestimation tools for svy
estat	Postestimation statistics for survey data, such as design effects
svy brr	Balanced repeated replication for survey data
brr_options	More options for BRR variance estimation
svy jackknife	Jackknife estimation for survey data
jackknife_options	More options for jackknife variance estimation

Survey data concepts

variance estimation	Variance estimation for survey data
subpopulation estimation	Subpopulation estimation for survey data
direct standardization	Direct standardization of means, proportions, and ratios
poststratification	Poststratification for survey data

Tools for programmers of new survey commands

ml for svy	Maximum pseudolikelihood estimation for survey data
svymarkout	Mark observations for exclusion on the basis of survey characteristics

Remarks

Remarks are presented under the following headings:

> *Introduction*
> *Survey design tools*
> *Survey data analysis tools*
> *Survey data concepts*
> *Tools for programmers of new survey commands*

Introduction

Stata's facilities for survey data analysis are centered around the svy prefix command. After you identify the survey design characteristics with the svyset command, prefix the estimation commands in your data analysis with "svy:". For example, where you would normally use the regress command to fit a linear regression model for nonsurvey data, use svy: regress to fit a linear regression model for your survey data.

Why should you use the svy prefix command when you have survey data? To answer this question, we need to discuss some of the characteristics of survey design and survey data collection because these characteristics affect how we must perform our analysis if we want to get it right.

Survey data are characterized by the following:

- Sampling weights, also called probability weights—pweights in Stata's terminology
- Cluster sampling
- Stratification

These features arise from the design and details of the data collection procedure. Here's a brief description of how these design features affect the analysis of the data:

- *Sampling weights.* In sample surveys, observations are selected through a random process, but different observations may have different probabilities of selection. Weights are equal to (or proportional to) the inverse of the probability of being sampled. Various postsampling adjustments to the weights are sometimes made, as well. A weight of w_j for the jth observation means, roughly speaking, that the jth observation represents w_j elements in the population from which the sample was drawn.

  Omitting weights from the analysis results in estimates that may be biased, sometimes seriously so. Sampling weights also play a role in estimating standard errors.

- *Clustering.* Individuals are not sampled independently in most survey designs. Collections of individuals (for example, counties, city blocks, or households) are typically sampled as a group, known as a *cluster.*

  There may also be further subsampling within the clusters. For example, counties may be sampled, then city blocks within counties, then households within city blocks, and then finally persons within households. The clusters at the first level of sampling are called *primary sampling units* (PSUs)—in this example, counties are the PSUs. In the absence of clustering, the PSUs are defined to be the individuals, or, equivalently, clusters, each of size one.

  Cluster sampling typically results in larger sample-to-sample variability than sampling individuals directly. This increased variability must be accounted for in standard error estimates, hypothesis testing, and other forms of inference.

- *Stratification.* In surveys, different groups of clusters are often sampled separately. These groups are called *strata.* For example, the 254 counties of a state might be divided into two strata, say, urban counties and rural counties. Then 10 counties might be sampled from the urban stratum, and 15 from the rural stratum.

  Sampling is done independently across strata; the stratum divisions are fixed in advance. Thus strata are statistically independent and can be analyzed as such. When the individual strata are more homogeneous than the population as a whole, the homogeneity can be exploited to produce smaller (and honestly so) estimates of standard errors.

To put it succinctly: using sampling weights is important to get the point estimates right. We must consider the weighting, clustering, and stratification of the survey design to get the standard errors right. If our analysis ignores the clustering in our design, we would probably produce standard errors that are smaller than they should be. Stratification can be used to get smaller standard errors for a given overall sample size.

For more detailed introductions to complex survey data analysis, see Cochran (1977); Kish (1965); Levy and Lemeshow (2008); Scheaffer, Mendenhall III, and Ott (2005); Skinner, Holt, and Smith (1989); Stuart (1984); Thompson (2002); and Williams (1978).

Survey design tools

Before using svy, first take a quick look at [SVY] **svyset**. Use the svyset command to specify the variables that identify the survey design characteristics and default method for estimating standard errors. Once set, svy will automatically use these design specifications until they are cleared or changed or a new dataset is loaded into memory.

As the following two examples illustrate, svyset allows you to identify a wide range of complex sampling designs. First, we show a simple single-stage design and then a complex multistage design.

▷ Example 1: Survey data from a one-stage design

A commonly used single-stage survey design uses clustered sampling across several strata, where the clusters are sampled without replacement. In a Stata dataset composed of survey data from this design, the survey design variables identify information about the strata, PSUs (clusters), sampling weights, and finite population correction. Here we use svyset to specify these variables, respectively named strata, su1, pw, and fpc1.

```
. use http://www.stata-press.com/data/r11/stage5a
. svyset su1 [pweight=pw], strata(strata) fpc(fpc1)
        pweight: pw
            VCE: linearized
  Single unit: missing
     Strata 1: strata
         SU 1: su1
        FPC 1: fpc1
```

In addition to the variables we specified, svyset reports that the default method for estimating standard errors is Taylor linearization and that svy will report missing values for the standard errors when it encounters a stratum with one sampling unit (also called singleton strata).

◁

▷ Example 2: Multistage survey data

We have (fictional) data on American high school seniors (12th graders), and the data were collected according to the following multistage design. In the first stage, counties were independently selected within each state. In the second stage, schools were selected within each chosen county. Within each chosen school, a questionnaire was filled out by every attending high school senior. We have entered all the information into a Stata dataset called multistage.dta.

The survey design variables are as follows:

- state contains the stratum identifiers.

- county contains the first-stage sampling units.

- ncounties contains the total number of counties within each state.

- school contains the second-stage sampling units.

- nschools contains the total number of schools within each county.

- sampwgt contains the sampling weight for each sampled individual.

Here we load the dataset into memory and use svyset with the above variables to declare that these data are survey data.

```
. use http://www.stata-press.com/data/r11/multistage
. svyset county [pw=sampwgt], strata(state) fpc(ncounties) || school, fpc(nschools)

      pweight: sampwgt
          VCE: linearized
  Single unit: missing
     Strata 1: state
         SU 1: county
        FPC 1: ncounties
     Strata 2: <one>
         SU 2: school
        FPC 2: nschools
. save highschool
file highschool.dta saved
```

We saved the svyset dataset to highschool.dta. We can now use this new dataset without having to worry about respecifying the design characteristics.

```
. clear
. describe
Contains data
  obs:           0
  vars:          0
  size:          0 (100.0% of memory free)
Sorted by:
. use highschool

. svyset

      pweight: sampwgt
          VCE: linearized
  Single unit: missing
     Strata 1: state
         SU 1: county
        FPC 1: ncounties
     Strata 2: <one>
         SU 2: school
        FPC 2: nschools
```

◁

After the design characteristics have been svyset, you should also look at [SVY] **svydescribe**. Use svydescribe to browse each stage of your survey data; svydescribe reports useful information on sampling unit counts, missing data, and singleton strata.

▷ Example 3: Survey describe

Here we use svydescribe to describe the first stage of our survey dataset of sampled high school seniors. We specified the weight variable to get svydescribe to report on where it contains missing values and how this affects the estimation sample.

```
. svydescribe weight

Survey: Describing stage 1 sampling units

      pweight: sampwgt
          VCE: linearized
  Single unit: missing
     Strata 1: state
        SU 1: county
        FPC 1: ncounties
     Strata 2: <one>
        SU 2: school
        FPC 2: nschools
```

Stratum	#Units included	#Units omitted	#Obs with complete data	#Obs with missing data	#Obs per included Unit min	mean	max
1	2	0	92	0	34	46.0	58
2	2	0	112	0	51	56.0	61
3	2	0	43	0	18	21.5	25
4	2	0	37	0	14	18.5	23
5	2	0	96	0	38	48.0	58
(output omitted)							
46	2	0	115	0	56	57.5	59
47	2	0	67	0	28	33.5	39
48	2	0	56	0	23	28.0	33
49	2	0	78	0	39	39.0	39
50	2	0	64	0	31	32.0	33
50	100	0	4071	0	14	40.7	81

4071

From the output, we gather that there are 50 strata, each stratum contains two PSUs, the PSUs vary in size, and the total sample size is 4,071 students. We can also see that there are no missing data in the weight variable.

◁

Survey data analysis tools

Stata's suite of survey data commands is governed by the svy prefix command; see [SVY] **svy** and [SVY] **svy estimation**. svy runs the supplied estimation command while accounting for the survey design characteristics in the point estimates and variance estimation method. The three available variance estimation methods are balanced repeated replication (BRR), the jackknife, and first-order Taylor linearization. By default, svy computes standard errors by using the linearized variance estimator—so called because it is based on a first-order Taylor series linear approximation (Wolter 2007). In the nonsurvey context, we refer to this variance estimator as the *robust* variance estimator, otherwise known in Stata as the Huber/White/sandwich estimator; see [P] **_robust**.

> ## Example 4: Estimating a population mean

Here we use the svy prefix with the mean command to estimate the average weight of high school seniors in our population.

```
. svy: mean weight
(running mean on estimation sample)

Survey: Mean estimation

Number of strata =      50        Number of obs      =       4071
Number of PSUs   =     100        Population size    =    8000000
                                  Design df          =         50
```

	Mean	Linearized Std. Err.	[95% Conf. Interval]
weight	160.2863	.7412512	158.7974 161.7751

In its header, svy reports the number of strata and PSUs from the first stage, the sample size, an estimate of population size, and the design degrees of freedom. Just like the standard output from the mean command, the table of estimation results contains the estimated mean and its standard error as well as a confidence interval.

◁

> ## Example 5: Survey regression

Here we use the svy prefix with the regress command to model the association between weight and height in our population of high school seniors.

```
. svy: regress weight height
(running regress on estimation sample)

Survey: Linear regression

Number of strata   =      50        Number of obs      =       4071
Number of PSUs     =     100        Population size    =    8000000
                                    Design df          =         50
                                    F(   1,    50)     =     593.99
                                    Prob > F           =     0.0000
                                    R-squared          =     0.2787
```

weight	Coef.	Linearized Std. Err.	t	P>|t|	[95% Conf. Interval]
height	.7163115	.0293908	24.37	0.000	.6572784 .7753447
_cons	-149.6183	12.57265	-11.90	0.000	-174.8712 -124.3654

In addition to the header elements we saw in the previous example using svy: mean, the command svy: regress also reports a model F test and estimated R^2. Although many of Stata's model-fitting commands report Z statistics for testing coefficients against zero, svy always reports t statistics and uses the design degrees of freedom to compute p-values.

◁

The svy prefix can be used with many estimation commands in Stata. Here is the list of estimation commands that support the svy prefix.

Descriptive statistics

mean	[R] **mean** — Estimate means
proportion	[R] **proportion** — Estimate proportions
ratio	[R] **ratio** — Estimate ratios
total	[R] **total** — Estimate totals

Linear regression models

cnsreg	[R] **cnsreg** — Constrained linear regression
glm	[R] **glm** — Generalized linear models
intreg	[R] **intreg** — Interval regression
nl	[R] **nl** — Nonlinear least-squares estimation
regress	[R] **regress** — Linear regression
tobit	[R] **tobit** — Tobit regression
treatreg	[R] **treatreg** — Treatment-effects model
truncreg	[R] **truncreg** — Truncated regression

Survival-data regression models

stcox	[ST] **stcox** — Cox proportional hazards model
streg	[ST] **streg** — Parametric survival models

Binary-response regression models

biprobit	[R] **biprobit** — Bivariate probit regression
cloglog	[R] **cloglog** — Complementary log-log regression
hetprob	[R] **hetprob** — Heteroskedastic probit model
logistic	[R] **logistic** — Logistic regression, reporting odds ratios
logit	[R] **logit** — Logistic regression, reporting coefficients
probit	[R] **probit** — Probit regression
scobit	[R] **scobit** — Skewed logistic regression

Discrete-response regression models

clogit	[R] **clogit** — Conditional (fixed-effects) logistic regression
mlogit	[R] **mlogit** — Multinomial (polytomous) logistic regression
mprobit	[R] **mprobit** — Multinomial probit regression
ologit	[R] **ologit** — Ordered logistic regression
oprobit	[R] **oprobit** — Ordered probit regression
slogit	[R] **slogit** — Stereotype logistic regression

Poisson regression models

gnbreg	Generalized negative binomial regression in [R] **nbreg**
nbreg	[R] **nbreg** — Negative binomial regression
poisson	[R] **poisson** — Poisson regression
zinb	[R] **zinb** — Zero-inflated negative binomial regression
zip	[R] **zip** — Zero-inflated Poisson regression
ztnb	[R] **ztnb** — Zero-truncated negative binomial regression
ztp	[R] **ztp** — Zero-truncated Poisson regression

Instrumental-variables regression models

ivprobit	[R] **ivprobit** — Probit model with continuous endogenous regressors
ivregress	[R] **ivregress** — Single-equation instrumental-variables regression
ivtobit	[R] **ivtobit** — Tobit model with continuous endogenous regressors

Regression models with selection

heckman	[R] **heckman** — Heckman selection model
heckprob	[R] **heckprob** — Probit model with sample selection

> ## Example 6: Cox's proportional hazards model

Suppose that we want to model the incidence of lung cancer by using three risk factors: smoking status, sex, and place of residence. Our dataset comes from a longitudinal health survey: the First National Health and Nutrition Examination Survey (NHANES I) (Miller 1973; Engel et al. 1978) and its 1992 Epidemiologic Follow-up Study (NHEFS) (Cox et al. 1997); see the National Center for Health Statistics web site at http://www.cdc.gov/nchs/. We will be using data from the samples identified by NHANES I examination locations 1–65 and 66–100; thus we will svyset the revised pseudo-PSU and strata variables associated with these locations. Similarly, our pweight variable was generated using the sampling weights for the nutrition and detailed samples for locations 1–65 and the weights for the detailed sample for locations 66–100.

```
. use http://www.stata-press.com/data/r11/nhefs
. svyset psu2 [pw=swgt2], strata(strata2)
       pweight: swgt2
           VCE: linearized
   Single unit: missing
      Strata 1: strata2
          SU 1: psu2
         FPC 1: <zero>
```

The lung cancer information was taken from the 1992 NHEFS interview data. We use the participants' ages for the time scale. Participants who never had lung cancer and were alive for the 1992 interview were considered censored. Participants who never had lung cancer and died before the 1992 interview were also considered censored at their age of death.

```
. stset age_lung_cancer [pw=swgt2], fail(lung_cancer)

      failure event:  lung_cancer != 0 & lung_cancer < .
 obs. time interval:  (0, age_lung_cancer]
 exit on or before:  failure
             weight:  [pweight=swgt2]
```

```
   14407  total obs.
    5126  event time missing (age_lung_cancer>=.)           PROBABLE ERROR

    9281  obs. remaining, representing
      83  failures in single record/single failure data
  599691  total analysis time at risk, at risk from t =         0
                          earliest observed entry t =           0
                             last observed exit t =            97
```

Although stset warns us that it is a "probable error" to have 5,126 observations with missing event times, we can verify from the 1992 NHEFS documentation that there were indeed 9,281 participants with complete information.

For our proportional hazards model, we pulled the risk factor information from the NHANES I and 1992 NHEFS datasets. Smoking status was taken from the 1992 NHEFS interview data, but we filled in all but 132 missing values by using the general medical history supplement data in NHANES I. Smoking status is represented by separate indicator variables for former smokers and current smokers; the base comparison group is nonsmokers. Sex was determined using the 1992 NHEFS vitality data and is represented by an indicator variable for males. Place-of-residence information was taken from the medical history questionnaire in NHANES I and is represented by separate indicator variables for rural and heavily populated (more than 1 million people) urban residences; the base comparison group is urban residences with populations of fewer than 1 million people.

```
. svy: stcox former_smoker smoker male urban1 rural
(running stcox on estimation sample)

Survey: Cox regression

Number of strata   =        35          Number of obs    =        9149
Number of PSUs     =       105          Population size  =   151327827
                                        Design df        =          70
                                        F(   5,     66)  =       14.07
                                        Prob > F         =      0.0000
```

_t	Haz. Ratio	Linearized Std. Err.	t	P>|t|	[95% Conf. Interval]	
former_smo~r	2.788113	.6205102	4.61	0.000	1.788705	4.345923
smoker	7.849483	2.593249	6.24	0.000	4.061457	15.17051
male	1.187611	.3445315	0.59	0.555	.6658757	2.118142
urban1	.8035074	.3285144	-0.54	0.594	.3555123	1.816039
rural	1.581674	.5281859	1.37	0.174	.8125799	3.078702

From the above results, we can see that both former and current smokers have a significantly higher risk for developing lung cancer than do nonsmokers.

◁

svy: tabulate can be used to produce one-way and two-way tables with survey data and can produce survey-adjusted tests of independence for two-way contingency tables; see [SVY] **svy: tabulate oneway** and [SVY] **svy: tabulate twoway**.

▷ Example 7: Two-way tables for survey data

With data from the Second National Health and Nutrition Examination Survey (NHANES II) (McDowell et al. 1981), we use svy: tabulate to produce a two-way table of cell proportions along with their standard errors and confidence intervals (the survey design characteristics have already been svyset). We also use the format() option to get svy: tabulate to report the cell values and marginals to four decimal places.

```
. use http://www.stata-press.com/data/r11/nhanes2b
. svy: tabulate race diabetes, row se ci format(%7.4f)
(running tabulate on estimation sample)
Number of strata    =         31        Number of obs      =       10349
Number of PSUs      =         62        Population size    =   117131111
                                        Design df          =          31
```

1=white, 2=black, 3=other	diabetes, 1=yes, 0=no		
	0	1	Total
White	0.9680 (0.0020) [0.9638,0.9718]	0.0320 (0.0020) [0.0282,0.0362]	1.0000
Black	0.9410 (0.0061) [0.9271,0.9523]	0.0590 (0.0061) [0.0477,0.0729]	1.0000
Other	0.9797 (0.0076) [0.9566,0.9906]	0.0203 (0.0076) [0.0094,0.0434]	1.0000
Total	0.9658 (0.0018) [0.9619,0.9693]	0.0342 (0.0018) [0.0307,0.0381]	1.0000

```
Key:   row proportions
       (linearized standard errors of row proportions)
       [95% confidence intervals for row proportions]
Pearson:
  Uncorrected   chi2(2)        =    21.3483
  Design-based  F(1.52, 47.26) =    15.0056      P = 0.0000
```

svy: tabulate has many options, such as the format() option, for controlling how the table looks. See [SVY] **svy: tabulate twoway** for a discussion of the different design-based and unadjusted tests of association.

◁

All the standard postestimation commands (e.g., estimates, lincom, margins, nlcom, test, testnl) are also available after svy.

▷ Example 8: Comparing means

Going back to our high school survey data in example 2, we estimate the mean of weight (in pounds) for each subpopulation identified by the categories of the sex variable (male and female).

```
. use http://www.stata-press.com/data/r11/highschool
. svy: mean weight, over(sex)
(running mean on estimation sample)

Survey: Mean estimation

Number of strata =       50          Number of obs     =       4071
Number of PSUs   =      100          Population size   =    8000000
                                     Design df         =         50

            male: sex = male
          female: sex = female
```

Over	Mean	Linearized Std. Err.	[95% Conf. Interval]	
weight				
male	175.4809	1.116802	173.2377	177.7241
female	146.204	.9004157	144.3955	148.0125

Here we use the test command to test the hypothesis that the average male is 30 pounds heavier than the average female; from the results, we cannot reject this hypothesis at the 5% level.

```
. test [weight]male - [weight]female = 30

Adjusted Wald test

 ( 1)  [weight]male - [weight]female = 30

       F(  1,     50) =     0.23
            Prob > F =     0.6353
```
◁

estat has specific subroutines for use after svy; see [SVY] **estat**.

- estat svyset reports the survey design settings used to produce the current estimation results.

- estat effects and estat lceffects report a table of design and misspecification effects for point estimates and linear combinations of point estimates, respectively.

- estat size reports a table of sample and subpopulation sizes after svy: mean, svy: proportion, svy: ratio, and svy: total.

- estat sd reports subpopulation standard deviations on the basis of the estimation results from mean and svy: mean.

- estat strata reports the number of singleton and certainty strata within each sampling stage.

▷ Example 9: Design effects

Here we use `estat effects` to report the design effects DEFF and DEFT for the mean estimates from the previous example.

```
. estat effects
           male: sex = male
         female: sex = female
```

	Over	Mean	Linearized Std. Err.	DEFF	DEFT
weight					
	male	175.4809	1.116802	2.61016	1.61519
	female	146.204	.9004157	1.7328	1.31603

Note: weights must represent population totals for deff to
      be correct when using an FPC; however, deft is
      invariant to the scale of weights.

Now we use `estat lceffects` to report the design effects DEFF and DEFT for the difference of the mean estimates from the previous example.

```
. estat lceffects [weight]male - [weight]female
 ( 1)  [weight]male - [weight]female = 0
```

Mean	Coef.	Std. Err.	DEFF	DEFT
(1)	29.27691	1.515201	2.42759	1.55768

Note: weights must represent population totals for deff to
      be correct when using an FPC; however, deft is
      invariant to the scale of weights.

◁

The `svy brr` prefix command produces point and variance estimates by using the BRR method; see [SVY] **svy brr**. BRR was first introduced by McCarthy (1966, 1969a, and 1969b) as a method of variance estimation for designs with two PSUs in every stratum. The BRR variance estimator tends to give more reasonable variance estimates for this design than the linearized variance estimator, which can result in large values and undesirably wide confidence intervals.

The `svy jackknife` prefix command produces point and variance estimates by using the jackknife replication method; see [SVY] **svy jackknife**. The jackknife is a data-driven variance estimation method that can be used with model-fitting procedures for which the linearized variance estimator is not implemented, even though a linearized variance estimator is theoretically possible to derive (Shao and Tu 1995).

To protect the privacy of survey participants, public survey datasets may contain replicate-weight variables instead of variables that identify the PSUs and strata. These replicate-weight variables can be used with the appropriate replication method for variance estimation instead of the linearized variance estimator; see [SVY] **svyset**.

The `svy brr` and `svy jackknife` prefix commands can be used with those commands that may not be fully supported by svy but are compatible with the BRR and the jackknife replication methods. They can also be used to produce point estimates for expressions of estimation results from a prefixed command.

▷ Example 10: BRR and replicate-weight variables

The survey design for the NHANES II data (McDowell et al. 1981) is specifically suited to BRR: there are two PSUs in every stratum.

```
. use http://www.stata-press.com/data/r11/nhanes2
. svydescribe

Survey: Describing stage 1 sampling units
        pweight: finalwgt
            VCE: linearized
    Single unit: missing
      Strata 1: strata
          SU 1: psu
         FPC 1: <zero>
```

			#Obs per Unit		
Stratum	#Units	#Obs	min	mean	max
1	2	380	165	190.0	215
2	2	185	67	92.5	118
3	2	348	149	174.0	199
4	2	460	229	230.0	231
5	2	252	105	126.0	147
6	2	298	131	149.0	167
(output omitted)					
25	2	256	116	128.0	140
26	2	261	129	130.5	132
27	2	283	139	141.5	144
28	2	299	136	149.5	163
29	2	503	215	251.5	288
30	2	365	166	182.5	199
31	2	308	143	154.0	165
32	2	450	211	225.0	239
31	62	10351	67	167.0	288

Here is a privacy-conscious dataset equivalent to the one above; all the variables and values remain, except that strata and psu are replaced with BRR replicate-weight variables. The BRR replicate-weight variables are already svyset, and the default method for variance estimation is vce(brr).

```
. use http://www.stata-press.com/data/r11/nhanes2brr
. svyset
        pweight: finalwgt
            VCE: brr
            MSE: off
      brrweight: brr_1 brr_2 brr_3 brr_4 brr_5 brr_6 brr_7 brr_8 brr_9 brr_10
                 brr_11 brr_12 brr_13 brr_14 brr_15 brr_16 brr_17 brr_18 brr_19
                 brr_20 brr_21 brr_22 brr_23 brr_24 brr_25 brr_26 brr_27 brr_28
                 brr_29 brr_30 brr_31 brr_32
    Single unit: missing
      Strata 1: <one>
          SU 1: <observations>
         FPC 1: <zero>
```

Suppose that we were interested in the population ratio of weight to height. Here we use total to estimate the population totals of weight and height and the svy brr prefix to estimate their ratio and variance; we use total instead of ratio (which is otherwise preferable here) to show how to specify an expression when using svy: brr.

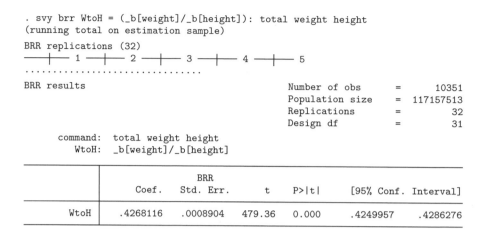

```
. svy brr WtoH = (_b[weight]/_b[height]): total weight height
(running total on estimation sample)
BRR replications (32)
──────┼──── 1 ──┼──── 2 ──┼──── 3 ──┼──── 4 ──┼──── 5
.............................
BRR results                          Number of obs    =       10351
                                     Population size  =   117157513
                                     Replications     =          32
                                     Design df        =          31

     command:  total weight height
        WtoH:  _b[weight]/_b[height]
```

	Coef.	BRR Std. Err.	t	P>|t|	[95% Conf. Interval]	
WtoH	.4268116	.0008904	479.36	0.000	.4249957	.4286276

◁

Survey data concepts

The variance estimation methods that Stata uses are discussed in [SVY] **variance estimation**.

Subpopulation estimation involves computing point and variance estimates for part of the population. This method is not the same as restricting the estimation sample to the collection of observations within the subpopulation because variance estimation for survey data measures sample-to-sample variability, assuming that the same survey design is used to collect the data. Use the subpop() option of the svy prefix to perform subpopulation estimation, and use if and in only when you need to make restrictions on the estimation sample; see [SVY] **subpopulation estimation**.

▷ Example 11: Subpopulation estimation

Here we will use our svyset high school data to model the association between weight and height in the subpopulation of male high school seniors. First, we describe the sex variable to determine how to identify the males in the dataset. We then use label list to verify that the variable label agrees with the value labels.

```
. use http://www.stata-press.com/data/r11/highschool
. describe sex
```

variable name	storage type	display format	value label	variable label
sex	byte	%9.0g	sex	1=male, 2=female

```
. label list sex
sex:
         1 male
         2 female
```

Here we generate a variable named male so that we can easily identify the male high school seniors. We specified if !missing(sex); doing so will cause the generated male variable to contain a missing value at each observation where the sex variable does. This is done on purpose (although it is not necessary if sex is free of missing values) because missing values should not be misinterpreted to imply female.

```
. gen male = sex == 1 if !missing(sex)
```

Now we specify `subpop(male)` as an option to the `svy` prefix in our model fit.

```
. svy, subpop(male): regress weight height
(running regress on estimation sample)

Survey: Linear regression

Number of strata   =          50          Number of obs     =        4071
Number of PSUs     =         100          Population size   =     8000000
                                          Subpop. no. of obs =        1938
                                          Subpop. size      = 3848021.4
                                          Design df         =          50
                                          F(  1,      50)    =      225.38
                                          Prob > F          =      0.0000
                                          R-squared         =      0.2347
```

weight	Coef.	Linearized Std. Err.	t	P>|t|	[95% Conf. Interval]	
height	.7632911	.0508432	15.01	0.000	.6611696	.8654127
_cons	-168.6532	22.5708	-7.47	0.000	-213.988	-123.3184

Although the table of estimation results contains the same columns as earlier, `svy` reports some extra subpopulation information in the header. Here the extra header information tells us that 1,938 of the 4,071 sampled high school seniors are male, and the estimated number of male high school seniors in the population is 3,848,021 (rounded down).

◁

Direct standardization is an estimation method that allows comparing rates that come from different frequency distributions; see [SVY] **direct standardization**. In direct standardization, estimated rates (means, proportions, and ratios) are adjusted according to the frequency distribution of a standard population. The standard population is partitioned into categories, called standard strata. The stratum frequencies for the standard population are called standard weights. In the standardizing frequency distribution, the standard strata are most commonly identified by demographic information such as age, sex, and ethnicity. The standardized rate estimate is the weighted sum of unadjusted rates, where the weights are the relative frequencies taken from the standardizing frequency distribution. Direct standardization is available with `svy: mean`, `svy: proportion`, and `svy: ratio`.

▷ Example 12: Standardized rates

Table 3.12-6 of Korn and Graubard (1999, 156) contains enumerated data for two districts of London for the years 1840–1841. The `age` variable identifies the age groups in 5-year increments, `bgliving` contains the number of people living in the Bethnal Green district at the beginning of 1840, `bgdeaths` contains the number of people who died in Bethnal Green that year, `hsliving` contains the number of people living in St. George's Hanover Square at the beginning of 1840, and `hsdeaths` contains the number of people who died in Hanover Square that year.

(Continued on next page)

```
. use http://www.stata-press.com/data/r11/stdize, clear
. list, noobs sep(0) sum
```

age	bgliving	bgdeaths	hsliving	hsdeaths
0-5	10739	850	5738	463
5-10	9180	76	4591	55
10-15	8006	38	4148	28
15-20	7096	37	6168	36
20-25	6579	38	9440	68
25-30	5829	51	8675	78
30-35	5749	51	7513	64
35-40	4490	56	5091	78
40-45	4385	47	4930	85
45-50	2955	66	2883	66
50-55	2995	74	2711	77
55-60	1644	67	1275	55
60-65	1835	64	1469	61
65-70	1042	64	649	55
70-75	879	68	619	58
75-80	366	47	233	51
80-85	173	39	136	20
85-90	71	22	48	15
90-95	21	6	10	4
95-100	4	2	2	1
unknown	50	1	124	0
Sum	74088	1764	66453	1418

We can use svy: ratio to compute the death rates for each district in 1840. Because this dataset is identified as census data, we will create an FPC variable that will contain a sampling rate of 100%. This method will result in zero standard errors, which are interpreted to mean no variability—appropriate because our point estimates came from the entire population.

```
. gen fpc = 1
. svyset, fpc(fpc)
      pweight: <none>
          VCE: linearized
  Single unit: missing
     Strata 1: <one>
        SU 1: <observations>
       FPC 1: fpc
. svy: ratio (Bethnal: bgdeaths/bgliving) (Hanover: hsdeaths/hsliving)
(running ratio on estimation sample)
Survey: Ratio estimation
Number of strata =        1        Number of obs    =       21
Number of PSUs   =       21        Population size  =       21
                                   Design df        =       20

      Bethnal: bgdeaths/bgliving
      Hanover: hsdeaths/hsliving
```

	Ratio	Linearized Std. Err.	[95% Conf. Interval]	
Bethnal	.0238095	0	.	.
Hanover	.0213384	0	.	.

```
Note: zero standard errors because of 100% sampling rate
      detected for FPC in the first stage.
```

The death rates are 2.38% for Bethnal Green and 2.13% for St. George's Hanover Square. These observed death rates are not really comparable because they come from two different age distributions. We can standardize based on the age distribution from Bethnal Green. Here age identifies our standard strata and bgliving contains the associated population sizes.

```
. svy: ratio (Bethnal: bgdeaths/bgliving) (Hanover: hsdeaths/hsliving),
> stdize(age) stdweight(bgliving)
(running ratio on estimation sample)

Survey: Ratio estimation

Number of strata =        1      Number of obs    =       21
Number of PSUs   =       21      Population size  =       21
N. of std strata =       21      Design df        =       20

          Bethnal: bgdeaths/bgliving
          Hanover: hsdeaths/hsliving
```

	Ratio	Linearized Std. Err.	[95% Conf. Interval]	
Bethnal	.0238095	0	.	.
Hanover	.0266409	0	.	.

```
Note: zero standard errors because of 100% sampling rate
      detected for FPC in the first stage.
```

The standardized death rate for St. George's Hanover Square, 2.66%, is larger than the death rate for Bethnal Green.

◁

Poststratification is a method for adjusting the sampling weights, usually to account for underrepresented groups in the population; see [SVY] **poststratification**. This method usually results in decreasing bias because of nonresponse and underrepresented groups in the population. It also tends to result in smaller variance estimates. Poststratification is available for all survey estimation commands and is specified using svyset; see [SVY] **svyset**.

▷ Example 13: Poststratified mean

Levy and Lemeshow (2008, sec. 6.6) give an example of poststratification by using simple survey data from a veterinarian's client list. The data in poststrata.dta were collected using simple random sampling (SRS) without replacement. The totexp variable contains the total expenses to the client, type identifies the cats and dogs, postwgt contains the poststratum sizes (450 for cats and 850 for dogs), and fpc contains the total number of clients ($850 + 450 = 1,300$).

```
. use http://www.stata-press.com/data/r11/poststrata, clear

. svyset, poststrata(type) postweight(postwgt) fpc(fpc)

       pweight: <none>
           VCE: linearized
    Poststrata: type
    Postweight: postwgt
   Single unit: missing
       Strata 1: <one>
           SU 1: <observations>
          FPC 1: fpc
```

```
. svy: mean totexp
(running mean on estimation sample)

Survey: Mean estimation

Number of strata =        1        Number of obs     =       50
Number of PSUs   =       50        Population size   =     1300
N. of poststrata =        2        Design df         =       49
```

		Linearized		
	Mean	Std. Err.	[95% Conf. Interval]	
totexp	40.11513	1.163498	37.77699	42.45327

The mean total expenses is \$40.12 with a standard error of \$1.16. In the following, we omit the poststratification information from svyset, resulting in mean total expenses of \$39.73 with standard error \$2.22. The difference between the mean estimates is explained by the facts that expenses tend to be larger for dogs than for cats and that the dogs were slightly underrepresented in the sample ($850/1{,}300 \approx 0.65$ for the population; $32/50 = 0.64$ for the sample). This reasoning also explains why the variance estimate from the poststratified mean is smaller than the one that was not poststratified.

```
. svyset, fpc(fpc)

      pweight: <none>
          VCE: linearized
  Single unit: missing
     Strata 1: <one>
        SU 1: <observations>
       FPC 1: fpc

. svy: mean totexp
(running mean on estimation sample)

Survey: Mean estimation

Number of strata =        1        Number of obs     =       50
Number of PSUs   =       50        Population size   =       50
                                   Design df         =       49
```

		Linearized		
	Mean	Std. Err.	[95% Conf. Interval]	
totexp	39.7254	2.221747	35.26063	44.19017

◁

Tools for programmers of new survey commands

The ml command can be used to fit a model by the method of maximum likelihood. When the svy option is specified, ml performs maximum pseudolikelihood, applying sampling weights and design-based linearization automatically; see [R] **ml** and Gould, Pitblado, and Sribney (2006).

▷ Example 14

The `ml` command requires a program that computes likelihood values to perform maximum likelihood. Here is a likelihood evaluator used in Gould, Pitblado, and Sribney (2006) to fit linear regression models using the likelihood from the normal distribution.

```
program mynormal_lf
        version 11
        args lnf mu lnsigma
        quietly replace 'lnf' = ln(normalden($ML_y1,'mu',exp('lnsigma')))
end
```

Back in example 5, we fit a linear regression model using the high school survey data. Here we use `ml` and `mynormal_lf` to fit the same survey regression model.

```
. use http://www.stata-press.com/data/r11/highschool

. ml model lf mynormal_lf (mu: weight = height) /lnsigma, svy

. ml max
initial:      log pseudolikelihood =    -<inf>  (could not be evaluated)
feasible:     log pseudolikelihood = -7.301e+08
rescale:      log pseudolikelihood = -51944380
rescale eq:   log pseudolikelihood = -47565331
Iteration 0:  log pseudolikelihood = -47565331
Iteration 1:  log pseudolikelihood = -41226725  (not concave)
Iteration 2:  log pseudolikelihood = -41221650  (not concave)
Iteration 3:  log pseudolikelihood = -41176159  (not concave)
Iteration 4:  log pseudolikelihood = -41154139  (not concave)
Iteration 5:  log pseudolikelihood = -41052368
Iteration 6:  log pseudolikelihood = -39379181  (backed up)
Iteration 7:  log pseudolikelihood = -38333242
Iteration 8:  log pseudolikelihood = -38328742
Iteration 9:  log pseudolikelihood = -38328739
```

Number of strata	=	50	Number of obs	=	4071
Number of PSUs	=	100	Population size	=	8000000
			Design df	=	50
			F(1, 50)	=	593.99
			Prob > F	=	0.0000

weight	Coef.	Linearized Std. Err.	t	P>|t|	[95% Conf. Interval]
mu					
height	.716311	.0293908	24.37	0.000	.6572778 .7753442
_cons	-149.6181	12.57266	-11.90	0.000	-174.871 -124.3652
lnsigma					
_cons	3.372153	.0180777	186.54	0.000	3.335843 3.408464

◁

`svymarkout` is a programmer's command that resets the values in a variable that identifies the estimation sample, dropping observations for which any of the survey characteristic variables contain missing values. This tool is most helpful for developing estimation commands that use `ml` to fit models using maximum pseudolikelihood directly, instead of relying on the `svy` prefix.

Acknowledgments

Many of the `svy` commands were developed in collaboration with John L. Eltinge, Bureau of Labor Statistics. We thank him for his invaluable assistance.

We thank Wayne Johnson of the National Center for Health Statistics for providing the NHANES II dataset.

We thank Nicholas Winter, Department of Government, Cornell University, for his diligent efforts to keep Stata up to date with mainstream variance estimation methods for survey data, as well as for providing versions of `svy brr` and `svy jackknife`.

William Gemmell Cochran (1909–1980) was born in Rutherglen, Scotland, and educated at the Universities of Glasgow and Cambridge. He accepted a post at Rothamsted before finishing his doctorate. Cochran emigrated to the United States in 1939 and worked at Iowa State, North Carolina State, Johns Hopkins, and Harvard. He made many major contributions across several fields of statistics, including experimental design, the analysis of counted data, sample surveys, and observational studies, and was author or coauthor (with Gertrude M. Cox and George W. Snedecor) of various widely used texts.

Leslie Kish (1910–2000) was born in Poprad, Hungary, and entered the United States with his family in 1926. He worked as a lab assistant at the Rockefeller Institute for Medical Research and studied at the College of the City of New York, fighting in the Spanish Civil War before receiving his first degree in mathematics. Kish worked for the Bureau of the Census, the Department of Agriculture, the Army Air Corps, and the University of Michigan. He carried out pioneering work in the theory and practice of survey sampling, including design effects, BRR, response errors, rolling samples and censuses, controlled selection, multipurpose designs, and small-area estimation.

References

Cochran, W. G. 1977. *Sampling Techniques*. 3rd ed. New York: Wiley.

Cox, C. S., M. E. Mussolino, S. T. Rothwell, M. A. Lane, C. D. Golden, J. H. Madans, and J. J. Feldman. 1997. Plan and operation of the NHANES I Epidemiologic Followup Study, 1992. In *Vital and Health Statistics*, vol. 1. Hyattsville, MD: National Center for Health Statistics.

Engel, A., R. S. Murphy, K. Maurer, and E. Collins. 1978. Plan and operation of the HANES I augmentation survey of adults 25–74 years. In *Vital and Health Statistics*, vol. 1. Hyattsville, MD: National Center for Health Statistics.

Gould, W. W., J. S. Pitblado, and W. M. Sribney. 2006. *Maximum Likelihood Estimation with Stata*. 3rd ed. College Station, TX: Stata Press.

Kish, L. 1965. *Survey Sampling*. New York: Wiley.

Korn, E. L., and B. I. Graubard. 1999. *Analysis of Health Surveys*. New York: Wiley.

Kreuter, F., and R. Valliant. 2007. A survey on survey statistics: What is done and can be done in Stata. *Stata Journal* 7: 1–21.

Levy, P. S., and S. Lemeshow. 2008. *Sampling of Populations: Methods and Applications*. 4th ed. Hoboken, NJ: Wiley.

McCarthy, P. J. 1966. Replication: An approach to the analysis of data from complex surveys. In *Vital and Health Statistics*, series 2. Hyattsville, MD: National Center for Health Statistics.

———. 1969a. Pseudoreplication: Further evaluation and application of the balanced half-sample technique. In *Vital and Health Statistics*, series 2. Hyattsville, MD: National Center for Health Statistics.

———. 1969b. Pseudo-replication: Half-samples. *Revue de l'Institut International de Statistique* 37: 239–264.

McDowell, A., A. Engel, J. T. Massey, and K. Maurer. 1981. Plan and operation of the Second National Health and Nutrition Examination Survey, 1976–1980. *Vital and Health Statistics* 1(15): 1–144.

Miller, H. W. 1973. Plan and operation of the Health and Nutrition Examination Survey: United States 1971–1973. *Vital and Health Statistics* 1(10a): 1–46.

Scheaffer, R. L., W. Mendenhall III, and R. L. Ott. 2005. *Elementary Survey Sampling.* 6th ed. Boston: Duxbury.

Shao, J., and D. Tu. 1995. *The Jackknife and Bootstrap.* New York: Springer.

Skinner, C. J., D. Holt, and T. M. F. Smith, ed. 1989. *Analysis of Complex Surveys.* New York: Wiley.

Stuart, A. 1984. *The Ideas of Sampling.* 3rd ed. New York: Griffin.

Thompson, S. K. 2002. *Sampling.* 2nd ed. New York: Wiley.

Williams, B. 1978. *A Sampler on Sampling.* New York: Wiley.

Wolter, K. M. 2007. *Introduction to Variance Estimation.* 2nd ed. New York: Springer.

Also see

[SVY] **svyset** — Declare survey design for dataset

[SVY] **svy** — The survey prefix command

[SVY] **svy estimation** — Estimation commands for survey data

[P] **_robust** — Robust variance estimates

Title

> *brr_options* — More options for BRR variance estimation

Syntax

brr_options	description
SE	
mse	use MSE formula for variance
nodots	suppress replication dots
<u>h</u>adamard(*matrix*)	Hadamard matrix
fay(*#*)	Fay's adjustment
[†] <u>saving</u>(*filename*, ...)	save results to *filename*
[†] <u>v</u>erbose	display the full table legend
[†] <u>noi</u>sily	display any output from *command*
[†] <u>trace</u>	trace the *command*
[†] <u>title</u>(*text*)	use *text* as the title for results
[†] nodrop	do not drop observations
[†] reject(*exp*)	identify invalid results

[†] These options are not shown in the dialog boxes for estimation commands.

Description

svy accepts more options when performing BRR variance estimation. See [SVY] **svy brr** for a complete discussion.

Options

┌─ SE ┐

mse specifies that svy compute the variance by using deviations of the replicates from the observed value of the statistics based on the entire dataset. By default, svy computes the variance by using deviations of the replicates from their mean.

nodots suppresses display of the replication dots. By default, one dot character is printed for each successful replication. A red 'x' is displayed if *command* returns with an error, and 'e' is displayed if at least one of the values in the *exp_list* is missing.

hadamard(*matrix*) specifies the Hadamard matrix to be used to determine which PSUs are chosen for each replicate.

fay(*#*) specifies Fay's adjustment. This option overrides the fay(*#*) option of svyset; see [SVY] **svyset**.

saving(), verbose, noisily, trace, title(), nodrop, reject(); see [SVY] **svy brr**.

Also see

[SVY] **svy** — The survey prefix command

[SVY] **svy brr** — Balanced repeated replication for survey data

Title

> **direct standardization** — Direct standardization of means, proportions, and ratios

Description

Direct standardization is an estimation method that allows comparing rates that come from different frequency distributions. The `mean`, `proportion`, and `ratio` commands can estimate means, proportions, and ratios by using direct standardization.

See [SVY] **poststratification** for a similar estimation method given population sizes for strata not used in the sampling design.

Remarks

In direct standardization, estimated rates (means, proportions, and ratios) are adjusted according to the frequency distribution of a standard population. The standard population is partitioned into categories, called standard strata. The stratum frequencies for the standard population are called standard weights. In the standardizing frequency distribution, the standard strata are most commonly identified by demographic information such as age, sex, and ethnicity.

Stata's `mean`, `proportion`, and `ratio` estimation commands have options for estimating means, proportions, and ratios by using direct standardization. The `stdize()` option takes a variable that identifies the standard strata, and the `stdweight()` option takes a variable that contains the standard weights.

The standard strata (specified using `stdize()`) from the standardizing population are not the same as the strata (specified using `svyset`'s `strata()` option) from the sampling design. In the output header, "Number of strata" is the number of strata in the first stage of the sampling design, and "N. of std strata" is the number of standard strata.

In the following example, we use direct standardization to compare the death rates between two districts of London in 1840.

▷ Example 1: Standardized rates

Table 3.12-6 of Korn and Graubard (1999, 156) contains enumerated data for two districts of London for the years 1840–1841. The `age` variable identifies the age groups in 5-year increments, `bgliving` contains the number of people living in the Bethnal Green district at the beginning of 1840, `bgdeaths` contains the number of people who died in Bethnal Green that year, `hsliving` contains the number of people living in St. George's Hanover Square at the beginning of 1840, and `hsdeaths` contains the number of people who died in Hanover Square that year.

```
. use http://www.stata-press.com/data/r11/stdize
. list, noobs sep(0) sum
```

	age	bgliving	bgdeaths	hsliving	hsdeaths
	0-5	10739	850	5738	463
	5-10	9180	76	4591	55
	10-15	8006	38	4148	28
	15-20	7096	37	6168	36
	20-25	6579	38	9440	68
	25-30	5829	51	8675	78
	30-35	5749	51	7513	64
	35-40	4490	56	5091	78
	40-45	4385	47	4930	85
	45-50	2955	66	2883	66
	50-55	2995	74	2711	77
	55-60	1644	67	1275	55
	60-65	1835	64	1469	61
	65-70	1042	64	649	55
	70-75	879	68	619	58
	75-80	366	47	233	51
	80-85	173	39	136	20
	85-90	71	22	48	15
	90-95	21	6	10	4
	95-100	4	2	2	1
	unknown	50	1	124	0
Sum		74088	1764	66453	1418

We can use svy: ratio to compute the death rates for each district in 1840. Because this dataset is identified as census data, we will create an FPC variable that will contain a sampling rate of 100%. This method will result in zero standard errors, which are interpreted to mean no variability—appropriate because our point estimates came from the entire population.

```
. gen fpc = 1
. svyset, fpc(fpc)
      pweight: <none>
          VCE: linearized
  Single unit: missing
     Strata 1: <one>
        SU 1: <observations>
       FPC 1: fpc
. svy: ratio (Bethnal: bgdeaths/bgliving) (Hanover: hsdeaths/hsliving)
(running ratio on estimation sample)
Survey: Ratio estimation

Number of strata =       1          Number of obs    =      21
Number of PSUs   =      21          Population size  =      21
                                    Design df        =      20

     Bethnal: bgdeaths/bgliving
     Hanover: hsdeaths/hsliving
```

		Linearized		
	Ratio	Std. Err.	[95% Conf. Interval]	
Bethnal	.0238095	0	.	.
Hanover	.0213384	0	.	.

```
Note: zero standard errors because of 100% sampling rate
      detected for FPC in the first stage.
```

The death rates are 2.38% for Bethnal Green and 2.13% for St. George's Hanover Square. These observed death rates are not really comparable because they come from two different age distributions. We can standardize based on the age distribution from Bethnal Green. Here `age` identifies our standard strata and `bgliving` contains the associated population sizes.

```
. svy: ratio (Bethnal: bgdeaths/bgliving) (Hanover: hsdeaths/hsliving),
> stdize(age) stdweight(bgliving)
(running ratio on estimation sample)

Survey: Ratio estimation

Number of strata =        1        Number of obs    =       21
Number of PSUs   =       21        Population size  =       21
N. of std strata =       21        Design df        =       20

        Bethnal: bgdeaths/bgliving
        Hanover: hsdeaths/hsliving
```

	Ratio	Linearized Std. Err.	[95% Conf. Interval]	
Bethnal	.0238095	0	.	.
Hanover	.0266409	0	.	.

```
Note: zero standard errors because of 100% sampling rate
      detected for FPC in the first stage.
```

The standardized death rate for St. George's Hanover Square, 2.66%, is larger than the death rate for Bethnal Green.

For this example, we could have used `dstdize` to compute the death rates; however, `dstdize` will not compute the correct standard errors for survey data. Furthermore, `dstdize` is not an estimation command, so `test` and the other postestimation commands are not available.

◁

❏ Technical note

The values in the variable supplied to the `stdweight()` option are normalized so that (1) is true; see *Methods and formulas*. Thus the `stdweight()` variable can contain either population sizes or population proportions for the associated standard strata.

❏

Methods and formulas

The following discussion assumes that you are already familiar with the topics discussed in [SVY] **variance estimation**.

In direct standardization, a weighted sum of the point estimates from the standard strata is used to produce an overall point estimate for the population. This section will show how direct standardization affects the ratio estimator. The mean and proportion estimators are special cases of the ratio estimator.

Suppose that you used a complex survey design to sample m individuals from a population of size M. Let D_g be the set of individuals in the sample that belong to the gth standard stratum, and let $I_{D_g}(j)$ indicate if the jth individual is in standard stratum g, where

$$I_{D_g}(j) = \begin{cases} 1, & \text{if } j \in D_g \\ 0, & \text{otherwise} \end{cases}$$

Also let L_D be the number of standard strata, and let π_g be the proportion of the population that belongs to standard stratum g.

$$\sum_{g=1}^{L_D} \pi_g = 1 \tag{1}$$

In subpopulation estimation, π_g is set to zero if none of the individuals in standard stratum g are in the subpopulation. Then the standard stratum proportions are renormalized.

Let y_j and x_j be the items of interest and w_j be the sampling weight for the jth sampled individual. The estimator for the standardized ratio of $R = Y/X$ is

$$\widehat{R}^D = \sum_{g=1}^{L_D} \pi_g \frac{\widehat{Y}_g}{\widehat{X}_g}$$

where

$$\widehat{Y}_g = \sum_{j=1}^{m} I_{D_g}(j)\, w_j y_j$$

with $\widehat{X}_g$ similarly defined.

For replication-based variance estimation, replicates of the standardized values are used in the variance formulas.

The score variable for the linearized variance estimator of the standardized ratio is

$$z_j(\widehat{R}^D) = \sum_{g=1}^{L_D} \pi_g I_{D_g}(j) \frac{\widehat{X}_g y_j - \widehat{Y}_g x_j}{\widehat{X}_g^2}$$

This score variable was derived using the method described in [SVY] **variance estimation** and is a direct result of the methods described in Deville (1999), Demnati and Rao (2004), and Shah (2004).

For the `mean` and `proportion` commands, the mean estimator is a ratio estimator with the denominator variable equal to one ($x_j = 1$) and the proportion estimator is the mean estimator with an indicator variable in the numerator ($y_j \in \{0, 1\}$).

References

Demnati, A., and J. N. K. Rao. 2004. Linearization variance estimators for survey data. *Survey Methodology* 30: 17–26.

Deville, J.-C. 1999. Variance estimation for complex statistics and estimators: Linearization and residual techniques. *Survey Methodology* 25: 193–203.

Korn, E. L., and B. I. Graubard. 1999. *Analysis of Health Surveys*. New York: Wiley.

Shah, B. V. 2004. Comment [on Demnati and Rao (2004)]. *Survey Methodology* 30: 29.

Also see

[SVY] **svy** — The survey prefix command

[SVY] **svyset** — Declare survey design for dataset

[SVY] **poststratification** — Poststratification for survey data

[SVY] **survey** — Introduction to survey commands

Title

> **estat** — Postestimation statistics for survey data

Syntax

Survey design characteristics

    estat svyset

Design and misspecification effects for point estimates

    estat <u>eff</u>ects [, *estat_effects_options*]

Design and misspecification effects for linear combinations of point estimates

    estat <u>lceff</u>ects *exp* [, *estat_lceffects_options*]

Subpopulation sizes

    estat size [, *estat_size_options*]

Subpopulation standard-deviation estimates

    estat sd [, *estat_sd_options*]

Singleton and certainty strata

    estat strata

Display covariance matrix estimates

    estat vce [, *estat_vce_options*]

estat_effects_options	description
deff	report DEFF design effects
deft	report DEFT design effects
<u>srs</u>subpop	report design effects, assuming SRS within subpopulation
meff	report MEFF design effects
meft	report MEFT design effects
display_options	control spacing and display of omitted variables and base and empty cells

estat_lceffects_options	description
deff	report DEFF design effects
deft	report DEFT design effects
srssubpop	report design effects, assuming SRS within subpopulation
meff	report MEFF design effects
meft	report MEFT design effects

estat_size_options	description
obs	report number of observations (within subpopulation)
size	report subpopulation sizes

estat_sd_options	description
variance	report subpopulation variances instead of standard deviations
srssubpop	report standard deviation, assuming SRS within subpopulation

estat_vce_options	description
covariance	display as covariance matrix; the default
correlation	display as correlation matrix
equation(spec)	display only specified equations
block	display submatrices by equation
diag	display submatrices by equation; diagonal blocks only
format(%fmt)	display format for covariances and correlations
nolines	suppress lines between equations
display_options	control display of omitted variables and base and empty cells

Menu

Statistics > Survey data analysis > DEFF, MEFF, and other statistics

Description

estat svyset reports the survey design characteristics associated with the current estimation results.

estat effects displays a table of design and misspecification effects for each estimated parameter.

estat lceffects displays a table of design and misspecification effects for a user-specified linear combination of the parameter estimates.

estat size displays a table of sample and subpopulation sizes for each estimated subpopulation mean, proportion, ratio, or total. This command is available only after svy: mean, svy: proportion, svy: ratio, and svy: total.

estat sd reports subpopulation standard deviations based on the estimation results from mean and svy: mean. estat sd is not appropriate with estimation results that used direct standardization or poststratification.

estat strata displays a table of the number of singleton and certainty strata within each sampling stage. The variance scaling factors are also displayed for estimation results where singleunit(scaled) was svyset.

estat vce displays the covariance or correlation matrix of the parameter estimates of the previous model. See [R] **estat** for examples.

Options for estat effects

deff and deft request that the design-effect measures DEFF and DEFT be displayed. This is the default, unless direct standardization or poststratification was used.

The deff and deft options are not allowed with estimation results that used direct standardization or poststratification. These methods obscure the measure of design effect because they adjust the frequency distribution of the target population.

srssubpop requests that DEFF and DEFT be computed using an estimate of simple random sampling (SRS) variance for sampling within a subpopulation. By default, DEFF and DEFT are computed using an estimate of the SRS variance for sampling from the entire population. Typically, srssubpop is used when computing subpopulation estimates by strata or by groups of strata.

meff and meft request that the misspecification-effect measures MEFF and MEFT be displayed.

display_options: <u>noomit</u>ted, vsquish, <u>noempty</u>cells, <u>base</u>levels, <u>allbase</u>levels; see [R] **estimation options**.

Options for estat lceffects

deff and deft request that the design-effect measures DEFF and DEFT be displayed. This is the default, unless direct standardization or poststratification was used.

The deff and deft options are not allowed with estimation results that used direct standardization or poststratification. These methods obscure the measure of design effect because they adjust the frequency distribution of the target population.

srssubpop requests that DEFF and DEFT be computed using an estimate of simple random sampling (SRS) variance for sampling within a subpopulation. By default, DEFF and DEFT are computed using an estimate of the SRS variance for sampling from the entire population. Typically, srssubpop is used when computing subpopulation estimates by strata or by groups of strata.

meff and meft request that the misspecification-effect measures MEFF and MEFT be displayed.

Options for estat size

obs requests that the number of observations used to compute the estimate be displayed for each row of estimates.

size requests that the estimate of the subpopulation size be displayed for each row of estimates. The subpopulation size estimate equals the sum of the weights for those observations in the estimation sample that are also in the specified subpopulation. The estimated population size is reported when a subpopulation is not specified.

Options for estat sd

variance requests that the subpopulation variance be displayed instead of the standard deviation.

srssubpop requests that the standard deviation be computed using an estimate of SRS variance for sampling within a subpopulation. By default, the standard deviation is computed using an estimate of the SRS variance for sampling from the entire population. Typically, srssubpop is given when computing subpopulation estimates by strata or by groups of strata.

Options for estat vce

covariance displays the matrix as a variance–covariance matrix; this is the default.

correlation displays the matrix as a correlation matrix rather than a variance–covariance matrix. rho is a synonym for correlation.

equation(*spec*) selects the part of the VCE to be displayed. If *spec* = *eqlist*, the VCE for the listed equations is displayed. If *spec* = *eqlist1* \ *eqlist2*, the part of the VCE associated with the equations in *eqlist1* (rowwise) and *eqlist2* (columnwise) is displayed. * is shorthand for all equations. equation() implies block if diag is not specified.

block displays the submatrices pertaining to distinct equations separately.

diag displays the diagonal submatrices pertaining to distinct equations separately.

format(%*fmt*) specifies the display format for displaying the elements of the matrix. The default is format(%10.0g) for covariances and format(%8.4f) for correlations. See [U] **12.5 Formats: Controlling how data are displayed** for more information.

nolines suppresses lines between equations.

display_options: noomitted, noemptycells, baselevels, allbaselevels; see [R] **estimation options**.

Remarks

▷ Example 1

Using data from the Second National Health and Nutrition Examination Survey (NHANES II) (McDowell et al. 1981), let's estimate the population means for total serum cholesterol (tcresult) and for serum triglycerides (tgresult).

```
. use http://www.stata-press.com/data/r11/nhanes2
. svy: mean tcresult tgresult
(running mean on estimation sample)
Survey: Mean estimation
Number of strata =        31        Number of obs     =       5050
Number of PSUs   =        62        Population size   =   56820832
                                    Design df         =         31
```

	Mean	Linearized Std. Err.	[95% Conf. Interval]	
tcresult	211.3975	1.252274	208.8435	213.9515
tgresult	138.576	2.071934	134.3503	142.8018

We can use estat svyset to remind us of the survey design characteristics that were used to produce these results.

```
. estat svyset
      pweight: finalwgt
          VCE: linearized
  Single unit: missing
     Strata 1: strata
        SU 1: psu
       FPC 1: <zero>
```

estat effects reports a table of design and misspecification effects for each mean we estimated.

```
. estat effects, deff deft meff meft
```

	Mean	Linearized Std. Err.	DEFF	DEFT	MEFF	MEFT
tcresult	211.3975	1.252274	3.57141	1.88982	3.46105	1.86039
tgresult	138.576	2.071934	2.35697	1.53524	2.32821	1.52585

estat size reports a table that contains sample and population sizes.

```
. estat size
```

	Mean	Linearized Std. Err.	Obs	Size
tcresult	211.3975	1.252274	5050	56820832
tgresult	138.576	2.071934	5050	56820832

estat size can also report a table of subpopulation sizes.

```
. svy: mean tcresult, over(sex)
(output omitted)
. estat size
        Male: sex = Male
      Female: sex = Female
```

Over	Mean	Linearized Std. Err.	Obs	Size
tcresult				
Male	210.7937	1.312967	4915	56159480
Female	215.2188	1.193853	5436	60998033

estat sd reports a table of subpopulation standard deviations.

```
. estat sd
        Male: sex = Male
      Female: sex = Female
```

Over	Mean	Std. Dev.
tcresult		
Male	210.7937	45.79065
Female	215.2188	50.72563

◁

▷ Example 2: Design effects with subpopulations

When there are subpopulations, `estat effects` can compute design effects with respect to one of two different hypothetical SRS designs. The default design is one in which SRS is conducted across the full population. The alternate design is one in which SRS is conducted entirely within the subpopulation of interest. This alternate design is used when the `srssubpop` option is specified.

Deciding which design is preferable depends on the nature of the subpopulations. If we can imagine identifying members of the subpopulations before sampling them, the alternate design is preferable. This case arises primarily when the subpopulations are strata or groups of strata. Otherwise, we may prefer to use the default.

Here is an example using the default with the NHANES II data.

```
. use http://www.stata-press.com/data/r11/nhanes2b
. svy: mean iron, over(sex)
(output omitted )
. estat effects
        Male: sex = Male
      Female: sex = Female
```

	Over	Mean	Linearized Std. Err.	DEFF	DEFT
iron					
	Male	104.7969	.557267	1.36097	1.16661
	Female	97.16247	.6743344	2.01403	1.41916

Thus the design-based variance estimate is about 36% larger than the estimate from the hypothetical SRS design including the full population. We can get DEFF and DEFT for the alternate SRS design by using the `srssubpop` option.

```
. estat effects, srssubpop
        Male: sex = Male
      Female: sex = Female
```

	Over	Mean	Linearized Std. Err.	DEFF	DEFT
iron					
	Male	104.7969	.557267	1.348	1.16104
	Female	97.16247	.6743344	2.03132	1.42524

Because the NHANES II did not stratify on sex, we think it problematic to consider design effects with respect to SRS of the female (or male) subpopulation. Consequently, we would prefer to use the default here, although the values of DEFF differ little between the two in this case.

For other examples (generally involving heavy oversampling or undersampling of specified subpopulations), the differences in DEFF for the two schemes can be much more dramatic.

Consider the NMIHS data (Gonzalez Jr., Krauss, and Scott 1992), and compute the mean of `birthwgt` over `race`:

```
. use http://www.stata-press.com/data/r11/nmihs
. svy: mean birthwgt, over(race)
(output omitted )
```

```
. estat effects
     nonblack: race = nonblack
        black: race = black
```

Over	Mean	Linearized Std. Err.	DEFF	DEFT
birthwgt				
nonblack	3402.32	7.609532	1.44376	1.20157
black	3127.834	6.529814	.172041	.414778

```
. estat effects, srssubpop
     nonblack: race = nonblack
        black: race = black
```

Over	Mean	Linearized Std. Err.	DEFF	DEFT
birthwgt				
nonblack	3402.32	7.609532	.826842	.909308
black	3127.834	6.529814	.528963	.727298

Because the NMIHS survey was stratified on race, marital status, age, and birthweight, we believe it reasonable to consider design effects computed with respect to SRS within an individual race group. Consequently, we would recommend here the alternative hypothetical design for computing design effects; i.e., we would use the `srssubpop` option.

◁

▷ Example 3: Misspecification effects

Misspecification effects assess biases in variance estimators that are computed under the wrong assumptions. The survey literature (e.g., Scott and Holt 1982, 850; Skinner 1989) defines misspecification effects with respect to a general set of "wrong" variance estimators. `estat effects` considers only one specific form: variance estimators computed under the incorrect assumption that our *observed* sample was selected through SRS.

The resulting "misspecification effect" measure is informative primarily when an unweighted point estimator is approximately unbiased for the parameter of interest. See Eltinge and Sribney (1996a) for a detailed discussion of extensions of misspecification effects that are appropriate for *biased* point estimators.

Note the difference between a misspecification effect and a design effect. For a design effect, we compare our complex-design–based variance estimate with an estimate of the true variance that we would have obtained under a hypothetical true simple random sample. For a misspecification effect, we compare our complex-design–based variance estimate with an estimate of the variance from fitting the same model without weighting, clustering, or stratification.

`estat effects` defines MEFF and MEFT as

$$\text{MEFF} = \widehat{V}/\widehat{V}_{\text{msp}}$$

$$\text{MEFT} = \sqrt{\text{MEFF}}$$

where $\widehat{V}$ is the appropriate design-based estimate of variance and $\widehat{V}_{\text{msp}}$ is the variance estimate computed with a misspecified design—ignoring the sampling weights, stratification, and clustering.

Here we request that the misspecification effects be displayed for the estimation of mean zinc levels from our NHANES II data.

```
. use http://www.stata-press.com/data/r11/nhanes2b
. svy: mean zinc, over(sex)
  (output omitted )
. estat effects, meff meft
        Male: sex = Male
      Female: sex = Female
```

Over	Mean	Linearized Std. Err.	MEFF	MEFT
zinc				
Male	90.74543	.5850741	6.28254	2.5065
Female	83.8635	.4689532	6.32648	2.51525

If we run `ci` without weights, we get the standard errors that are $(\widehat{V}_{\mathrm{msp}})^{1/2}$.

```
. sort sex
. ci zinc if sex == "Male":sex
```

Variable	Obs	Mean	Std. Err.	[95% Conf. Interval]
zinc	4375	89.53143	.2334228	89.0738 89.98906

```
. display [zinc]_se[Male]/r(se)
2.5064994
. display ([zinc]_se[Male]/r(se))^2
6.2825393
. ci zinc if sex == "Female":sex
```

Variable	Obs	Mean	Std. Err.	[95% Conf. Interval]
zinc	4827	83.76652	.186444	83.40101 84.13204

```
. display [zinc]_se[Female]/r(se)
2.515249
. display ([zinc]_se[Female]/r(se))^2
6.3264774
```

◁

▷ Example 4: Design and misspecification effects for linear combinations

Let's compare the mean of total serum cholesterol (`tcresult`) between men and women in the NHANES II dataset.

(Continued on next page)

```
. use http://www.stata-press.com/data/r11/nhanes2

. svy: mean tcresult, over(sex)
(running mean on estimation sample)
Survey: Mean estimation

Number of strata =       31       Number of obs   =       10351
Number of PSUs   =       62       Population size  = 117157513
                                  Design df        =          31

          Male: sex = Male
        Female: sex = Female
```

Over	Mean	Linearized Std. Err.	[95% Conf. Interval]	
tcresult				
Male	210.7937	1.312967	208.1159	213.4715
Female	215.2188	1.193853	212.784	217.6537

We can use `estat lceffects` to report the standard error, design effects, and misspecification effects of the difference between the above means.

```
. estat lceffects [tcresult]Male - [tcresult]Female, deff deft meff meft
 ( 1)  [tcresult]Male - [tcresult]Female = 0
```

Mean	Coef.	Std. Err.	DEFF	DEFT	MEFF	MEFT
(1)	-4.425109	1.086786	1.31241	1.1456	1.27473	1.12904

◁

▷ Example 5: Using survey data to determine Neyman allocation

Suppose that we have partitioned our population into L strata and stratum h contains N_h individuals. Also let σ_h represent the standard deviation of a quantity we wish to sample from the population. According to Cochran (1977, sec. 5.5), we can minimize the variance of the stratified mean estimator, for a fixed sample size n, if we choose the stratum sample sizes according to Neyman allocation:

$$n_h = n\frac{N_h\sigma_h}{\sum_{i=1}^{L} N_i\sigma_i} \tag{1}$$

We can use `estat sd` with our current survey data to produce a table of subpopulation standard-deviation estimates. Then we could plug these estimates into (1) to improve our survey design for the next time we sample from our population.

Here is an example using birthweight from the NMIHS data. First, we need estimation results from `svy: mean` over the strata.

```
. use http://www.stata-press.com/data/r11/nmihs

. svyset [pw=finwgt], strata(stratan)
      pweight: finwgt
          VCE: linearized
  Single unit: missing
     Strata 1: stratan
         SU 1: <observations>
        FPC 1: <zero>

. svy: mean birthwgt, over(stratan)
  (output omitted )
```

Next we will use `estat size` to report the table of stratum sizes. We will also generate matrix `p_obs` to contain the observed percent allocations for each stratum. In the matrix expression, `r(_N)` is a row vector of stratum sample sizes and `e(N)` contains the total sample size. `r(_N_subp)` is a row vector of the estimated population stratum sizes.

```
. estat size
                 1: stratan = 1
                 2: stratan = 2
                 3: stratan = 3
                 4: stratan = 4
                 5: stratan = 5
                 6: stratan = 6
```

Over	Mean	Linearized Std. Err.	Obs	Size
birthwgt				
1	1049.434	19.00149	841	18402.98161
2	2189.561	9.162736	803	67650.95932
3	3303.492	7.38429	3578	579104.6188
4	1036.626	12.32294	710	29814.93215
5	2211.217	9.864682	714	153379.07445
6	3485.42	8.057648	3300	3047209.10519

```
. matrix p_obs = 100 * r(_N)/e(N)
. matrix nsubp = r(_N_subp)
```

Now we call `estat sd` to report the stratum standard-deviation estimates and generate matrix `p_neyman` to contain the percent allocations according to (1). In the matrix expression, `r(sd)` is a vector of the stratum standard deviations.

```
. estat sd
                 1: stratan = 1
                 2: stratan = 2
                 3: stratan = 3
                 4: stratan = 4
                 5: stratan = 5
                 6: stratan = 6
```

Over	Mean	Std. Dev.
birthwgt		
1	1049.434	2305.931
2	2189.561	555.7971
3	3303.492	687.3575
4	1036.626	999.0867
5	2211.217	349.8068
6	3485.42	300.6945

```
. matrix p_neyman = 100 * hadamard(nsubp,r(sd))/el(nsubp*r(sd)',1,1)
. matrix list p_obs, format(%4.1f)

p_obs[1,6]
        birthwgt:  birthwgt:  birthwgt:  birthwgt:  birthwgt:  birthwgt:
               1          2          3          4          5          6
    r1       8.5        8.1       36.0        7.1        7.2       33.2
```

```
. matrix list p_neyman, format(%4.1f)
```

```
p_neyman[1,6]
       birthwgt:  birthwgt:  birthwgt:  birthwgt:  birthwgt:  birthwgt:
           1          2          3          4          5          6
    r1       2.9        2.5       26.9        2.0        3.6       62.0
```

We can see that strata 3 and 6 each contain about one-third of the observed data, with the rest of the observations spread out roughly equally to the remaining strata. However, plugging our sample estimates into (1) indicates that stratum 6 should get 62% of the sampling units, stratum 3 should get about 27%, and the remaining strata should get a roughly equal distribution of sampling units.

◁

▷ Example 6: Summarizing singleton and certainty strata

Use `estat strata` with `svy` estimation results to produce a table that reports the number of singleton and certainty strata in each sampling stage. Here is an example using (fictional) data from a complex survey with five sampling stages (the dataset is already `svyset`). If singleton strata are present, `estat strata` will report their effect on the standard errors.

```
. use http://www.stata-press.com/data/r11/strata5
. svy: total y
(output omitted )
. estat strata
```

Stage	Singleton strata	Certainty strata	Total strata
1	0	1	4
2	1	0	10
3	0	3	29
4	2	0	110
5	204	311	865

```
Note: missing standard error because of
      stratum with single sampling unit.
```

`estat strata` also reports the scale factor used when the `singleunit(scaled)` option is `svyset`. Of the 865 strata in the last stage, 204 are singleton strata and 311 are certainty strata. Thus the scaling factor for the last stage is

$$\frac{865 - 311}{865 - 311 - 204} \approx 1.58$$

```
. svyset, singleunit(scaled) noclear
(output omitted )
. svy: total y
(output omitted )
```

```
. estat strata
```

Stage	Singleton strata	Certainty strata	Total strata	Scale factor
1	0	1	4	1
2	1	0	10	1.11
3	0	3	29	1
4	2	0	110	1.02
5	204	311	865	1.58

Note: variances scaled within each stage to handle
       strata with a single sampling unit.

The singleunit(scaled) option of svyset is one of three methods in which Stata's svy commands can automatically handle singleton strata when performing variance estimation; see [SVY] **variance estimation** for a brief discussion of these methods.

◁

Saved results

estat svyset saves the following in r():

Scalars
    r(stages)   number of sampling stages

Macros
    r(wtype)   weight type
    r(wexp)   weight expression
    r(wvar)   weight variable name
    r(su#)   variable identifying sampling units for stage #
    r(strata#)   variable identifying strata for stage #
    r(fpc#)   FPC for stage #
    r(brrweight)   brrweight() variable list
    r(fay)   Fay's adjustment
    r(jkrweight)   jkrweight() variable list
    r(vce)   *vcetype* specified in vce()
    r(mse)   mse, if specified
    r(poststrata)   poststrata() variable
    r(postweight)   postweight() variable
    r(settings)   svyset arguments to reproduce the current settings
    r(singleunit) singleunit() setting

estat strata saves the following in r():

Matrices
    r(_N_strata_single)   number of strata with one sampling unit
    r(_N_strata_certain) number of certainty strata
    r(_N_strata)   number of strata
    r(scale)   variance scale factors used when singleunit(scaled) is svyset

estat effects saves the following in r():

Matrices

r(deff)	vector of DEFF estimates
r(deft)	vector of DEFT estimates
r(deffsub)	vector of DEFF estimates for srssubpop
r(deftsub)	vector of DEFT estimates for srssubpop
r(meff)	vector of MEFF estimates
r(meft)	vector of MEFT estimates

estat lceffects saves the following in r():

Scalars

r(estimate)	point estimate
r(se)	estimate of standard error
r(df)	degrees of freedom
r(deff)	DEFF estimate
r(deft)	DEFT estimate
r(deffsub)	DEFF estimate for srssubpop
r(deftsub)	DEFT estimate for srssubpop
r(meff)	MEFF estimate
r(meft)	MEFT estimate

estat size saves the following in r():

Matrices

r(_N)	vector of numbers of nonmissing observations
r(_N_subp)	vector of subpopulation size estimates

estat sd saves the following in r():

Macros

r(srssubpop)	srssubpop, if specified

Matrices

r(mean)	vector of subpopulation mean estimates
r(sd)	vector of subpopulation standard-deviation estimates
r(variance)	vector of subpopulation variance estimates

estat vce saves the following in r():

Matrices

r(V)	VCE or correlation matrix

Methods and formulas

estat is implemented as an ado-file.

Methods and formulas are presented under the following headings:

Design effects
Linear combinations
Misspecification effects
Population and subpopulation standard deviations

Design effects

estat effects produces two estimators of design effect, DEFF and DEFT.

DEFF is estimated as described in Kish (1965) as

$$
\text{DEFF} = \frac{\widehat{V}(\widehat{\theta})}{\widehat{V}_{\text{srswor}}(\widetilde{\theta}_{\text{srs}})}
$$

where $\widehat{V}(\widehat{\theta})$ is the design-based estimate of variance for a parameter, θ, and $\widehat{V}_{\text{srswor}}(\widetilde{\theta}_{\text{srs}})$ is an estimate of the variance for an estimator, $\widetilde{\theta}_{\text{srs}}$, that would be obtained from a similar hypothetical survey conducted using SRS without replacement (wor) and with the same number of sample elements, m, as in the actual survey. For example, if θ is a total Y, then

$$
\widehat{V}_{\text{srswor}}(\widetilde{\theta}_{\text{srs}}) = (1 - f)\frac{\widehat{M}}{m - 1}\sum_{j=1}^{m} w_j\left(y_j - \widehat{\overline{Y}}\right)^2 \tag{1}
$$

where $\widehat{\overline{Y}} = \widehat{Y}/\widehat{M}$. The factor $(1 - f)$ is a finite population correction. If the user sets an FPC for the first stage, $f = m/\widehat{M}$ is used; otherwise, $f = 0$.

DEFT is estimated as described in Kish (1987, 41) as

$$
\text{DEFT} = \sqrt{\frac{\widehat{V}(\widehat{\theta})}{\widehat{V}_{\text{srswr}}(\widetilde{\theta}_{\text{srs}})}}
$$

where $\widehat{V}_{\text{srswr}}(\widetilde{\theta}_{\text{srs}})$ is an estimate of the variance for an estimator, $\widetilde{\theta}_{\text{srs}}$, obtained from a similar survey conducted using SRS with replacement (wr). $\widehat{V}_{\text{srswr}}(\widetilde{\theta}_{\text{srs}})$ is computed using (1) with $f = 0$.

When computing estimates for a subpopulation, $\mathcal{S}$, and the srssubpop option is *not* specified (i.e., the default), (1) is used with $w_{\mathcal{S}j} = I_{\mathcal{S}}(j)\,w_j$ in place of w_j, where

$$
I_{\mathcal{S}}(j) = \begin{cases} 1, & \text{if } j \in \mathcal{S} \\ 0, & \text{otherwise} \end{cases}
$$

The sums in (1) are still calculated over all elements in the sample, regardless of whether they belong to the subpopulation: by default, the SRS is assumed to be done across the full population.

When the srssubpop option is specified, the SRS is carried out within subpopulation $\mathcal{S}$. Here (1) is used with the sums restricted to those elements belonging to the subpopulation; m is replaced with $m_{\mathcal{S}}$, the number of sample elements from the subpopulation; $\widehat{M}$ is replaced with $\widehat{M}_{\mathcal{S}}$, the sum of the weights from the subpopulation; and $\widehat{\overline{Y}}$ is replaced with $\widehat{\overline{Y}}_{\mathcal{S}} = \widehat{Y}_{\mathcal{S}}/\widehat{M}_{\mathcal{S}}$, the weighted mean across the subpopulation.

Linear combinations

estat lceffects estimates $\eta = C\theta$, where θ is a $q \times 1$ vector of parameters (e.g., population means or population regression coefficients) and C is any $1 \times q$ vector of constants. The estimate of η is $\widehat{\eta} = C\widehat{\theta}$, and its variance estimate is

$$\widehat{V}(\widehat{\eta}) = C\widehat{V}(\widehat{\theta})C'$$

Similarly, the SRS without replacement (srswor) variance estimator used in the computation of DEFF is

$$\widehat{V}_{\text{srswor}}(\widetilde{\eta}_{\text{srs}}) = C\widehat{V}_{\text{srswor}}(\widehat{\theta}_{\text{srs}})C'$$

and the SRS with replacement (srswr) variance estimator used in the computation of DEFT is

$$\widehat{V}_{\text{srswr}}(\widetilde{\eta}_{\text{srs}}) = C\widehat{V}_{\text{srswr}}(\widehat{\theta}_{\text{srs}})C'$$

The variance estimator used in computing MEFF and MEFT is

$$\widehat{V}_{\text{msp}}(\widetilde{\eta}_{\text{msp}}) = C\widehat{V}_{\text{msp}}(\widehat{\theta}_{\text{msp}})C'$$

estat lceffects was originally developed under a different command name; see Eltinge and Sribney (1996b).

Misspecification effects

estat effects produces two estimators of misspecification effect, MEFF and MEFT.

$$\text{MEFF} = \frac{\widehat{V}(\widehat{\theta})}{\widehat{V}_{\text{msp}}(\widehat{\theta}_{\text{msp}})}$$

$$\text{MEFT} = \sqrt{\text{MEFF}}$$

where $\widehat{V}(\widehat{\theta})$ is the design-based estimate of variance for a parameter, θ, and $\widehat{V}_{\text{msp}}(\widehat{\theta}_{\text{msp}})$ is the variance estimate for $\widehat{\theta}_{\text{msp}}$. These estimators, $\widehat{\theta}_{\text{msp}}$ and $\widehat{V}_{\text{msp}}(\widehat{\theta}_{\text{msp}})$, are based on the incorrect assumption that the observations were obtained through SRS with replacement: they are the estimators obtained by simply ignoring weights, stratification, and clustering. When θ is a total Y, the estimator and its variance estimate are computed using the standard formulas for an unweighted total:

$$\widehat{Y}_{\text{msp}} = \widehat{M}\,\overline{y} = \frac{\widehat{M}}{m}\sum_{j=1}^{m} y_j$$

$$\widehat{V}_{\text{msp}}(\widehat{Y}_{\text{msp}}) = \frac{\widehat{M}^2}{m(m-1)}\sum_{j=1}^{m}(y_j - \overline{y})^2$$

When computing MEFF and MEFT for a subpopulation, sums are restricted to those elements belonging to the subpopulation, and m_S and $\widehat{M}_S$ are used in place of m and $\widehat{M}$.

Population and subpopulation standard deviations

For srswr designs, the variance of the mean estimator is

$$V_{\mathrm{srswr}}(\overline{y}) = \sigma^2/n$$

where n is the sample size and σ is the population standard deviation. estat sd uses this formula and the results from mean and svy: mean to estimate the population standard deviation via

$$\widehat{\sigma} = \sqrt{n \ \widehat{V}_{\mathrm{srswr}}(\overline{y})}$$

Subpopulation standard deviations are computed similarly, using the corresponding variance estimate and sample size.

References

Cochran, W. G. 1977. *Sampling Techniques*. 3rd ed. New York: Wiley.

Eltinge, J. L., and W. M. Sribney. 1996a. Accounting for point-estimation bias in assessment of misspecification effects, confidence-set coverage rates and test sizes. Unpublished manuscript, Department of Statistics, Texas A&M University.

———. 1996b. svy5: Estimates of linear combinations and hypothesis tests for survey data. *Stata Technical Bulletin* 31: 31–42. Reprinted in *Stata Technical Bulletin Reprints*, vol. 6, pp. 246–259. College Station, TX: Stata Press.

Gonzalez Jr., J. F., N. Krauss, and C. Scott. 1992. Estimation in the 1988 National Maternal and Infant Health Survey. *Proceedings of the Section on Statistics Education, American Statistical Association* 343–348.

Kish, L. 1965. *Survey Sampling*. New York: Wiley.

———. 1987. *Statistical Design for Research*. New York: Wiley.

McDowell, A., A. Engel, J. T. Massey, and K. Maurer. 1981. Plan and operation of the Second National Health and Nutrition Examination Survey, 1976–1980. *Vital and Health Statistics* 1(15): 1–144.

Scott, A. J., and D. Holt. 1982. The effect of two-stage sampling on ordinary least squares methods. *Journal of the American Statistical Association* 77: 848–854.

Skinner, C. J. 1989. Introduction to part A. In *Analysis of Complex Surveys*, ed. C. J. Skinner, D. Holt, and T. M. F. Smith, 23–58. New York: Wiley.

Also see

[SVY] **svy postestimation** — Postestimation tools for svy

[SVY] **svy estimation** — Estimation commands for survey data

[SVY] **subpopulation estimation** — Subpopulation estimation for survey data

[SVY] **variance estimation** — Variance estimation for survey data

Title

> *jackknife_options* — More options for jackknife variance estimation

Syntax

jackknife_options	description
SE	
mse	use MSE formula for variance
nodots	suppress replication dots
†saving(*filename*, ...)	save results to *filename*
†keep	keep pseudovalues
†verbose	display the full table legend
†noisily	display any output from *command*
†trace	trace the *command*
†title(*text*)	use *text* as the title for results
†nodrop	do not drop observations
†reject(*exp*)	identify invalid results

†These options are not shown in the dialog boxes for estimation commands.

Description

svy accepts more options when performing jackknife variance estimation.

Options

SE

mse indicates that svy compute the variance by using deviations of the replicates from the observed value of the statistic based on the entire dataset. By default, svy computes the variance by using deviations of the pseudovalues from their mean.

nodots suppresses display of the replication dots. By default, one dot character is printed for each successful replication. A red 'x' is displayed if *command* returns with an error, 'e' is displayed if at least one of the values in the *exp_list* is missing, and 'n' is displayed if the sample size is not correct.

saving(), keep, verbose, noisily, trace, title(), nodrop, reject(); see [SVY] **svy jackknife**.

Also see

[SVY] **svy** — The survey prefix command

[SVY] **svy jackknife** — Jackknife estimation for survey data

Title

> **ml for svy** — Maximum pseudolikelihood estimation for survey data

Remarks

Stata's `ml` command can fit maximum likelihood–based models for survey data. Many `ml`-based estimators can now be modified to handle one or more stages of clustering, stratification, sampling weights, finite population correction, poststratification, and subpopulation estimation. See [R] **ml** for details.

See [P] **program properties** for a discussion of the programming requirements for an estimation command to work with the `svy` prefix. See Gould, Pitblado, and Sribney (2006) for examples of user-written estimation commands that support the `svy` prefix.

▷ Example 1: User-written survey regression

The `ml` command requires a program that computes likelihood values to perform maximum likelihood. Here is a likelihood evaluator used in Gould, Pitblado, and Sribney (2006) to fit linear regression models using likelihood from the normal distribution.

```
program mynormal_lf
        version 11
        args lnf mu lnsigma
        quietly replace 'lnf' = ln(normalden($ML_y1,'mu',exp('lnsigma')))
end
```

Here we fit a survey regression model using a multistage survey dataset with `ml` and the above likelihood evaluator.

```
. use http://www.stata-press.com/data/r11/multistage
. svyset county [pw=sampwgt], strata(state) fpc(ncounties) || school, fpc(nschools)

        pweight: sampwgt
            VCE: linearized
    Single unit: missing
      Strata 1: state
          SU 1: county
         FPC 1: ncounties
      Strata 2: <one>
          SU 2: school
         FPC 2: nschools
. ml model lf mynormal_lf (mu: weight = height) /lnsigma, svy
```

```
. ml max
initial:       log pseudolikelihood =      -<inf>  (could not be evaluated)
feasible:      log pseudolikelihood = -7.301e+08
rescale:       log pseudolikelihood =  -51944380
rescale eq:    log pseudolikelihood =  -47565331
Iteration 0:   log pseudolikelihood =  -47565331
Iteration 1:   log pseudolikelihood =  -41226725  (not concave)
Iteration 2:   log pseudolikelihood =  -41221650  (not concave)
Iteration 3:   log pseudolikelihood =  -41176159  (not concave)
Iteration 4:   log pseudolikelihood =  -41154139  (not concave)
Iteration 5:   log pseudolikelihood =  -41052368
Iteration 6:   log pseudolikelihood =  -39379181  (backed up)
Iteration 7:   log pseudolikelihood =  -38333242
Iteration 8:   log pseudolikelihood =  -38328742
Iteration 9:   log pseudolikelihood =  -38328739
```

Number of strata	=	50		Number of obs	=	4071
Number of PSUs	=	100		Population size	=	8000000
				Design df	=	50
				F(1, 50)	=	593.99
				Prob > F	=	0.0000

weight	Coef.	Linearized Std. Err.	t	P>|t|	[95% Conf. Interval]	
mu						
height	.716311	.0293908	24.37	0.000	.6572778	.7753442
_cons	-149.6181	12.57266	-11.90	0.000	-174.871	-124.3652
lnsigma						
_cons	3.372153	.0180777	186.54	0.000	3.335843	3.408464

◁

Reference

Gould, W. W., J. S. Pitblado, and W. M. Sribney. 2006. *Maximum Likelihood Estimation with Stata.* 3rd ed. College Station, TX: Stata Press.

Also see

[P] **program properties** — Properties of user-defined programs

[R] **maximize** — Details of iterative maximization

[R] **ml** — Maximum likelihood estimation

[SVY] **survey** — Introduction to survey commands

Title

poststratification — Poststratification for survey data

Description

Poststratification is a method for adjusting the sampling weights, usually to account for underrepresented groups in the population.

See [SVY] **direct standardization** for a similar method of adjustment that allows the comparison of rates that come from different frequency distributions.

Remarks

Poststratification involves adjusting the sampling weights so that they sum to the population sizes within each poststratum. This usually results in decreasing bias because of nonresponse and underrepresented groups in the population. Poststratification also tends to result in smaller variance estimates.

The svyset command has options to set variables for applying poststratification adjustments to the sampling weights. The poststrata() option takes a variable that contains poststratum identifiers, and the postweight() option takes a variable that contains the poststratum population sizes.

In the following example, we use an example from Levy and Lemeshow (2008) to show how poststratification affects the point estimates and their variance.

▷ Example 1: Poststratified mean

Levy and Lemeshow (2008, sec. 6.6) give an example of poststratification by using simple survey data from a veterinarian's client list. The data in poststrata.dta were collected using simple random sampling without replacement. The totexp variable contains the total expenses to the client, type identifies the cats and dogs, postwgt contains the poststratum sizes (450 for cats and 850 for dogs), and fpc contains the total number of clients ($850 + 450 = 1300$).

```
. use http://www.stata-press.com/data/r11/poststrata
. svyset, poststrata(type) postweight(postwgt) fpc(fpc)
      pweight: <none>
          VCE: linearized
   Poststrata: type
   Postweight: postwgt
  Single unit: missing
      Strata 1: <one>
         SU 1: <observations>
        FPC 1: fpc
```

```
. svy: mean totexp
(running mean on estimation sample)

Survey: Mean estimation

Number of strata =      1          Number of obs    =      50
Number of PSUs   =     50          Population size  =    1300
N. of poststrata =      2          Design df        =      49
```

	Mean	Linearized Std. Err.	[95% Conf. Interval]
totexp	40.11513	1.163498	37.77699 42.45327

The mean total expenses is \$40.12 with a standard error of \$1.16. In the following, we omit the poststratification information from svyset, resulting in mean total expenses of \$39.73 with standard error \$2.22. The difference between the mean estimates is explained by the facts that expenses tend to be larger for dogs than for cats and that the dogs were slightly underrepresented in the sample ($850/1{,}300 \approx 0.65$ for the population; $32/50 = 0.64$ for the sample). This reasoning also explains why the variance estimate from the poststratified mean is smaller than the one that was not poststratified.

```
. svyset, fpc(fpc)

      pweight: <none>
          VCE: linearized
  Single unit: missing
      Strata 1: <one>
          SU 1: <observations>
         FPC 1: fpc

. svy: mean totexp
(running mean on estimation sample)

Survey: Mean estimation

Number of strata =      1          Number of obs    =      50
Number of PSUs   =     50          Population size  =      50
                                   Design df        =      49
```

	Mean	Linearized Std. Err.	[95% Conf. Interval]
totexp	39.7254	2.221747	35.26063 44.19017

◁

Methods and formulas

The following discussion assumes that you are already familiar with the topics discussed in [SVY] **variance estimation**.

Suppose that you used a complex survey design to sample m individuals from a population of size M. Let P_k be the set of individuals in the sample that belong to poststratum k, and let $I_{P_k}(j)$ indicate if the jth individual is in poststratum k, where

$$I_{P_k}(j) = \begin{cases} 1, & \text{if } j \in P_k \\ 0, & \text{otherwise} \end{cases}$$

Also let L_P be the number of poststrata and M_k be the population size for poststratum k.

If w_j is the unadjusted sampling weight for the jth sampled individual, the poststratification adjusted sampling weight is

$$w_j^* = \sum_{k=1}^{L_P} I_{P_k}(j) \frac{M_k}{\widehat{M}_k} w_j$$

where $\widehat{M}_k$ is

$$\widehat{M}_k = \sum_{j=1}^{m} I_{P_k}(j) w_j$$

The point estimates are computed using these adjusted weights. For example, the poststratified total estimator is

$$\widehat{Y}^P = \sum_{j=1}^{m} w_j^* y_j$$

where y_j is an item from the jth sampled individual.

For replication-based variance estimation, the BRR and jackknife replicate-weight variables are similarly adjusted to produce the replicate values used in the respective variance formulas.

The score variable for the linearized variance estimator of a poststratified total is

$$z_j(\widehat{Y}^P) = \sum_{k=1}^{L_P} I_{P_k}(j) \frac{M_k}{\widehat{M}_k} \left(y_j - \frac{\widehat{Y}_k}{\widehat{M}_k} \right) \tag{1}$$

where $\widehat{Y}_k$ is the total estimator for the kth poststratum,

$$\widehat{Y}_k = \sum_{j=1}^{m} I_{P_k}(j) w_j y_j$$

For the poststratified ratio estimator, the score variable is

$$z_j(\widehat{R}^P) = \frac{\widehat{X}^P z_j(\widehat{Y}^P) - \widehat{Y}^P z_j(\widehat{X}^P)}{(\widehat{X}^P)^2} \tag{2}$$

where $\widehat{X}^P$ is the poststratified total estimator for item x_j. For regression models, the equation-level scores are adjusted as in (1). These score variables were derived using the method described in [SVY] **variance estimation** for the ratio estimator and are a direct result of the methods described in Deville (1999), Demnati and Rao (2004), and Shah (2004).

References

Demnati, A., and J. N. K. Rao. 2004. Linearization variance estimators for survey data. *Survey Methodology* 30: 17–26.

Deville, J.-C. 1999. Variance estimation for complex statistics and estimators: Linearization and residual techniques. *Survey Methodology* 25: 193–203.

Levy, P. S., and S. Lemeshow. 2008. *Sampling of Populations: Methods and Applications*. 4th ed. Hoboken, NJ: Wiley.

Shah, B. V. 2004. Comment [on Demnati and Rao (2004)]. *Survey Methodology* 30: 29.

Also see

[SVY] **svy** — The survey prefix command

[SVY] **svyset** — Declare survey design for dataset

[SVY] **survey** — Introduction to survey commands

Title

---
subpopulation estimation — Subpopulation estimation for survey data
---

Description

Subpopulation estimation focuses on part of the population. This entry discusses subpopulation estimation and explains why you should use the subpop() option instead of if and in for your survey data analysis.

Remarks

Subpopulation estimation involves computing point and variance estimates for part of the population. This is not the same as restricting the estimation sample to the collection of observations within the subpopulation because variance estimation for survey data measures sample-to-sample variability, assuming that the same survey design is used to collect the data; see *Methods and formulas* for a detailed explanation. West, Berglund, and Heeringa (2008) provides further information on subpopulation analysis.

The svy prefix command's subpop() option performs subpopulation estimation. The svy: mean, svy: proportion, svy: ratio, and svy: total commands also have the over() option to perform estimation for multiple subpopulations.

The following examples illustrate how to use the subpop() and over() options.

▷ Example 1

Suppose that we are interested in estimating the proportion of women in our population who have had a heart attack. In our NHANES II dataset (McDowell et al. 1981), the female participants can be identified using the female variable, and the heartatk variable indicates whether an individual has ever had a heart attack. Below we use svy: mean with the heartatk variable to estimate the proportion of individuals who have had a heart attack, and we use subpop(female) to identify our subpopulation of interest.

```
. use http://www.stata-press.com/data/r11/nhanes2d

. svy, subpop(female): mean heartatk
(running mean on estimation sample)

Survey: Mean estimation

Number of strata =      31     Number of obs     =       10349
Number of PSUs   =      62     Population size   =   117131111
                               Subpop. no. obs   =        5434
                               Subpop. size      =    60971631
                               Design df         =          31
```

	Mean	Linearized Std. Err.	[95% Conf. Interval]
heartatk	.0193276	.0017021	.0158562 .0227991

The subpop(*varname*) option takes a 0/1 variable, and the subpopulation of interest is defined by *varname* = 1. All other members of the sample not in the subpopulation are indicated by *varname* = 0.

If a person's subpopulation status is unknown, *varname* should be set to missing (.), so those observations will be omitted from the analysis. For instance, in the preceding analysis, if a person's sex was not recorded, `female` should be coded as missing rather than as male (`female` = 0).

◁

❑ Technical note

Actually, the subpop(*varname*) option takes a zero/nonzero variable, and the subpopulation is defined by *varname* ≠ 0 and not missing. All other members of the sample not in the subpopulation are indicated by *varname* = 0, but 0, 1, and missing are typically the only values used for the subpop() variable.

Furthermore, you can specify an `if` qualifier within subpop() to identify a subpopulation. The result is the same as generating a variable equal to the conditional expression and supplying it as the subpop() variable. If a *varname* and an `if` qualifier are specified within the subpop() option, the subpopulation is identified by their logical conjunction (logical *and*), and observations with missing values in either are dropped from the estimation sample.

❑

⊳ Example 2: Multiple subpopulation estimation

Means, proportions, ratios, and totals for multiple subpopulations can be estimated using the over() option with svy: mean, svy: proportion, svy: ratio, and svy: total, respectively. Here is an example using the NMIHS data (Gonzalez Jr., Krauss, and Scott 1992), estimating mean birthweight over the categories of the race variable.

```
. use http://www.stata-press.com/data/r11/nmihs
. svy: mean birthwgt, over(race)
(running mean on estimation sample)

Survey: Mean estimation

Number of strata =       6          Number of obs    =      9946
Number of PSUs   =    9946          Population size  =   3895562
                                    Design df        =      9940

         nonblack: race = nonblack
            black: race = black
```

		Linearized		
Over	Mean	Std. Err.	[95% Conf.	Interval]
birthwgt				
nonblack	3402.32	7.609532	3387.404	3417.236
black	3127.834	6.529814	3115.035	3140.634

More than one variable can be used in the over() option.

```
. svy: mean birthwgt, over(race marital)
(running mean on estimation sample)

Survey: Mean estimation

Number of strata =        6         Number of obs    =     9946
Number of PSUs   =     9946         Population size  =  3895562
                                    Design df        =     9940

            Over: race marital
       _subpop_1: nonblack single
       _subpop_2: nonblack married
       _subpop_3: black single
       _subpop_4: black married
```

		Linearized		
Over	Mean	Std. Err.	[95% Conf. Interval]	
birthwgt				
_subpop_1	3291.045	20.18795	3251.472	3330.617
_subpop_2	3426.407	8.379497	3409.982	3442.833
_subpop_3	3073.122	8.752553	3055.965	3090.279
_subpop_4	3221.616	12.42687	3197.257	3245.975

Here the race and marital variables have value labels. race has the value 0 labeled "nonblack" (i.e., white and other) and 1 labeled "black"; marital has the value 0 labeled "single" and 1 labeled "married". Value labels on the over() variables make for a more informative legend above the table of point estimates. See [U] **12.6.3 Value labels** for information on creating value labels.

We can also combine the subpop() option with the over() option.

```
. generate nonblack = (race == 0) if !missing(race)

. svy, subpop(nonblack): mean birthwgt, over(marital age20)
(running mean on estimation sample)

Survey: Mean estimation

Number of strata =        3         Number of obs    =     4724
Number of PSUs   =     4724         Population size  =  3230403
                                    Subpop. no. obs  =     4724
                                    Subpop. size     =  3230403
                                    Design df        =     4721

            Over: marital age20
       _subpop_1: single age20+
       _subpop_2: single age<20
       _subpop_3: married age20+
       _subpop_4: married age<20
```

		Linearized		
Over	Mean	Std. Err.	[95% Conf. Interval]	
birthwgt				
_subpop_1	3312.012	24.2869	3264.398	3359.625
_subpop_2	3244.709	36.85934	3172.448	3316.971
_subpop_3	3434.923	8.674633	3417.916	3451.929
_subpop_4	3287.301	34.15988	3220.332	3354.271

```
Note: 3 strata omitted because they contain no subpopulation
      members.
```

This time, we estimated means for the marital status and age (<20 or ≥ 20) subpopulations for race == 0 (nonblack) only. We carefully define nonblack so that it is missing when race is missing.

If we omitted the `if !missing(race)` in our `generate` statement, then `nonblack` would be 0 when `race` was missing. This would improperly assume that all individuals with a missing value for `race` were black and could cause our results to have incorrect standard errors. The standard errors could be incorrect because those observations for which `race` is missing would be counted as part of the estimation sample, potentially inflating the number of PSUs used in the formula for the variance estimator. For this reason, observations with missing values for any of the `over()` variables are omitted from the analysis.

◁

Methods and formulas

The following discussion assumes that you are already familiar with the topics discussed in [SVY] **variance estimation**.

Cochran (1977, sec. 2.13) discusses a method by which you can derive estimates for subpopulation totals. This section uses this method to derive the formulas for a subpopulation total from a simple random sample (without replacement) to explain how the `subpop()` option works, shows why this method will often produce different results from those produced using an equivalent `if` (or `in`) qualifier (outside the `subpop()` option), and discusses how this method applies to subpopulation means, proportions, ratios, and regression models.

Methods and formulas are presented under the following headings:

> *Subpopulation totals*
> *Subpopulation estimates other than the total*
> *Subpopulation with replication methods*

Subpopulation totals

Let Y_j be a survey item for individual j in the population, where $j = 1, \ldots, N$ and N is the population size. Let S be a subset of individuals in the population and $I_S(j)$ indicate if the jth individual is in S, where

$$I_S(j) = \begin{cases} 1, \text{ if } j \in S \\ 0, \text{ otherwise} \end{cases}$$

The subpopulation total is

$$Y_S = \sum_{j=1}^{N} I_S(j) Y_j$$

and the subpopulation size is

$$N_S = \sum_{j=1}^{N} I_S(j)$$

Let y_j be the items for those individuals selected in the sample, where $j = 1, \ldots, n$ and n is the sample size. The number of individuals sampled from the subpopulation is

$$n_S = \sum_{j=1}^{n} I_S(j)$$

The estimator for the subpopulation total is

$$\widehat{Y}_S = \sum_{j=1}^{n} I_S(j) w_j y_j \tag{1}$$

where $w_j = N/n$ is the unadjusted sampling weight for this design. The estimator for N_S is

$$\widehat{N}_S = \sum_{j=1}^{n} I_S(j) w_j$$

The replicate values for the BRR and jackknife variance estimators are computed using the same method.

The linearized variance estimator for $\widehat{Y}_S$ is

$$\widehat{V}(\widehat{Y}_S) = \left(1 - \frac{n}{N}\right) \frac{n}{n-1} \sum_{j=1}^{n} \left\{ I_S(j) y_j - \frac{1}{n}\widehat{Y}_S \right\}^2 \tag{2}$$

The covariance estimator for the subpopulation totals $\widehat{Y}_S$ and $\widehat{X}_S$ (notation for X_S is defined similarly to that of Y_S) is

$$\widehat{\mathrm{Cov}}(\widehat{Y}_S, \widehat{X}_S) = \left(1 - \frac{n}{N}\right) \frac{n}{n-1} \sum_{j=1}^{n} \left\{ I_S(j) y_j - \frac{1}{n}\widehat{Y}_S \right\} \left\{ I_S(j) x_j - \frac{1}{n}\widehat{X}_S \right\} \tag{3}$$

Equation (2) is not the same formula that results from restricting the estimation sample to the observations within S. The formula using this restricted sample (assuming a svyset with the corresponding FPC) is

$$\widetilde{V}(\widehat{Y}_S) = \left(1 - \frac{n_S}{\widehat{N}_S}\right) \frac{n_S}{n_S-1} \sum_{j=1}^{n} I_S(j) \left\{ y_j - \frac{1}{n_S}\widehat{Y}_S \right\}^2 \tag{4}$$

These variance estimators, (2) and (4), assume two different survey designs. In (2), n individuals are sampled without replacement from the population comprising the N_S values from the subpopulation with $N - N_S$ additional zeros. In (4), n_S individuals are sampled without replacement from the subpopulation of N_S values. We discourage using (4) by warning against using the if and in qualifiers for subpopulation estimation because this variance estimator does not accurately measure the sample-to-sample variability of the subpopulation estimates for the survey design that was used to collect the data.

For survey data, there are only a few circumstances that require using the if qualifier. For example, if you suspected laboratory error for a certain set of measurements, then using the if qualifier to omit these observations from the analysis might be proper.

Subpopulation estimates other than the total

To generalize the above results, note that the other point estimators—such as means, proportions, ratios, and regression coefficients—yield a linearized variance estimator based on one or more (equation level) score variables. For example, the weighted sample estimation equations of a regression model for a given subpopulation (see (3) from [SVY] **variance estimation**) is

$$\widehat{G}(\boldsymbol{\beta}_S) = \sum_{j=1}^{n} I_S(j) w_j S(\boldsymbol{\beta}_S; y_j, \mathbf{x}_j) = 0 \tag{5}$$

You can write $\widehat{G}(\boldsymbol{\beta}_S)$ as

$$\widehat{G}(\boldsymbol{\beta}_S) = \sum_{j=1}^{n} I_S(j) w_j \mathbf{d}_j$$

which is an estimator for the subpopulation total $G(\boldsymbol{\beta}_S)$, so its variance estimator can be computed using the design-based variance estimator for a subpopulation total.

Subpopulation with replication methods

The above comparison between the variance estimator from the subpop() option and the variance estimator from the if and in qualifiers is also true for the replication methods.

For the BRR method, the same number of replicates is produced with or without the subpop() option. The difference is how the replicate values are computed. Using the if and in qualifiers may cause an error because svy brr checks that there are two PSUs in every stratum within the restricted sample.

For the jackknife method, every PSU produces a replicate, even if it does not contain an observation within the subpopulation specified using the subpop() option. When the if and in qualifiers are used, only the PSUs that have at least 1 observation within the restricted sample will produce a replicate.

References

Cochran, W. G. 1977. *Sampling Techniques*. 3rd ed. New York: Wiley.

Gonzalez Jr., J. F., N. Krauss, and C. Scott. 1992. Estimation in the 1988 National Maternal and Infant Health Survey. *Proceedings of the Section on Statistics Education, American Statistical Association* 343–348.

McDowell, A., A. Engel, J. T. Massey, and K. Maurer. 1981. Plan and operation of the Second National Health and Nutrition Examination Survey, 1976–1980. *Vital and Health Statistics* 1(15): 1–144.

West, B. T., P. Berglund, and S. G. Heeringa. 2008. A closer examination of subpopulation analysis of complex-sample survey data. *Stata Journal* 8: 520–531.

Also see

[SVY] **svy postestimation** — Postestimation tools for svy

[SVY] **svy** — The survey prefix command

[SVY] **svyset** — Declare survey design for dataset

[SVY] **survey** — Introduction to survey commands

Title

svy — The survey prefix command

Syntax

svy $\left[\,vcetype\,\right]$ $\left[\,,\,svy\_options\ eform\_option\,\right]$: *command*

vcetype	description
SE	
linearized	Taylor linearized variance estimation
brr	BRR variance estimation; see [SVY] **svy brr**
jackknife	jackknife variance estimation; see [SVY] **svy jackknife**

Specifying a *vcetype* overrides the default from svyset.

svy_options	description
if/in	
subpop($\left[\,varname\,\right]$ $\left[\,if\,\right]$)	identify a subpopulation
SE	
brr_options	more options allowed with BRR variance estimation; see [SVY] ***brr_options***
jackknife_options	more options allowed with jackknife variance estimation; see [SVY] ***jackknife_options***
Reporting	
level(#)	set confidence level; default is level(95)
nocnsreport	do not display constraints
display_options	control spacing and display of omitted variables and base and empty cells
[†]noheader	suppress table header
[†]nolegend	suppress table legend
[†]noadjust	do not adjust model Wald statistic
[†]noisily	display any output from *command*
[†]trace	trace the *command*
[†]coeflegend	display coefficients' legend instead of coefficient table

[†]noheader, nolegend, noadjust, noisily, trace, and coeflegend are not shown in the dialog boxes for estimation commands.

svy requires that the survey design variables be identified using svyset; see [SVY] **svyset**.

mi estimate may be used with svy linearized if the estimation command allows mi estimate; it may not be used with svy brr or svy jackknife.

See [U] **20 Estimation and postestimation commands** for more capabilities of estimation commands.

Warning: Using if or in restrictions will often not produce correct variance estimates for subpopulations. To compute estimates for a subpopulation, use the subpop() option.

Description

svy fits statistical models for complex survey data. Typing

. svy: *command*

executes *command* while accounting for the survey settings identified by svyset.

command defines the estimation command to be executed. Not all estimation commands are supported by svy. See [SVY] **svy estimation** for a list of Stata's estimation commands that are supported by svy. See [P] **program properties** for a discussion of what is required for svy to support an estimation command. The by prefix may not be part of *command*.

Options

<u>　　　　┌ if/in ┐</u>

subpop(*subpop*) specifies that estimates be computed for the single subpopulation identified by *subpop*, which is

$\left[\, varname \,\right]\ \left[\, if \,\right]$

Thus the subpopulation is defined by the observations for which *varname* $\neq 0$ that also meet the if conditions. Typically, *varname* $= 1$ defines the subpopulation, and *varname* $= 0$ indicates observations not belonging to the subpopulation. For observations whose subpopulation status is uncertain, *varname* should be set to a missing value; such observations are dropped from the estimation sample.

See [SVY] **subpopulation estimation** and [SVY] **estat**.

<u>　　　　┌ SE ┐</u>

brr_options are other options that are allowed with BRR variance estimation specified by svy brr or specified as svyset using the vce(brr) option; see [SVY] *brr_options*.

jackknife_options are other options that are allowed with jackknife variance estimation specified by svy jackknife or specified as svyset using the vce(jackknife) option; see [SVY] *jackknife_options*.

<u>　　　　┌ Reporting ┐</u>

level(*#*) specifies the confidence level, as a percentage, for confidence intervals. The default is level(95) or as set by set level; see [U] **20.7 Specifying the width of confidence intervals**.

nocnsreport; see [R] **estimation options**.

display_options: <u>noomit</u>ted, vsquish, noemptycells, <u>base</u>levels, <u>allbase</u>levels; see [R] **estimation options**.

The following options are available with svy but are not shown in the dialog boxes:

noheader prevents the table header from being displayed. This option implies nolegend.

nolegend prevents the table legend identifying the subpopulations from being displayed.

noadjust specifies that the model Wald test be carried out as $W/k \sim F(k, d)$, where W is the Wald test statistic, k is the number of terms in the model excluding the constant term, d is the total number of sampled PSUs minus the total number of strata, and $F(k, d)$ is an F distribution with k numerator degrees of freedom and d denominator degrees of freedom. By default, an adjusted Wald test is conducted: $(d - k + 1)W/(kd) \sim F(k, d - k + 1)$.

See Korn and Graubard (1990) for a discussion of the Wald test and the adjustments thereof. Using the noadjust option is not recommended.

noisily requests that any output from *command* be displayed.

trace causes a trace of the execution of *command* to be displayed.

coeflegend; see [R] **estimation options**.

The following option is usually available with svy at the time of estimation or on replay but is not shown in all dialog boxes:

eform_option; see [R] ***eform_option***.

Remarks

The svy prefix is designed for use with complex survey data. Typical survey design characteristics include sampling weights, one or more stages of clustered sampling, and stratification. For a general discussion of various aspects of survey designs, including multistage designs, see [SVY] **svyset**.

Below we present an example of the effects of weights, clustering, and stratification. This is a typical case, but drawing general rules from any one example is still dangerous. You could find particular analyses from other surveys that are counterexamples for each of the trends for standard errors exhibited here.

▷ Example 1: The effects of weights, clustering, and stratification

We use data from the Second National Health and Nutrition Examination Survey (NHANES II) (McDowell et al. 1981) as our example. This is a national survey, and the dataset has sampling weights, strata, and clustering. In this example, we will consider the estimation of the mean serum zinc level of all adults in the United States.

First, consider a proper design-based analysis, which accounts for weighting, clustering, and stratification. Before we issue our svy estimation command, we set the weight, strata, and PSU identifier variables:

```
. use http://www.stata-press.com/data/r11/nhanes2f
. svyset psuid [pweight=finalwgt], strata(stratid)
      pweight: finalwgt
          VCE: linearized
  Single unit: missing
     Strata 1: stratid
         SU 1: psuid
        FPC 1: <zero>
```

We now estimate the mean by using the proper design-based analysis:

```
. svy: mean zinc
(running mean on estimation sample)

Survey: Mean estimation

Number of strata =      31      Number of obs    =       9189
Number of PSUs   =      62      Population size  =  104176071
                                Design df        =         31
```

	Mean	Linearized Std. Err.	[95% Conf. Interval]	
zinc	87.18207	.4944827	86.17356	88.19057

If we ignore the survey design and use `mean` to estimate the mean, we get

```
. mean zinc
Mean estimation                    Number of obs    =      9189
```

	Mean	Std. Err.	[95% Conf. Interval]
zinc	86.51518	.1510744	86.21904 86.81132

The point estimate from the unweighted analysis is smaller by more than one standard error than the proper design-based estimate. Also, design-based analysis produced a standard error that is 3.27 times larger than the standard error produced by our incorrect analysis.

◁

▷ Example 2: Halfway is not enough—the importance of stratification and clustering

When some people analyze survey data, they say, "I know I have to use my survey weights, but I will just ignore the stratification and clustering information." If we follow this strategy, we will obtain the proper design-based point estimates, but our standard errors, confidence intervals, and test statistics will usually be wrong.

To illustrate this effect, suppose that we used the `svy: mean` procedure with `pweights` only.

```
. svyset [pweight=finalwgt]
      pweight: finalwgt
          VCE: linearized
  Single unit: missing
     Strata 1: <one>
        SU 1: <observations>
       FPC 1: <zero>
. svy: mean zinc
(running mean on estimation sample)

Survey: Mean estimation

Number of strata =        1          Number of obs    =       9189
Number of PSUs   =     9189          Population size  =  104176071
                                     Design df        =       9188
```

		Linearized	
	Mean	Std. Err.	[95% Conf. Interval]
zinc	87.18207	.1828747	86.82359 87.54054

This approach gives us the same point estimate as our design-based analysis, but the reported standard error is less than one-half the design-based standard error. If we accounted only for clustering and weights and ignored stratification in NHANES II, we would obtain the following analysis:

```
. svyset psuid [pweight=finalwgt]
      pweight: finalwgt
          VCE: linearized
  Single unit: missing
     Strata 1: <one>
        SU 1: psuid
       FPC 1: <zero>
```

```
. svy: mean zinc
(running mean on estimation sample)

Survey: Mean estimation

Number of strata =          1      Number of obs     =       9189
Number of PSUs   =          2      Population size   =  104176071
                                   Design df         =          1
```

		Linearized		
	Mean	Std. Err.	[95% Conf. Interval]	
zinc	87.18207	.7426221	77.74616	96.61798

Here our standard error is about 50% larger than what we obtained in our proper design-based analysis.

◁

▷ Example 3

Let's look at a regression. We model zinc on the basis of age, weight, sex, race, and rural or urban residence. We compare a proper design-based analysis with an ordinary regression (which assumes independent and identically distributed error).

Here is our design-based analysis:

```
. svyset psuid [pweight=finalwgt], strata(stratid)

      pweight: finalwgt
          VCE: linearized
  Single unit: missing
      Strata 1: stratid
          SU 1: psuid
         FPC 1: <zero>

. svy: regress zinc age c.age#c.age weight female black orace rural
(running regress on estimation sample)

Survey: Linear regression

Number of strata   =         31      Number of obs     =       9189
Number of PSUs     =         62      Population size   =  104176071
                                     Design df         =         31
                                     F(  7,    25)     =      62.50
                                     Prob > F          =     0.0000
                                     R-squared         =     0.0698
```

zinc	Coef.	Linearized Std. Err.	t	P>|t|	[95% Conf. Interval]	
age	-.1701161	.0844192	-2.02	0.053	-.3422901	.002058
c.age#c.age	.0008744	.0008655	1.01	0.320	-.0008907	.0026396
weight	.0535225	.0139115	3.85	0.001	.0251499	.0818951
female	-6.134161	.4403625	-13.93	0.000	-7.032286	-5.236035
black	-2.881813	1.075958	-2.68	0.012	-5.076244	-.687381
orace	-4.118051	1.621121	-2.54	0.016	-7.424349	-.8117528
rural	-.5386327	.6171836	-0.87	0.390	-1.797387	.7201216
_cons	92.47495	2.228263	41.50	0.000	87.93038	97.01952

If we had improperly ignored our survey weights, stratification, and clustering (i.e., if we had used the usual Stata regress command), we would have obtained the following results:

```
. regress zinc age c.age#c.age weight female black orace rural
```

Source	SS	df	MS
Model	110417.827	7	15773.9753
Residual	1816535.3	9181	197.85811
Total	1926953.13	9188	209.724982

```
Number of obs =    9189
F(  7,  9181) =   79.72
Prob > F      =  0.0000
R-squared     =  0.0573
Adj R-squared =  0.0566
Root MSE      =  14.066
```

zinc	Coef.	Std. Err.	t	P>|t|	[95% Conf. Interval]	
age	-.090298	.0638452	-1.41	0.157	-.2154488	.0348528
c.age#c.age	-.0000324	.0006788	-0.05	0.962	-.0013631	.0012983
weight	.0606481	.0105986	5.72	0.000	.0398725	.0814237
female	-5.021949	.3194705	-15.72	0.000	-5.648182	-4.395716
black	-2.311753	.5073536	-4.56	0.000	-3.306279	-1.317227
orace	-3.390879	1.060981	-3.20	0.001	-5.470637	-1.311121
rural	-.0966462	.3098948	-0.31	0.755	-.7041089	.5108166
_cons	89.49465	1.477528	60.57	0.000	86.59836	92.39093

The point estimates differ by 3%–100%, and the standard errors for the proper designed-based analysis are 30%–110% larger. The differences are not as dramatic as we saw with the estimation of the mean, but they are still substantial.

◁

Saved results

svy saves the following in e():

Scalars

e(N)	number of observations	e(df_r)	variance degrees of freedom
e(N_sub)	subpopulation observations	e(N_pop)	estimate of population size
e(N_strata)	number of strata	e(N_subpop)	estimate of subpopulation size
e(N_strata_omit)	number of strata omitted	e(N_psu)	number of sampled PSUs
e(singleton)	indicates singleton strata	e(k_eq)	number of equations
e(census)	indicates census data	e(k_aux)	number of ancillary parameters
e(F)	model F statistic	e(p)	p-value
e(df_m)	model degrees of freedom	e(rank)	rank of e(V)

Macros

e(prefix)	svy	e(fpc)	fpc() variable
e(cmdname)	command name from *command*	e(fpc#)	FPC for stage #
e(cmd)	same as e(cmdname) or e(vce)	e(title)	title in estimation output
e(command)	*command*	e(poststrata)	poststrata() variable
e(cmdline)	command as typed	e(postweight)	postweight() variable
e(wtype)	weight type	e(vce)	*vcetype* specified in vce()
e(wexp)	weight expression	e(vcetype)	title used to label Std. Err.
e(wvar)	weight variable name	e(mse)	mse, if specified
e(singleunit)	singleunit() setting	e(subpop)	*subpop* from subpop()
e(strata)	strata() variable	e(adjust)	noadjust, if specified
e(strata#)	variable identifying strata for stage #	e(properties)	b V
		e(estat_cmd)	program used to implement estat
e(psu)	psu() variable	e(predict)	program used to implement
e(su#)	variable identifying sampling units for stage #		predict

Matrices

e(b)	estimates
e(V)	design-based variance
e(V_srs)	simple-random-sampling-without-replacement variance, $\widehat{V}_{\mathrm{srswor}}$
e(V_srssub)	subpopulation simple-random-sampling-without-replacement variance, $\widehat{V}_{\mathrm{srswor}}$ (created only when subpop() is specified)
e(V_srswr)	simple-random-sampling-with-replacement variance, $\widehat{V}_{\mathrm{srswr}}$ (created only when fpc() option is svyset)
e(V_srssubwr)	subpopulation simple-random-sampling-with-replacement variance, $\widehat{V}_{\mathrm{srswr}}$ (created only when subpop() is specified)
e(V_modelbased)	model-based variance
e(V_msp)	variance from misspecified model fit, $\widehat{V}_{\mathrm{msp}}$
e(_N_strata_single)	number of strata with one sampling unit
e(_N_strata_certain)	number of certainty strata
e(_N_strata)	number of strata

Functions

e(sample)	marks estimation sample

svy also carries forward most of the results already in e() from *command*.

Methods and formulas

svy is implemented as an ado-file.

See [SVY] **variance estimation** for all the details behind the point estimate and variance calculations made by svy.

References

Korn, E. L., and B. I. Graubard. 1990. Simultaneous testing of regression coefficients with complex survey data: Use of Bonferroni *t* statistics. *American Statistician* 44: 270–276.

McDowell, A., A. Engel, J. T. Massey, and K. Maurer. 1981. Plan and operation of the Second National Health and Nutrition Examination Survey, 1976–1980. *Vital and Health Statistics* 1(15): 1–144.

Also see

[SVY] **svy estimation** — Estimation commands for survey data

[SVY] **svy postestimation** — Postestimation tools for svy

[SVY] **svy brr** — Balanced repeated replication for survey data

[SVY] **svy jackknife** — Jackknife estimation for survey data

[SVY] **svyset** — Declare survey design for dataset

[P] **_robust** — Robust variance estimates

[U] **20 Estimation and postestimation commands**

[SVY] **poststratification** — Poststratification for survey data

[SVY] **subpopulation estimation** — Subpopulation estimation for survey data

[SVY] **variance estimation** — Variance estimation for survey data

[P] **program properties** — Properties of user-defined programs

Title

svy brr — Balanced repeated replication for survey data

Syntax

$\left[\text{svy}\right]$ brr *exp_list* $\left[\,,\ \textit{svy_options}\ \textit{brr_options}\ \textit{eform_option}\right]$: *command*

svy_options	description
if/in	
<u>sub</u>pop($\left[\textit{varname}\right]\left[\textit{if}\right]$)	identify a subpopulation
Reporting	
<u>l</u>evel(#)	set confidence level; default is level(95)
<u>noh</u>eader	suppress table header
<u>nol</u>egend	suppress table legend
<u>noadj</u>ust	do not adjust model Wald statistic
<u>nocns</u>report	do not display constraints
display_options	control spacing and display of omitted variables and base and empty cells
[†]<u>coefl</u>egend	display coefficients' legend instead of coefficient table

[†]<u>coefl</u>egend is not shown in the dialog boxes for estimation commands.

brr_options	description
Main	
<u>had</u>amard(*matrix*)	Hadamard matrix
<u>fay</u>(#)	Fay's adjustment
Options	
<u>sa</u>ving(*filename*$\left[\,,\ \dots\right]$)	save results to *filename*; save statistics in double precision; save results to *filename* every # replications
mse	use MSE formula for variance
Reporting	
<u>v</u>erbose	display the full table legend
<u>nod</u>ots	suppress replication dots
<u>noi</u>sily	display any output from *command*
<u>tr</u>ace	trace the *command*
<u>tit</u>le(*text*)	use *text* as title for BRR results
Advanced	
nodrop	do not drop observations
reject(*exp*)	identify invalid results

svy requires that the survey design variables be identified using svyset; see [SVY] **svyset**.

See [U] **20 Estimation and postestimation commands** for more capabilities of estimation commands.

Warning: Using if or in restrictions will often not produce correct variance estimates for subpopulations. To compute estimates for a subpopulation, use the subpop() option.

exp_list contains	(*name* : *elist*)
	elist
	eexp
elist contains	*newvarname* = (*exp*)
	(*exp*)
eexp is	*specname*
	[*eqno*]*specname*
specname is	_b
	_b[]
	_se
	_se[]
eqno is	# #
	name

exp is a standard Stata expression; see [U] **13 Functions and expressions**.

Distinguish between [ ], which are to be typed, and [ ], which indicate optional arguments.

Menu

Statistics > Survey data analysis > Resampling > Balanced repeated replications estimation

Description

svy brr performs balanced repeated replication (BRR) for complex survey data. Typing

. svy brr *exp_list* : *command*

executes *command* once for each replicate, using sampling weights that are adjusted according to the BRR methodology.

command defines the statistical command to be executed. Most Stata commands and user-written programs can be used with svy brr as long as they follow standard Stata syntax, allow the if qualifier, and allow pweights and iweights; see [U] **11 Language syntax**. The by prefix may not be part of *command*.

exp_list specifies the statistics to be collected from the execution of *command*. *exp_list* is required unless *command* has the svyb program property, in which case *exp_list* defaults to _b; see [P] **program properties**.

Options

svy_options; see [SVY] **svy**.

$\lceil$ Main $\rceil$

hadamard(*matrix*) specifies the Hadamard matrix to be used to determine which PSUs are chosen for each replicate.

fay(#) specifies Fay's adjustment (Judkins 1990). This option overrides the fay(#) option of svyset; see [SVY] **svyset**.

saving(*filename* [, *suboptions*]) creates a Stata data file (.dta file) consisting of, for each statistic in *exp_list*, a variable containing the replicates.

> double specifies that the results for each replication be stored as doubles, meaning 8-byte reals. By default, they are stored as floats, meaning 4-byte reals. This option may be used without the saving() option to compute the variance estimates by using double precision.

> every(*#*) specifies that results be written to disk every #th replication. every() should be specified in conjunction with saving() only when *command* takes a long time for each replication. This will allow recovery of partial results should some other software crash your computer. See [P] **postfile**.

> replace indicates that *filename* be overwritten if it exists. This option is not shown on the dialog box.

mse indicates that svy brr compute the variance by using deviations of the replicates from the observed value of the statistics based on the entire dataset. By default, svy brr computes the variance by using deviations of the replicates from their mean.

verbose requests that the full table legend be displayed. By default, coefficients and standard errors are not displayed.

nodots suppresses display of the replication dots. By default, one dot character is printed for each successful replication. A red 'x' is printed if *command* returns with an error, and 'e' is printed if one of the values in *exp_list* is missing.

noisily requests that any output from *command* be displayed. This option implies the nodots option.

trace causes a trace of the execution of *command* to be displayed. This option implies the noisily option.

title(*text*) specifies a title to be displayed above the table of BRR results; the default title is "BRR results".

nodrop prevents observations outside e(sample) and the if and in qualifiers from being dropped before the data are resampled.

reject(*exp*) identifies an expression that indicates when results should be rejected. When *exp* is true, the resulting values are reset to missing values.

The following option is usually available with svy brr at the time of estimation or on replay but is not shown in the dialog box:

eform_option; see [R] *eform_option*. This option is ignored if *exp_list* is not _b.

Remarks

BRR was first introduced by McCarthy (1966, 1969a, 1969b) as a method of variance estimation for designs with two PSUs in every stratum. The BRR variance estimator tends to give more reasonable variance estimates for this design than the linearized variance estimator, which can result in large values and undesirably wide confidence intervals.

In BRR, the model is fit multiple times, once for each of a balanced set of combinations where one PSU is dropped from each stratum. The variance is estimated using the resulting replicated point estimates. Although the BRR method has since been generalized to include other designs, Stata's implementation of BRR requires two PSUs per stratum.

To protect the privacy of survey participants, public survey datasets may contain replicate-weight variables instead of variables that identify the PSUs and strata. These replicate-weight variables are adjusted copies of the sampling weights. For BRR, the sampling weights are adjusted for dropping one PSU from each stratum; see [SVY] **variance estimation** for more details.

▷ Example 1: BRR replicate-weight variables

The survey design for the NHANES II data (McDowell et al. 1981) is specifically suited to BRR; there are two PSUs in every stratum.

```
. use http://www.stata-press.com/data/r11/nhanes2
. svydescribe
Survey: Describing stage 1 sampling units

      pweight: finalwgt
          VCE: linearized
  Single unit: missing
     Strata 1: strata
         SU 1: psu
        FPC 1: <zero>
```

			#Obs per Unit		
Stratum	#Units	#Obs	min	mean	max
1	2	380	165	190.0	215
2	2	185	67	92.5	118
3	2	348	149	174.0	199
4	2	460	229	230.0	231
5	2	252	105	126.0	147
(output omitted)					
29	2	503	215	251.5	288
30	2	365	166	182.5	199
31	2	308	143	154.0	165
32	2	450	211	225.0	239
31	62	10351	67	167.0	288

Here is a privacy-conscious dataset equivalent to the one above; all the variables and values remain, except `strata` and `psu` are replaced with BRR replicate-weight variables. The BRR replicate-weight variables are already `svyset`, and the default method for variance estimation is `vce(brr)`.

```
. use http://www.stata-press.com/data/r11/nhanes2brr
. svyset
      pweight: finalwgt
          VCE: brr
          MSE: off
    brrweight: brr_1 brr_2 brr_3 brr_4 brr_5 brr_6 brr_7 brr_8 brr_9 brr_10
               brr_11 brr_12 brr_13 brr_14 brr_15 brr_16 brr_17 brr_18 brr_19
               brr_20 brr_21 brr_22 brr_23 brr_24 brr_25 brr_26 brr_27 brr_28
               brr_29 brr_30 brr_31 brr_32
  Single unit: missing
     Strata 1: <one>
         SU 1: <observations>
        FPC 1: <zero>
```

Suppose that we were interested in the population ratio of weight to height. Here we use `total` to estimate the population totals of `weight` and `height` and the `svy brr` prefix to estimate their ratio and variance; we use `total` instead of `ratio` (which is otherwise preferable here) to illustrate how to specify an *exp_list*.

```
. svy brr WtoH = (_b[weight]/_b[height]): total weight height
(running total on estimation sample)

BRR replications (32)
————+— 1 ——+— 2 ——+— 3 ——+— 4 ——+— 5
.............................

BRR results                        Number of obs     =      10351
                                   Population size    =  117157513
                                   Replications       =         32
                                   Design df          =         31

      command: total weight height
         WtoH: _b[weight]/_b[height]
```

		BRR			
	Coef.	Std. Err.	t	P>|t|	[95% Conf. Interval]
WtoH	.4268116	.0008904	479.36	0.000	.4249957 .4286276

The `mse` option causes `svy brr` to use the MSE form of the BRR variance estimator. This variance estimator will tend to be larger than the previous because of the addition of the familiar squared bias term in the MSE; see [SVY] **variance estimation** for more details. The header for the column of standard errors in the table of results is BRR * for the BRR variance estimator using the MSE formula.

```
. svy brr WtoH = (_b[weight]/_b[height]), mse: total weight height
(running total on estimation sample)

BRR replications (32)
————+— 1 ——+— 2 ——+— 3 ——+— 4 ——+— 5
.............................

BRR results                        Number of obs     =      10351
                                   Population size    =  117157513
                                   Replications       =         32
                                   Design df          =         31

      command: total weight height
         WtoH: _b[weight]/_b[height]
```

		BRR *			
	Coef.	Std. Err.	t	P>|t|	[95% Conf. Interval]
WtoH	.4268116	.0008904	479.36	0.000	.4249957 .4286276

The bias term here is too small to see any difference in the standard errors.

◁

▷ Example 2: Survey data without replicate-weight variables

For survey data with the PSU and strata variables but no replication weights, `svy brr` can compute adjusted sampling weights within its replication loop. Here the `hadamard()` option must be supplied with the name of a Stata matrix that is a Hadamard matrix of appropriate order for the number of strata in your dataset (see the following technical note for a quick introduction to Hadamard matrices).

There are 31 strata in nhanes2.dta, so we need a Hadamard matrix of order 32 (or more) to use svy brr with this dataset. Here we use h32 (from the following technical note) to estimate the population ratio of weight to height by using the BRR variance estimator.

```
. use http://www.stata-press.com/data/r11/nhanes2
. svy brr, hadamard(h32): ratio (WtoH: weight/height)
(running ratio on estimation sample)

BRR replications (32)
————+— 1 —+— 2 —+— 3 —+— 4 —+— 5
..............................

Survey: Ratio estimation

Number of strata =       31        Number of obs    =       10351
Number of PSUs   =       62        Population size  =   117157513
                                   Replications     =          32
                                   Design df        =          31

          WtoH: weight/height
```

	Ratio	BRR Std. Err.	[95% Conf. Interval]	
WtoH	.4268116	.0008904	.4249957	.4286276

◁

❏ Technical note

A Hadamard matrix is a square matrix with r rows and columns that has the property

$$H_r' H_r = r I_r$$

where I_r is the identity matrix of order r. Generating a Hadamard matrix with order $r = 2^p$ is easily accomplished. Start with a Hadamard matrix of order 2 (H_2), and build your H_r by repeatedly applying Kronecker products with H_2. Here is the Stata code to generate the Hadamard matrix for the previous example.

```
matrix h2 = (-1, 1 \ 1, 1)
matrix h32 = h2
forvalues i = 1/4 {
        matrix h32 = h2 # h32
}
```

❏

Saved results

In addition to the results documented in [SVY] **svy**, svy brr saves the following in e():

Scalars
e(N_reps)	number of replications
e(fay)	Fay's adjustment

Macros
e(cmdname)	command name from *command*
e(cmd)	same as e(cmdname) or brr
e(vce)	brr
e(brrweight)	brrweight() variable list

Matrices
e(b_brr)	BRR means
e(V)	BRR variance estimates

When *exp_list* is _b, svy brr will also carry forward most of the results already in e() from *command*.

Methods and formulas

svy brr is implemented as an ado-file.

See [SVY] **variance estimation** for details regarding BRR variance estimation.

References

Judkins, D. R. 1990. Fay's method for variance estimation. *Journal of Official Statistics* 6: 223–239.

McCarthy, P. J. 1966. Replication: An approach to the analysis of data from complex surveys. In *Vital and Health Statistics*, series 2. Hyattsville, MD: National Center for Health Statistics.

———. 1969a. Pseudoreplication: Further evaluation and application of the balanced half-sample technique. In *Vital and Health Statistics*, series 2. Hyattsville, MD: National Center for Health Statistics.

———. 1969b. Pseudo-replication: Half-samples. *Revue de l'Institut International de Statistique* 37: 239–264.

McDowell, A., A. Engel, J. T. Massey, and K. Maurer. 1981. Plan and operation of the Second National Health and Nutrition Examination Survey, 1976–1980. *Vital and Health Statistics* 1(15): 1–144.

Also see

[SVY] **svy postestimation** — Postestimation tools for svy

[SVY] **svy jackknife** — Jackknife estimation for survey data

[U] **20 Estimation and postestimation commands**

[SVY] **poststratification** — Poststratification for survey data

[SVY] **subpopulation estimation** — Subpopulation estimation for survey data

[SVY] **variance estimation** — Variance estimation for survey data

Title

svy estimation — Estimation commands for survey data

Description

Survey data analysis in Stata is essentially the same as standard data analysis. The standard syntax applies; you just need to also remember the following:

- Use svyset to identify the survey design characteristics.
- Prefix the estimation commands with "svy:".

For example,

```
. use http://www.stata-press.com/data/r11/nhanes2f
. svyset psuid [pweight=finalwgt], strata(stratid)
. svy: regress zinc age c.age#c.age weight female black orace rural
```

See [SVY] **svyset** and [SVY] **svy**.

The following estimation commands support the svy prefix:

Descriptive statistics

mean	[R] **mean** — Estimate means	
proportion	[R] **proportion** — Estimate proportions	
ratio	[R] **ratio** — Estimate ratios	
total	[R] **total** — Estimate totals	

Linear regression models

cnsreg	[R] **cnsreg** — Constrained linear regression
glm	[R] **glm** — Generalized linear models
intreg	[R] **intreg** — Interval regression
nl	[R] **nl** — Nonlinear least-squares estimation
regress	[R] **regress** — Linear regression
tobit	[R] **tobit** — Tobit regression
treatreg	[R] **treatreg** — Treatment-effects model
truncreg	[R] **truncreg** — Truncated regression

Survival-data regression models

stcox	[ST] **stcox** — Cox proportional hazards model
streg	[ST] **streg** — Parametric survival models

Binary-response regression models

biprobit	[R] **biprobit** — Bivariate probit regression
cloglog	[R] **cloglog** — Complementary log-log regression
hetprob	[R] **hetprob** — Heteroskedastic probit model
logistic	[R] **logistic** — Logistic regression, reporting odds ratios
logit	[R] **logit** — Logistic regression, reporting coefficients
probit	[R] **probit** — Probit regression
scobit	[R] **scobit** — Skewed logistic regression

Discrete-response regression models

clogit	[R] **clogit** — Conditional (fixed-effects) logistic regression
mlogit	[R] **mlogit** — Multinomial (polytomous) logistic regression
mprobit	[R] **mprobit** — Multinomial probit regression
ologit	[R] **ologit** — Ordered logistic regression
oprobit	[R] **oprobit** — Ordered probit regression
slogit	[R] **slogit** — Stereotype logistic regression

Poisson regression models

gnbreg	Generalized negative binomial regression in [R] **nbreg**
nbreg	[R] **nbreg** — Negative binomial regression
poisson	[R] **poisson** — Poisson regression
zinb	[R] **zinb** — Zero-inflated negative binomial regression
zip	[R] **zip** — Zero-inflated Poisson regression
ztnb	[R] **ztnb** — Zero-truncated negative binomial regression
ztp	[R] **ztp** — Zero-truncated Poisson regression

Instrumental-variables regression models

ivprobit	[R] **ivprobit** — Probit model with continuous endogenous regressors
ivregress	[R] **ivregress** — Single-equation instrumental-variables regression
ivtobit	[R] **ivtobit** — Tobit model with continuous endogenous regressors

Regression models with selection

heckman	[R] **heckman** — Heckman selection model
heckprob	[R] **heckprob** — Probit model with sample selection

Menu

Statistics > Survey data analysis > ...

Dialog boxes for all statistical estimators that support svy can be found on the above menu path. In addition, you can access survey data estimation from standard dialog boxes on the **SE/Robust** or **SE/Cluster** tab.

Remarks

Remarks are presented under the following headings:

Overview of survey analysis in Stata
Descriptive statistics
Regression models
Health surveys

Overview of survey analysis in Stata

Many Stata commands estimate the parameters of a process or population by using sample data. For example, `mean` estimates means, `ratio` estimates ratios, `regress` fits linear regression models, `poisson` fits Poisson regression models, and `logistic` fits logistic regression models. Some of these *estimation commands* support the `svy` prefix, that is, they may be prefixed by `svy:` to produce results appropriate for complex survey data. Whereas `poisson` is used with standard, nonsurvey data, `svy: poisson` is used with survey data. In what follows, we refer to any estimation command not prefixed by `svy:` as the standard command. A standard command prefixed by `svy:` is referred to as a `svy` command.

Most standard commands (and all standard commands supported by `svy`) allow `pweights` and the `vce(cluster clustvar)` option, where *varname* corresponds to the PSU variable that you `svyset`. If your survey data exhibit only sampling weights or first-stage clusters (or both), you can get by with using the standard command with `pweights`, `vce(cluster clustvar)`, or both. Your parameter estimates will always be identical to those you would have obtained from the `svy` command, and the standard command uses the same robust (linearization) variance estimator as the `svy` command with a similarly `svyset` design.

Most standard commands are also fit using maximum likelihood. When used with independently distributed, nonweighted data, the likelihood to be maximized reflects the joint probability distribution of the data given the chosen model. With complex survey data, however, this interpretation of the likelihood is no longer valid, because survey data are weighted, not independently distributed, or both. Yet for survey data, (valid) parameter estimates for a given model can be obtained using the associated likelihood function with appropriate weighting. Because the probabilistic interpretation no longer holds, the likelihood here is instead called a *pseudolikelihood*, but likelihood-ratio tests are no longer valid. See Skinner (1989, sec. 3.4.4) for a discussion of maximum pseudolikelihood estimators.

Here we highlight the other features of `svy` commands:

- `svy` commands handle stratified sampling, but none of the standard commands do. Because stratification usually makes standard errors smaller, ignoring stratification is usually conservative. So not using `svy` with stratified sample data is not a terrible thing to do. However, to get the smallest possible "honest" standard-error estimates for stratified sampling, use `svy`.

- `svy` commands use t statistics with $n - L$ degrees of freedom to test the significance of coefficients, where n is the total number of sampled PSUs (clusters) and L is the number of strata in the first stage. Some of the standard commands use t statistics, but most use z statistics. If the standard command uses z statistics for its standard variance estimator, then it also uses z statistics with the robust (linearization) variance estimator. Strictly speaking, t statistics are appropriate with the robust (linearization) variance estimator; see [P] _robust for the theoretical rationale. But, using z rather than t statistics yields a nontrivial difference only when there is a small number of clusters (< 50). If a regression model command uses t statistics and the `vce(cluster clustvar)` option is specified, then the degrees of freedom used is the same as that of the `svy` command (in the absence of stratification).

- svy commands produce an adjusted Wald test for the model test, and `test` can be used to produce adjusted Wald tests for other hypotheses after `svy` commands. Only unadjusted Wald tests are available if the `svy` prefix is not used. The adjustment can be important when the degrees of freedom, $n - L$, is small relative to the dimension of the test. (If the dimension is one, then the adjusted and unadjusted Wald tests are identical.) This fact along with the point made in the second bullet make using the `svy` command important if the number of sampled PSUs (clusters) is small (< 50).

- `svy: regress` differs slightly from `regress` and `svy: ivregress` differs slightly from `ivregress` in that they use different multipliers for the variance estimator. `regress` and `ivregress` (when the `small` option is specified) use a multiplier of $\{(N-1)/(N-k)\}\{n/(n-1)\}$, where N is the number of observations, n is the number of clusters (PSUs), and k is the number of regressors including the constant. `svy: regress` and `svy: ivregress` use $n/(n-1)$ instead. Thus they produce slightly different standard errors. The $(N-1)/(N-k)$ is ad hoc and has no rigorous theoretical justification; hence, the purist `svy` commands do not use it. The `svy` commands tacitly assume that $N \gg k$. If $(N-1)/(N-k)$ is not close to 1, you may be well advised to use `regress` or `ivregress` so that some punishment is inflicted on your variance estimates. Maximum likelihood estimators in Stata (e.g., `logit`) do no such adjustment but rely on the sensibilities of the analyst to ensure that N is reasonably larger than k. Thus the maximum pseudolikelihood estimators (e.g., `svy: logit`) produce the same standard errors as the corresponding maximum likelihood commands (e.g., `logit`), but p-values are slightly different because of the point made in the second bullet.

- svy commands can produce proper estimates for subpopulations by using the `subpop()` option. Using an `if` restriction with `svy` or standard commands can yield incorrect standard-error estimates for subpopulations. Often an `if` restriction will yield the same standard error as `subpop()`; most other times, the two standard errors will be slightly different; but sometimes—usually for thinly sampled subpopulations—the standard errors can be appreciably different. Hence, the `svy` command with the `subpop()` option should be used to obtain estimates for thinly sampled subpopulations. See [SVY] **subpopulation estimation** for more information.

- svy commands handle zero sampling weights properly. Standard commands ignore any observation with a weight of zero. Usually, this will yield the same standard errors, but sometimes they will differ. Sampling weights of zero can arise from various postsampling adjustment procedures. If the sum of weights for one or more PSUs is zero, `svy` and standard commands will produce different standard errors, but usually this difference is very small.

- You can `svyset iweights` and let these weights be negative. Negative sampling weights can arise from various postsampling adjustment procedures. If you want to use negative sampling weights, then you must `svyset iweights` instead of `pweights`; no standard command will allow negative sampling weights.

- The `svy` commands compute finite population corrections (FPCs).

- After a `svy` command, `estat effects` will compute the design effects DEFF and DEFT and the misspecification effects MEFF and MEFT.

- svy commands can perform variance estimation that accounts for multiple stages of clustered sampling.

- svy commands can perform variance estimation that accounts for poststratification adjustments to the sampling weights.

- Some standard options are not allowed with the `svy` prefix. For example, `vce()` and weights cannot be specified when using the `svy` prefix because `svy` is already using the variance estimation and sampling weights identified by `svyset`. Some options are not valid with survey data, such as beta for standardized coefficients and noskip for producing optional likelihood-ratio tests. Other options are not allowed because they change how estimation results are reported (e.g., nodisplay, first, plus) or are not compatible with svy's variance estimation methods (e.g., irls, mse1, hc2, hc3).

- Estimation results are presented in the standard way, except that svy has its own table header: In addition to the sample size, model test, and R^2 (if present in the output from the standard command), svy will also report the following information in the header:

  a. number of strata and PSUs

  b. number of poststrata, if specified to svyset

  c. population size estimate

  d. subpopulation sizes, if the subpop() option was specified

  e. design degrees of freedom

Descriptive statistics

Use svy: mean, svy: ratio, svy: proportion, and svy: total to estimate finite population and subpopulation means, ratios, proportions, and totals, respectively. You can also estimate standardized means, ratios, and proportions for survey data; see [SVY] **direct standardization**. Estimates for multiple subpopulations can be obtained using the over() option; see [SVY] **subpopulation estimation**.

▷ Example 1

Suppose that we need to estimate the average birthweight for the population represented by the National Maternal and Infant Health Survey (NMIHS) (Gonzalez Jr., Krauss, and Scott 1992).

First, we gather the survey design information.

- Primary sampling units are mothers; i.e., PSUs are individual observations—there is no separate PSU variable.

- The finalwgt variable contains the sampling weights.

- The stratan variable identifies strata.

- There is no variable for the finite population correction.

Then we use svyset to identify the variables for sampling weights and stratification.

```
. use http://www.stata-press.com/data/r11/nmihs
. svyset [pweight=finwgt], strata(stratan)
      pweight: finwgt
          VCE: linearized
  Single unit: missing
     Strata 1: stratan
         SU 1: <observations>
        FPC 1: <zero>
```

Now we can use svy: mean to estimate the average birthweight for our population.

```
. svy: mean birthwgt
(running mean on estimation sample)

Survey: Mean estimation

Number of strata =        6        Number of obs    =       9946
Number of PSUs   =     9946        Population size  =    3895562
                                   Design df        =       9940
```

		Linearized		
	Mean	Std. Err.	[95% Conf. Interval]	
birthwgt	3355.452	6.402741	3342.902	3368.003

From these results, we are 95% confident that the mean birthweight for our population is between 3,343 and 3,368 grams.

◁

Regression models

As exhibited in the table at the beginning of this manual entry, many of Stata's regression model commands support the svy prefix. If you know how to use one of these commands with standard data, then you can also use the corresponding svy command with your survey data.

> Example 2

Let's model the incidence of high blood pressure with a dataset from the Second National Health and Nutrition Examination Survey (NHANES II) (McDowell et al. 1981). The survey design characteristics are already svyset, so we will just replay them.

```
. use http://www.stata-press.com/data/r11/nhanes2d
. svyset
      pweight: finalwgt
          VCE: linearized
  Single unit: missing
     Strata 1: strata
        SU 1: psu
       FPC 1: <zero>
```

Now we can use svy: logistic to model the incidence of high blood pressure as a function of height, weight, age, and sex (using the female indicator variable).

```
. svy: logistic highbp height weight age female
(running logistic on estimation sample)

Survey: Logistic regression

Number of strata =       31        Number of obs    =      10351
Number of PSUs   =       62        Population size  =  117157513
                                   Design df        =         31
                                   F(   4,     28)  =     178.69
                                   Prob > F         =     0.0000
```

highbp	Odds Ratio	Linearized Std. Err.	t	P>|t|	[95% Conf. Interval]	
height	.9688567	.0056822	-5.39	0.000	.9573369	.9805151
weight	1.052489	.0032829	16.40	0.000	1.045814	1.059205
age	1.050473	.0024816	20.84	0.000	1.045424	1.055547
female	.7250087	.0641188	-3.64	0.001	.605353	.8683158

The odds ratio for the `female` predictor is 0.73 (rounded to two decimal places) and is significantly less than 1. This finding implies that females have a lower incidence of high blood pressure than do males.

Here we use the `subpop()` option to model the incidence of high blood pressure in the subpopulation identified by the `female` variable.

```
. svy, subpop(female): logistic highbp height weight age
(running logistic on estimation sample)

Survey: Logistic regression

Number of strata   =       31              Number of obs     =       10351
Number of PSUs     =       62              Population size    =   117157513
                                           Subpop. no. of obs =        5436
                                           Subpop. size      =    60998033
                                           Design df         =          31
                                           F(   3,     29)   =      137.04
                                           Prob > F          =      0.0000
```

highbp	Odds Ratio	Linearized Std. Err.	t	P>|t|	[95% Conf. Interval]	
height	.9765379	.0092444	-2.51	0.018	.9578647	.9955752
weight	1.047845	.0044668	10.96	0.000	1.038774	1.056994
age	1.058105	.0035411	16.88	0.000	1.050907	1.065352

Because the odds ratio for the `age` predictor is significantly greater than 1, we can conclude that older females are more likely to have high blood pressure than are younger females.

◁

Health surveys

There are many sources of bias when modeling the association between a disease and its risk factors (Korn, Graubard, and Midthune 1997; Korn and Graubard 1999, sec. 3.7). In cross-sectional health surveys, inference is typically restricted to the target population as it stood when the data were collected. This type of survey cannot capture the fact that participants may change their habits over time. Some health surveys collect data retrospectively, relying on the participants to recall the status of risk factors as they stood in the past. This type of survey is vulnerable to recall bias.

Longitudinal surveys collect data over time, monitoring the survey participants over several years. Although the above biases are minimized, analysts are still faced with some tough choices/situations when modeling time-to-event data. For example:

- Time scale. When studying cancer, should we measure the time scale by using the participant's age or the initial date from which data were collected?

- Time-varying covariates. Were all relevant risk factors sampled over time, or do we have only the baseline measurement?

- Competing risks. When studying mortality, do we have the data specific to cause of death?

Binder (1983) provides the foundation for fitting most of the common parametric models by using survey data. Similarly, Lin and Wei (1989) provide the foundational theory for robust inference by using the proportional hazards model. Binder (1992) describes how to estimate standard errors for the proportional hazards model from survey data, and Lin (2000) provides a rigorous justification for Binder's method. Korn and Graubard (1999) discuss many aspects of model fitting by using data from health surveys. O'Donnell et al. (2008, chap. 10) use Stata survey commands to perform multivariate analysis using health survey data.

▷ Example 3: Cox's proportional hazards model

Suppose that we want to model the incidence of lung cancer by using three risk factors: smoking status, sex, and place of residence. Our dataset comes from a longitudinal health survey: the First National Health and Nutrition Examination Survey (NHANES I) (Miller 1973; Engel et al. 1978) and its 1992 Epidemiologic Follow-up Study (NHEFS) (Cox et al. 1997); see the National Center for Health Statistics web site at http://www.cdc.gov/nchs/. We will be using data from the samples identified by NHANES I examination locations 1–65 and 66–100; thus we will svyset the revised pseudo-PSU and strata variables associated with these locations. Similarly, our pweight variable was generated using the sampling weights for the nutrition and detailed samples for locations 1–65 and the weights for the detailed sample for locations 66–100.

```
. use http://www.stata-press.com/data/r11/nhefs
. svyset psu2 [pw=swgt2], strata(strata2)
      pweight: swgt2
          VCE: linearized
  Single unit: missing
     Strata 1: strata2
         SU 1: psu2
        FPC 1: <zero>
```

The lung cancer information was taken from the 1992 NHEFS interview data. We use the participants' ages for the time scale. Participants who never had lung cancer and were alive for the 1992 interview were considered censored. Participants who never had lung cancer and died before the 1992 interview were also considered censored at their age of death.

```
. stset age_lung_cancer [pw=swgt2], fail(lung_cancer)
      failure event:  lung_cancer != 0 & lung_cancer < .
 obs. time interval:  (0, age_lung_cancer]
 exit on or before:  failure
             weight:  [pweight=swgt2]
```

14407	total obs.	
5126	event time missing (age_lung_cancer>=.)	PROBABLE ERROR
9281	obs. remaining, representing	
83	failures in single record/single failure data	
599691	total analysis time at risk, at risk from t =	0
	earliest observed entry t =	0
	last observed exit t =	97

Although stset warns us that it is a "probable error" to have 5,126 observations with missing event times, we can verify from the 1992 NHEFS documentation that there were indeed 9,281 participants with complete information.

For our proportional hazards model, we pulled the risk factor information from the NHANES I and 1992 NHEFS datasets. Smoking status was taken from the 1992 NHEFS interview data, but we filled in all but 132 missing values by using the general medical history supplement data in NHANES I. Smoking status is represented by separate indicator variables for former smokers and current smokers; the base comparison group is nonsmokers. Sex was determined using the 1992 NHEFS vitality data and is represented by an indicator variable for males. Place-of-residence information was taken from the medical history questionnaire in NHANES I and is represented by separate indicator variables for rural and heavily populated (more than 1 million people) urban residences; the base comparison group is urban residences with populations of fewer than 1 million people.

```
. svy: stcox former_smoker smoker male urban1 rural
(running stcox on estimation sample)

Survey: Cox regression

Number of strata   =        35          Number of obs    =       9149
Number of PSUs     =       105          Population size  =  151327827
                                        Design df        =         70
                                        F(  5,     66)   =      14.07
                                        Prob > F         =     0.0000
```

_t	Haz. Ratio	Linearized Std. Err.	t	P>|t|	[95% Conf. Interval]	
former_smo~r	2.788113	.6205102	4.61	0.000	1.788705	4.345923
smoker	7.849483	2.593249	6.24	0.000	4.061457	15.17051
male	1.187611	.3445315	0.59	0.555	.6658757	2.118142
urban1	.8035074	.3285144	-0.54	0.594	.3555123	1.816039
rural	1.581674	.5281859	1.37	0.174	.8125799	3.078702

From the above results, we can see that both former and current smokers have a significantly higher risk for developing lung cancer than do nonsmokers.

◁

❑ Technical note

In the previous example, we specified a sampling weight variable in the calls to both svyset and stset. When the svy prefix is used with stcox and streg, it identifies the sampling weight variable by using the data characteristics from both svyset and stset. svy will report an error if the svyset pweight variable is different from the stset pweight variable. The svy prefix will use the specified pweight variable, even if it is svyset but not stset. If a pweight variable is stset but not svyset, svy will note that it will be using the stset pweight variable and then svyset it.

The standard st commands will not use the svyset pweight variable if it is not also stset.

❑

▷ Example 4: Multiple baseline hazards

We can assess the proportional-hazards assumption across the observed race categories for the model fit in the previous example. The race information in our 1992 NHEFS dataset is contained in the revised_race variable. We will use stphplot to produce a log-log plot for each category of revised_race. As described in [ST] **stcox PH-assumption tests**, if the plotted lines are reasonably parallel, the proportional-hazards assumption has not been violated. We will use the zero option to reset the risk factors to their base comparison group.

```
. stphplot, strata(revised_race) adjust(former_smoker smoker male urban1 rural)
> zero legend(col(1))

          failure _d:  lung_cancer
    analysis time _t:  age_lung_cancer
              weight:  [pweight=swgt2]
```

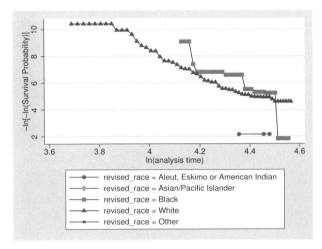

As we can see from the graph produced above, the lines for the black and white race categories intersect. This indicates a violation of the proportional-hazards assumption, so we should consider using separate baseline hazard functions for each race category in our model fit. We do this next, by specifying strata(revised_race) in our call to svy: stcox.

```
. svy: stcox former_smoker smoker male urban1 rural, strata(revised_race)
(running stcox on estimation sample)

Survey: Cox regression

Number of strata   =        35          Number of obs     =        9149
Number of PSUs     =       105          Population size    =   151327827
                                        Design df          =          70
                                        F(   5,     66)    =       13.95
                                        Prob > F           =      0.0000
```

_t	Haz. Ratio	Linearized Std. Err.	t	P>|t|	[95% Conf. Interval]	
former_smo~r	2.801797	.6280352	4.60	0.000	1.791761	4.381201
smoker	7.954921	2.640022	6.25	0.000	4.103709	15.42038
male	1.165724	.3390339	0.53	0.600	.6526527	2.082139
urban1	.784031	.3120525	-0.61	0.543	.3544764	1.73412
rural	1.490269	.5048569	1.18	0.243	.7582848	2.928851

Stratified by revised_race

◁

References

Binder, D. A. 1983. On the variances of asymptotically normal estimators from complex surveys. *International Statistical Review* 51: 279–292.

——. 1992. Fitting Cox's proportional hazards models for survey data. *Biometrika* 79: 139–147.

Cox, C. S., M. E. Mussolino, S. T. Rothwell, M. A. Lane, C. D. Golden, J. H. Madans, and J. J. Feldman. 1997. Plan and operation of the NHANES I Epidemiologic Followup Study, 1992. In *Vital and Health Statistics*, vol. 1. Hyattsville, MD: National Center for Health Statistics.

Engel, A., R. S. Murphy, K. Maurer, and E. Collins. 1978. Plan and operation of the HANES I augmentation survey of adults 25–74 years. In *Vital and Health Statistics*, vol. 1. Hyattsville, MD: National Center for Health Statistics.

Gonzalez Jr., J. F., N. Krauss, and C. Scott. 1992. Estimation in the 1988 National Maternal and Infant Health Survey. *Proceedings of the Section on Statistics Education, American Statistical Association* 343–348.

Korn, E. L., and B. I. Graubard. 1999. *Analysis of Health Surveys*. New York: Wiley.

Korn, E. L., B. I. Graubard, and D. Midthune. 1997. Time-to-event analysis of longitudinal follow-up of a survey: Choice of time-scale. *American Journal of Epidemiology* 145: 72–80.

Lin, D. Y. 2000. On fitting Cox's proportional hazards models to survey data. *Biometrika* 87: 37–47.

Lin, D. Y., and L. J. Wei. 1989. The robust inference for the Cox proportional hazards model. *Journal of the American Statistical Association* 84: 1074–1078.

McDowell, A., A. Engel, J. T. Massey, and K. Maurer. 1981. Plan and operation of the Second National Health and Nutrition Examination Survey, 1976–1980. *Vital and Health Statistics* 1(15): 1–144.

Miller, H. W. 1973. Plan and operation of the Health and Nutrition Examination Survey: United States 1971–1973. *Vital and Health Statistics* 1(10a): 1–46.

O'Donnell, O., E. van Doorslaer, A. Wagstaff, and M. Lindelow. 2008. *Analyzing Health Equity Using Household Survey Data: A Guide to Techniques and Their Implementation*. Washington, DC: The World Bank.

Skinner, C. J. 1989. Introduction to part A. In *Analysis of Complex Surveys*, ed. C. J. Skinner, D. Holt, and T. M. F. Smith, 23–58. New York: Wiley.

Also see

[SVY] **svy postestimation** — Postestimation tools for svy

[SVY] **estat** — Postestimation statistics for survey data

[SVY] **direct standardization** — Direct standardization of means, proportions, and ratios

[SVY] **poststratification** — Poststratification for survey data

[SVY] **subpopulation estimation** — Subpopulation estimation for survey data

[SVY] **variance estimation** — Variance estimation for survey data

[U] **20 Estimation and postestimation commands**

[SVY] **svyset** — Declare survey design for dataset

[SVY] **svy** — The survey prefix command

Title

svy jackknife — Jackknife estimation for survey data

Syntax

svy jackknife *exp_list* $\big[$, *svy_options jackknife_options eform_option* $\big]$: *command*

svy_options	description
if/in	
<u>sub</u>pop($\big[$ *varname* $\big]$ $\big[$ *if* $\big]$)	identify a subpopulation
Reporting	
<u>l</u>evel(#)	set confidence level; default is level(95)
<u>noh</u>eader	suppress table header
<u>nol</u>egend	suppress table legend
<u>noadj</u>ust	do not adjust model Wald statistic
<u>nocnsr</u>eport	do not display constraints
display_options	control spacing and display of omitted variables and base and empty cells
† coeflegend	display coefficients' legend instead of coefficient table

† coeflegend is not shown in the dialog boxes for estimation commands.

jackknife_options	description
Main	
<u>e</u>class	number of observations is in e(N)
<u>r</u>class	number of observations is in r(N)
n(*exp*)	specify *exp* that evaluates to number of observations used
Options	
<u>sa</u>ving(*filename*$\big[$, ... $\big]$)	save results to *filename*; save statistics in double precision; save results to *filename* every # replications
keep	keep pseudovalues
mse	use MSE formula for variance
Reporting	
<u>v</u>erbose	display the full table legend
nodots	suppress replication dots
<u>noi</u>sily	display any output from *command*
<u>trace</u>	trace the *command*
<u>tit</u>le(*text*)	use *text* as title for jackknife results
Advanced	
nodrop	do not drop observations
reject(*exp*)	identify invalid results

svy requires that the survey design variables be identified using svyset; see [SVY] **svyset**.

See [U] **20 Estimation and postestimation commands** for more capabilities of estimation commands.

Warning: Using if or in restrictions will often not produce correct variance estimates for subpopulations. To compute estimates for a subpopulation, use the subpop() option.

exp_list contains	(*name*: *elist*)
	elist
	eexp
elist contains	*newvarname* = (*exp*)
	(*exp*)
eexp is	*specname*
	[*eqno*]*specname*
specname is	_b
	_b[]
	_se
	_se[]
eqno is	# #
	name

exp is a standard Stata expression; see [U] **13 Functions and expressions**.

Distinguish between [], which are to be typed, and [ ], which indicate optional arguments.

Menu

Statistics > Survey data analysis > Resampling > Jackknife estimation

Description

svy jackknife performs jackknife estimation for complex survey data. Typing

> . svy jackknife *exp_list*: *command*

executes *command* once for each primary sampling unit (PSU) in the dataset, leaving the associated PSU out of the calculations that make up *exp_list*.

command defines the statistical command to be executed. Most Stata commands and user-written programs can be used with svy jackknife as long as they follow standard Stata syntax, allow the if qualifier, and allow pweights and iweights; see [U] **11 Language syntax**. The by prefix may not be part of *command*.

exp_list specifies the statistics to be collected from the execution of *command*. *exp_list* is required unless *command* has the svyj program property, in which case *exp_list* defaults to _b; see [P] **program properties**.

Options

svy_options; see [SVY] **svy**.

⌐ Main ⌐

eclass, rclass, and n(*exp*) specify where *command* saves the number of observations on which it based the calculated results. We strongly advise you to specify one of these options.

eclass specifies that *command* save the number of observations in e(N).

rclass specifies that *command* save the number of observations in r(N).

n(*exp*) allows you to specify an expression that evaluates to the number of observations used. Specifying n(r(N)) is equivalent to specifying the rclass option. Specifying n(e(N)) is equivalent to specifying the eclass option. If *command* saves the number of observations in r(N1), specify n(r(N1)).

If you specify none of these options, svy jackknife will assume eclass or rclass depending upon which of e(N) and r(N) is not missing (in that order). If both e(N) and r(N) are missing, svy jackknife assumes that all observations in the dataset contribute to the calculated result. If that assumption is incorrect, then the reported standard errors will be incorrect. For instance, say that you specify

        . svy jackknife coef=_b[x2]: myreg y x1 x2 x3

where myreg uses e(n) instead of e(N) to identify the number of observations used in calculations. Further assume that observation 42 in the dataset has x3 equal to missing. The 42nd observation plays no role in obtaining the estimates, but svy jackknife has no way of knowing that and will use the wrong N. If, on the other hand, you specify

        . svy jackknife coef=_b[x2], n(e(n)): myreg y x1 x2 x3

Then svy jackknife will notice that observation 42 plays no role. The n(e(n)) option is specified because myreg is an estimation command, but it saves the number of observations used in e(n) (instead of the standard e(N)). When svy jackknife runs the regression omitting the 42nd observation, svy jackknife will observe that e(n) has the same value as when svy jackknife previously ran the regression by using all the observations. Thus svy jackknife will know that myreg did not use the observation.

⌐ Options ⌐

saving(*filename*[, *suboptions*]) creates a Stata data file (.dta file) consisting of, for each statistic in *exp_list*, a variable containing the jackknife replicates.

double specifies that the results for each replication be stored as doubles, meaning 8-byte reals. By default, they are stored as floats, meaning 4-byte reals. This option may be used without the saving() option to compute the variance estimates by using double precision.

every(#) specifies that results be written to disk every #th replication. every() should be specified in conjunction with saving() only when *command* takes a long time for each replication. This will allow recovery of partial results should some other software crash your computer. See [P] **postfile**.

replace indicates that *filename* be overwritten if it exists. This option is not shown in the dialog box.

keep specifies that new variables be added to the dataset containing the pseudovalues of the requested statistics. For instance, if you typed

        . svy jackknife coef=_b[x2], eclass keep: regress y x1 x2 x3

Then the new variable coef would be added to the dataset containing the pseudovalues for _b[x2]. Let b be defined as the value of _b[x2] when all observations are used to fit the model, and let $b(j)$ be the value when the jth observation is omitted. The pseudovalues are defined as

$$\text{pseudovalue}_j = N \times \{b - b(j)\} + b(j)$$

where N is the number of observations used to produce b.

keep implies the nodrop option.

mse specifies that svy jackknife compute the variance by using deviations of the replicates from the observed value of the statistics based on the entire dataset. By default, svy jackknife computes the variance by using deviations of the pseudovalues from their mean.

⌐ Reporting ⌐

verbose requests that the full table legend be displayed. By default, coefficients and standard errors are not displayed.

nodots suppresses display of the replication dots. By default, one dot character is printed for each successful replication. A red 'x' is printed if *command* returns with an error, 'e' is printed if one of the values in *exp_list* is missing, and 'n' is printed if the sample size is not correct.

noisily requests that any output from *command* be displayed. This option implies the nodots option.

trace causes a trace of the execution of *command* to be displayed. This option implies the noisily option.

title(*text*) specifies a title to be displayed above the table of jackknife results; the default title is "Jackknife results".

⌐ Advanced ⌐

nodrop prevents observations outside e(sample) and the if and in options from being dropped before the data are resampled.

reject(*exp*) identifies an expression that indicates when results should be rejected. When *exp* is true, the resulting values are reset to missing values.

The following option is usually available with svy jackknife at the time of estimation or on replay but is not shown in the dialog box:

eform_option; see [R] ***eform_option***. This option is ignored if *exp_list* is not _b.

Remarks

The jackknife is

- an alternative, first-order unbiased estimator for a statistic;

- a data-dependent way to calculate the standard error of the statistic and to obtain significance levels and confidence intervals; and

- a way of producing measures called pseudovalues for each observation, reflecting the observation's influence on the overall statistic.

The idea behind the simplest form of the jackknife—the one implemented in [R] **jackknife**—is to repeatedly calculate the statistic in question, each time omitting just one of the dataset's observations. Assume that our statistic of interest is the sample mean. Let y_j be the jth observation of our data on some measurement y, where $j = 1, \ldots, N$ and N is the sample size. If $\overline{y}$ is the sample mean of y using the entire dataset and $\overline{y}_{(j)}$ is the mean when the jth observation is omitted, then

$$\overline{y} = \frac{(N-1)\,\overline{y}_{(j)} + y_j}{N}$$

Solving for y_j, we obtain

$$y_j = N\,\overline{y} - (N-1)\,\overline{y}_{(j)}$$

These are the pseudovalues that `svy: jackknife` calculates. To move this discussion beyond the sample mean, let $\widehat{\theta}$ be the value of our statistic (not necessarily the sample mean) using the entire dataset, and let $\widehat{\theta}_{(j)}$ be the computed value of our statistic with the jth observation omitted. The pseudovalue for the jth observation is

$$\widehat{\theta}_j^* = N\,\widehat{\theta} - (N-1)\,\widehat{\theta}_{(j)}$$

The mean of the pseudovalues is the alternative, first-order unbiased estimator mentioned above, and the standard error of the mean of the pseudovalues is an estimator for the standard error of $\widehat{\theta}$ (Tukey 1958, Shao and Tu 1995).

When the jackknife is applied to survey data, PSUs are omitted instead of observations, N is the number of PSUs instead of the sample size, and the sampling weights are adjusted owing to omitting PSUs; see [SVY] **variance estimation** for more details.

Because of privacy concerns, many public survey datasets contain jackknife replication-weight variables instead of variables containing information on the PSUs and strata. These replication-weight variables are the adjusted sampling weights, and there is one replication-weight variable for each omitted PSU.

▷ Example 1: Jackknife with information on PSUs and strata

Suppose that we were interested in a measure of association between the weight and height of individuals in the population represented by the NHANES II data (McDowell et al. 1981). To measure the association, we will use the slope estimate from a linear regression of `weight` on `height`. We also use `svy jackknife` to estimate the variance of the slope.

(Continued on next page) .

```
. use http://www.stata-press.com/data/r11/nhanes2

. svyset
      pweight: finalwgt
          VCE: linearized
  Single unit: missing
      Strata 1: strata
          SU 1: psu
         FPC 1: <zero>

. svy jackknife slope = _b[height]: regress weight height
(running regress on estimation sample)
Jackknife replications (62)
————+— 1 —+— 2 —+— 3 —+— 4 —+— 5
..................................................    50
...........

Linear regression

Number of strata   =         31          Number of obs    =      10351
Number of PSUs     =         62          Population size  =  117157513
                                         Replications     =         62
                                         Design df        =         31

      command:  regress weight height
        slope:  _b[height]
          n():  e(N)
```

		Jackknife			
	Coef.	Std. Err.	t	P>|t|	[95% Conf. Interval]
slope	.8014753	.0160281	50.00	0.000	.7687858 .8341648

◁

▷ Example 2: Jackknife replicate-weight variables

nhanes2jknife.dta is a privacy-conscious dataset equivalent to nhanes2.dta; all the variables and values remain, except that strata and psu are replaced with jackknife replicate-weight variables. The replicate-weight variables are already svyset, and the default method for variance estimation is vce(jackknife).

```
. use http://www.stata-press.com/data/r11/nhanes2jknife

. svyset
      pweight: finalwgt
          VCE: jackknife
          MSE: off
    jkrweight: jkw_1 jkw_2 jkw_3 jkw_4 jkw_5 jkw_6 jkw_7 jkw_8 jkw_9 jkw_10
               jkw_11 jkw_12 jkw_13 jkw_14 jkw_15 jkw_16 jkw_17 jkw_18 jkw_19
               jkw_20 jkw_21 jkw_22 jkw_23 jkw_24 jkw_25 jkw_26 jkw_27 jkw_28
               jkw_29 jkw_30 jkw_31 jkw_32 jkw_33 jkw_34 jkw_35 jkw_36 jkw_37
               jkw_38 jkw_39 jkw_40 jkw_41 jkw_42 jkw_43 jkw_44 jkw_45 jkw_46
               jkw_47 jkw_48 jkw_49 jkw_50 jkw_51 jkw_52 jkw_53 jkw_54 jkw_55
               jkw_56 jkw_57 jkw_58 jkw_59 jkw_60 jkw_61 jkw_62
  Single unit: missing
      Strata 1: <one>
          SU 1: <observations>
         FPC 1: <zero>
```

Here we perform the same analysis as in the previous example, using jackknife replication weights.

```
. svy jackknife slope = _b[height], nodots: regress weight height

Linear regression

Number of strata   =        31              Number of obs    =        10351
                                            Population size   =    117157513
                                            Replications      =           62
                                            Design df         =           31

        command:  regress weight height
          slope:  _b[height]
```

	Coef.	Jackknife Std. Err.	t	P>|t|	[95% Conf. Interval]
slope	.8014753	.0160281	50.00	0.000	.7687858 .8341648

The `mse` option causes `svy jackknife` to use the MSE form of the jackknife variance estimator. This variance estimator will tend to be larger than the previous because of the addition of the familiar squared bias term in the MSE; see [SVY] **variance estimation** for more details. The header for the column of standard errors in the table of results is `Jknife *` for the jackknife variance estimator, which uses the MSE formula.

```
. svy jackknife slope = _b[height], mse nodots: regress weight height

Linear regression

Number of strata   =        31              Number of obs    =        10351
                                            Population size   =    117157513
                                            Replications      =           62
                                            Design df         =           31

        command:  regress weight height
          slope:  _b[height]
```

	Coef.	Jknife * Std. Err.	t	P>|t|	[95% Conf. Interval]
slope	.8014753	.0160284	50.00	0.000	.7687852 .8341654

◁

(Continued on next page)

Saved results

In addition to the results documented in [SVY] **svy**, svy jackknife saves the following in e():

Scalars
e(N_reps)	number of replications
e(N_misreps)	number of replications with missing values
e(k_exp)	number of standard expressions
e(k_eexp)	number of _b/_se expressions
e(k_extra)	number of extra estimates added to _b

Macros
e(cmdname)	command name from *command*
e(cmd)	same as e(cmdname) or jackknife
e(vce)	jackknife
e(exp#)	#th expression
e(jkrweight)	jkrweight() variable list

Matrices
e(b_jk)	jackknife means
e(V)	jackknife variance estimates

When *exp_list* is _b, svy jackknife will also carry forward most of the results already in e() from *command*.

Methods and formulas

svy jackknife is implemented as an ado-file.

See [SVY] **variance estimation** for details on the jackknife variance estimator.

References

McDowell, A., A. Engel, J. T. Massey, and K. Maurer. 1981. Plan and operation of the Second National Health and Nutrition Examination Survey, 1976–1980. *Vital and Health Statistics* 1(15): 1–144.

Shao, J., and D. Tu. 1995. *The Jackknife and Bootstrap*. New York: Springer.

Tukey, J. W. 1958. Bias and confidence in not-quite large samples. Abstract in *Annals of Mathematical Statistics* 29: 614.

Also see

[SVY] **svy postestimation** — Postestimation tools for svy

[R] **jackknife** — Jackknife estimation

[SVY] **svy brr** — Balanced repeated replication for survey data

[U] **20 Estimation and postestimation commands**

[SVY] **poststratification** — Poststratification for survey data

[SVY] **subpopulation estimation** — Subpopulation estimation for survey data

[SVY] **variance estimation** — Variance estimation for survey data

Title

> **svy postestimation** — Postestimation tools for svy

Description

The following postestimation commands are available for svy:

command	description
estat (svy)	postestimation statistics for survey data
estimates	cataloging estimation results
lincom	point estimates, standard errors, testing, and inference for linear combinations of coefficients
margins	marginal means, predictive margins, marginal effects, and average marginal effects
nlcom	point estimates, standard errors, testing, and inference for nonlinear combinations of coefficients
predict	predictions, residuals, influence statistics, and other diagnostic measures
predictnl	point estimates, standard errors, testing, and inference for generalized predictions
suest	seemingly unrelated estimation
test	Wald tests of simple and composite linear hypotheses
testnl	Wald tests of nonlinear hypotheses

See [SVY] **estat**.

See the corresponding entries in the *Stata Base Reference Manual* for details.

Syntax for predict

The syntax of predict (and even if predict is allowed) after svy depends on the command used with svy. Specifically, predict is not allowed after svy: mean, svy: proportion, svy: ratio, svy: tabulate, or svy: total.

Remarks

What follows are some examples of applications of postestimation commands using survey data. The examples are meant only to introduce the commands in a survey context and explore a few of the possibilities for postestimation analysis. See the individual entries for each command in the *Base Reference Manual* for complete syntax and many more examples.

▷ Example 1: Linear and nonlinear combinations

lincom will display an estimate of a linear combination of parameters, along with its standard error, a confidence interval, and a test that the linear combination is zero. nlcom will do likewise for nonlinear combinations of parameters.

lincom is commonly used to compute the differences of two subpopulation means. For example, suppose that we wish to estimate the difference of zinc levels in white males versus black males in the population represented by the NHANES II data (McDowell et al. 1981). Because the survey design characteristics are already svyset in nhanes2.dta, we only need to generate a variable for identifying the male subpopulation before using svy: mean.

```
. use http://www.stata-press.com/data/r11/nhanes2

. generate male = (sex == 1)

. svy, subpop(male): mean zinc, over(race)
(running mean on estimation sample)
```

Survey: Mean estimation

Number of strata =	31	Number of obs	=	9811
Number of PSUs =	62	Population size	=	111127314
		Subpop. no. obs	=	4375
		Subpop. size	=	50129281
		Design df	=	31

```
                   White: race = White
                   Black: race = Black
                   Other: race = Other
```

		Linearized		
Over	Mean	Std. Err.	[95% Conf. Interval]	
zinc				
White	91.15725	.541625	90.0526	92.2619
Black	88.269	1.208336	85.80458	90.73342
Other	85.54716	2.608974	80.22612	90.8682

Then we run `lincom` to estimate the difference of zinc levels between the two subpopulations.

```
. lincom [zinc]White - [zinc]Black
 ( 1)  [zinc]White - [zinc]Black = 0
```

Mean	Coef.	Std. Err.	t	P>|t|	[95% Conf. Interval]	
(1)	2.888249	1.103999	2.62	0.014	.6366288	5.139868

The t statistic and its p-value give a survey analysis equivalent of a two-sample t test.

`lincom` and `nlcom` can be used after any of the estimation commands described in [SVY] **svy estimation**. `lincom` can, for example, display results as odds ratios after svy: `logit` and can be used to compute odds ratios for one covariate group relative to another. `nlcom` can display odds ratios, as well, and allows more general nonlinear combinations of the parameters. See [R] **lincom** and [R] **nlcom** for full details. Also see Eltinge and Sribney (1996) for an earlier implementation of `lincom` for survey data.

Finally, `lincom` and `nlcom` operate on the estimated parameters only. To obtain estimates and inference for functions of the parameters and of the data, such as for an exponentiated linear predictor or a predicted probability of success from a logit model, use `predictnl`; see [R] **predictnl**.

◁

▷ Example 2: Quadratic terms

From example 2 in [SVY] **svy estimation**, we modeled the incidence of high blood pressure as a function of height, weight, age, and sex (using the female indicator variable). Here we also include c.age#c.age, a squared term for age.

```
. use http://www.stata-press.com/data/r11/nhanes2d, clear
. svy: logistic highbp height weight age c.age#c.age female
(running logistic on estimation sample)
Survey: Logistic regression
```

```
Number of strata    =        31          Number of obs    =        10351
Number of PSUs      =        62          Population size  =    117157513
                                         Design df        =           31
                                         F(  5,    27)    =       108.92
                                         Prob > F         =       0.0000
```

highbp	Odds Ratio	Linearized Std. Err.	t	P>|t|	[95% Conf. Interval]	
height	.967517	.0057521	-5.55	0.000	.9558564	.9793199
weight	1.051088	.0034035	15.39	0.000	1.044169	1.058052
age	1.165921	.0242516	7.38	0.000	1.117494	1.216447
c.age#c.age	.9989282	.0002015	-5.32	0.000	.9985173	.9993392
female	.7091193	.0634648	-3.84	0.001	.590808	.8511227

Because our model includes a quadratic in the age variable, the peak incidence of high blood pressure with respect to age will occur at $-\_b[age]/(2*\_b[c.age\#c.age])$, which we can estimate, along with its standard error, using nlcom.

```
. nlcom peak: -_b[age]/(2*_b[c.age#c.age])
       peak:  -_b[age]/(2*_b[c.age#c.age])
```

highbp	Coef.	Std. Err.	t	P>|t|	[95% Conf. Interval]	
peak	71.57263	4.022564	17.79	0.000	63.36856	79.77671

Or we can use testnl to test that the peak incidence of high blood pressure in the population is 70 years.

```
. testnl -_b[age]/(2*_b[c.age#c.age]) = 70
  (1)  -_b[age]/(2*_b[c.age#c.age]) = 70
            F(1, 31) =        0.15
            Prob > F =        0.6985
```

These data do not reject our theory. testnl allows multiple hypotheses to be tested jointly and applies the degrees-of-freedom adjustment for survey results; see [R] **testnl**.

◁

▷ Example 3: Predictive margins

Changing our logistic regression for high blood pressure slightly, we add a factor variable for the levels of race. Level 1 of race represents whites, level 2 represents blacks, and level 3 represents others. We also specify that female is a factor variable, which does not change its coefficient but does increase its functionality with some postestimation commands.

```
. svy: logistic highbp height weight age c.age#c.age i.female i.race, baselevels
(running logistic on estimation sample)
Survey: Logistic regression

Number of strata   =       31          Number of obs    =      10351
Number of PSUs     =       62          Population size  =  117157513
                                       Design df        =         31
                                       F(   7,      25) =      72.33
                                       Prob > F         =     0.0000
```

highbp	Odds Ratio	Linearized Std. Err.	t	P>|t|	[95% Conf. Interval]	
height	.9683005	.0056137	−5.56	0.000	.9569187	.9798177
weight	1.050374	.0033535	15.39	0.000	1.043557	1.057236
age	1.166568	.0242898	7.40	0.000	1.118066	1.217174
c.age#c.age	.9989275	.0002008	−5.34	0.000	.9985182	.9993371
female						
0	(base)					
1	.7044769	.060717	−4.06	0.000	.5909168	.8398605
race						
1	(base)					
2	1.413595	.2000043	2.45	0.020	1.059262	1.886454
3	1.162631	.5057044	0.35	0.731	.478819	2.82301

Our point estimates indicate that the odds of females having high blood pressure is about 70% of the odds for men and that the odds of blacks having high blood pressure is about 1.4 times that of whites. The odds ratios give us the relative effects of their covariates, but they do not give us any sense of the absolute size of the effects. The odds ratio comparing blacks with whites is clearly large and statistically significant, but does it represent a sizable change? One way to answer that question is to explore the probabilities of high blood pressure from our fitted model. Let's first look at the predictive margins of the probability of high blood pressure for the three levels of race.

```
. margins race, vce(svy)
Predictive margins                     Number of obs    =      10351
Expression   : Pr(highbp), predict()
```

	Margin	Linearized Std. Err.	t	P>|t|	[95% Conf. Interval]	
race						
1	.1024922	.0068574	14.95	0.000	.0885065	.1164779
2	.1337316	.0143502	9.32	0.000	.1044642	.162999
3	.1152981	.0380074	3.03	0.005	.0377814	.1928148

Because our response is a probability, these margins are sometimes called predicted marginal proportions or model-adjusted risks. They let us compare the effect of our three racial groups while controlling for the distribution of other covariates in the groups. Computationally, these predictive margins are the weighted average of the predicted probabilities for each observation in the estimation sample. The marginal probability for whites is the average probability, assuming that everyone in the sample is white; the margin for blacks assumes that everyone is black; and the margin for others assumes that everyone is something other than black or white.

There is a sizable difference in blood pressure between whites and blacks, with the marginal probability of high blood pressure for whites being about 10% and that for blacks being just over 13%. These are the adjusted probability levels. A more direct answer to our question about whether the odds ratios represent a substantial effect requires looking at the differences of these marginal probabilities. Researchers in the health-related sciences call such differences risk differences, whereas researchers in the social sciences usually call them average marginal effects or average partial effects.

Regardless of terminology, we are interested in the difference in the probability of blacks having high blood pressure as compared with whites, while adjusting for all other covariates in the model. We request risk differences by specifying the variables of interest in a dydx() option.

```
. margins, vce(svy) dydx(race)
Average marginal effects                        Number of obs    =      10351
Expression   : Pr(highbp), predict()
dy/dx w.r.t. : 2.race 3.race
```

	dy/dx	Linearized Std. Err.	t	P>|t|	[95% Conf. Interval]	
race						
2	.0312395	.0137273	2.28	0.030	.0032424	.0592366
3	.0128059	.0385697	0.33	0.742	-.0658575	.0914693

Note: dy/dx for factor levels is the discrete change from the base level.

Looking in the column labeled dy/dx, we see that the risk difference between blacks and whites is about 3.1% (0.0312). That is a sizable as well as significant difference.

Because they are population-weighted averages over the whole sample, these margins are estimates of the population average risk differences. And because we specified the vce(svy) option, their standard errors and confidence intervals can be used to make inferences about the population average risk differences. See *Methods and formulas* in [R] **margins** for details.

We can also compute margins or risk differences for subpopulations. To compute risk differences for the four subpopulations that are the regions of the United States—Northeast, Midwest, South, and West—we add the by(region) option.

(Continued on next page)

```
. margins, vce(svy) dydx(race) by(region)
Average marginal effects                      Number of obs    =      10351
Expression   : Pr(highbp), predict()
dy/dx w.r.t. : 2.race 3.race
By           : region
```

	dy/dx	Linearized Std. Err.	t	P>|t|	[95% Conf. Interval]	
2.race						
region						
1	.032436	.014278	2.27	0.030	.0033159	.0615561
2	.0304643	.0135598	2.25	0.032	.0028088	.0581197
3	.0325231	.0140719	2.31	0.028	.0038232	.061223
4	.0298228	.0131634	2.27	0.031	.0029759	.0566697
3.race						
region						
1	.0133025	.0400776	0.33	0.742	-.0684363	.0950413
2	.0124846	.0376194	0.33	0.742	-.0642407	.0892098
3	.0133421	.0401567	0.33	0.742	-.0685581	.0952422
4	.0122144	.0367734	0.33	0.742	-.0627855	.0872143

Note: dy/dx for factor levels is the discrete change from the base level.

The differences in the covariate distributions across the regions have little effect on the risk differences between blacks and whites, or between other races and whites.

Rather than explore the probabilities after logistic regression, we might have explored the hazards or mean survival times after fitting a survival model. See [R] **margins** for many more applications of margins.

◁

▷ Example 4: Nonlinear predictions and their standard errors

Continuing with the NHANES II data, we fit a linear regression of log of blood lead level on age, age-squared, gender, race, and region.

```
. use http://www.stata-press.com/data/r11/nhanes2d
. svy: regress loglead age c.age#c.age i.female i.race i.region
(running regress on estimation sample)

Survey: Linear regression
```

Number of strata	=	31	Number of obs	=	4948
Number of PSUs	=	62	Population size	=	56405414
			Design df	=	31
			F(8, 24)	=	156.24
			Prob > F	=	0.0000
			R-squared	=	0.2379

loglead	Coef.	Linearized Std. Err.	t	P>|t|	[95% Conf. Interval]	
age	.0158388	.0027352	5.79	0.000	.0102603	.0214173
c.age#c.age	-.0001464	.0000295	-4.96	0.000	-.0002066	-.0000862
1.female	-.3655338	.0116157	-31.47	0.000	-.3892242	-.3418434
race						
2	.178402	.0314173	5.68	0.000	.114326	.242478
3	-.0516952	.0402381	-1.28	0.208	-.1337614	.030371
region						
2	-.02283	.0389823	-0.59	0.562	-.1023349	.0566749
3	-.1685453	.056004	-3.01	0.005	-.2827662	-.0543244
4	-.0362295	.0387508	-0.93	0.357	-.1152623	.0428032
_cons	2.440671	.0627987	38.86	0.000	2.312592	2.568749

Given that we modeled the natural log of the lead measurement, we can use `predictnl` to compute the exponentiated linear prediction (in the original units of the `lead` variable), along with its standard error.

```
. predictnl leadhat = exp(xb()) if e(sample), se(leadhat_se)
(5403 missing values generated)
. sort lead leadhat
. gen showobs = inrange(_n,1,5) + inrange(_n,2501,2505) + inrange(_n,4945,4948)
```

(Continued on next page)

```
. list lead leadhat leadhat_se age c.age#c.age if showobs, abbrev(10)
```

	lead	leadhat	leadhat_se	age	c.age# c.age
1.	2	9.419804	.5433255	29	841
2.	3	8.966098	.5301117	23	529
3.	3	9.046788	.5298448	24	576
4.	3	9.046788	.5298448	24	576
5.	3	9.27693	.5347956	27	729
2501.	13	16.88317	.7728783	37	1369
2502.	13	16.90057	2.296082	71	5041
2503.	13	16.90057	2.296082	71	5041
2504.	13	16.90237	1.501056	48	2304
2505.	13	16.90852	2.018708	60	3600
4945.	61	17.18581	2.052034	58	3364
4946.	64	15.08437	.647629	24	576
4947.	66	17.78698	1.641349	56	3136
4948.	80	16.85864	1.333927	42	1764

◁

▷ Example 5: Multiple-hypothesis testing

Joint-hypothesis tests can be performed after svy commands with the test command. Using the results from the regression model fit in the previous example, we can use test to test the joint significance of 2.region, 3.region, and 4.region. (1.region is the Northeast, 2.region is the Midwest, 3.region is the South, and 4.region is the West.) We test the hypothesis that 2.region = 0, 3.region = 0, and 4.region = 0.

```
. test 2.region 3.region 4.region

Adjusted Wald test

 ( 1)   2.region = 0
 ( 2)   3.region = 0
 ( 3)   4.region = 0

       F(  3,    29) =    2.96
            Prob > F =    0.0486
```

The nosvyadjust option on test produces an unadjusted Wald test.

```
. test 2.region 3.region 4.region, nosvyadjust

Unadjusted Wald test

 ( 1)   2.region = 0
 ( 2)   3.region = 0
 ( 3)   4.region = 0

       F(  3,    31) =    3.17
            Prob > F =    0.0382
```

For one-dimensional tests, the adjusted and unadjusted F statistics are identical, but they differ for higher-dimensional tests. Using the nosvyadjust option is not recommended because the unadjusted F statistic can produce extremely anticonservative p-values (i.e., p-values that are too small) when the variance degrees of freedom (equal to the number of sampled PSUs minus the number of strata) is not large relative to the dimension of the test.

Bonferroni-adjusted p-values can also be computed:

```
. test 2.region 3.region 4.region, mtest(bonferroni)

Adjusted Wald test
 ( 1)   2.region = 0
 ( 2)   3.region = 0
 ( 3)   4.region = 0
```

	F(df,29)	df	p
(1)	0.34	1	1.0000 #
(2)	9.06	1	0.0155 #
(3)	0.87	1	1.0000 #
all	2.96	3	0.0486

```
# Bonferroni adjusted p-values
```

See Korn and Graubard (1990) for a discussion of these three different procedures for conducting joint-hypothesis tests. See Eltinge and Sribney (1996) for an earlier implementation of test for survey data.

◁

▷ Example 6: Using suest with survey data, the svy prefix

suest can be used to obtain the variance estimates for a series of estimators that used the svy prefix. To use suest for this purpose, perform the following steps:

1. Be sure to set the survey design characteristics correctly by using svyset. Do not use the vce() option to change the default variance estimator from the linearized variance estimator. vce(brr) and vce(jackknife) are not supported by suest.

2. Fit the model or models by using the svy prefix command, optionally including subpopulation estimation with the subpop() option.

3. Store the estimation results with estimates store *name*.

In the following, we illustrate how to use suest to compare the parameter estimates between two ordered logistic regression models.

In the NHANES II dataset, we have the variable health containing self-reported health status, which takes on the values 1–5, with 1 being "poor" and 5 being "excellent". Because this is an ordered categorical variable, it makes sense to model it by using svy: ologit. We use some basic demographic variables as predictors: female (an indicator of female individuals), black (an indicator for black individuals), age in years, and c.age#c.age (age squared).

```
. use http://www.stata-press.com/data/r11/nhanes2f, clear
. svyset psuid [pw=finalwgt], strata(stratid)
      pweight: finalwgt
          VCE: linearized
  Single unit: missing
     Strata 1: stratid
         SU 1: psuid
        FPC 1: <zero>
```

```
. svy: ologit health female black age c.age#c.age
(running ologit on estimation sample)

Survey: Ordered logistic regression

Number of strata  =         31          Number of obs    =       10335
Number of PSUs    =         62          Population size  =   116997257
                                        Design df        =          31
                                        F(   4,     28)  =      223.27
                                        Prob > F         =      0.0000
```

health	Coef.	Linearized Std. Err.	t	P>|t|	[95% Conf. Interval]	
female	-.1615219	.0523678	-3.08	0.004	-.2683267	-.054717
black	-.986568	.0790277	-12.48	0.000	-1.147746	-.8253899
age	-.0119491	.0082974	-1.44	0.160	-.0288717	.0049736
c.age#c.age	-.0003234	.000091	-3.55	0.001	-.000509	-.0001377
/cut1	-4.566229	.1632561	-27.97	0.000	-4.899192	-4.233266
/cut2	-3.057415	.1699944	-17.99	0.000	-3.404121	-2.710709
/cut3	-1.520596	.1714342	-8.87	0.000	-1.870239	-1.170954
/cut4	-.242785	.1703965	-1.42	0.164	-.590311	.104741

The self-reported `health` variable takes five categories. Categories 1 and 2 denote negative categories, whereas categories 4 and 5 denote positive categories. We wonder whether the distinctions between the two positive categories and between the two negative categories are produced in accordance with one latent dimension, which is an assumption of the ordered logistic model. To test one-dimensionality, we will collapse the five-point health measure into a three-point measure, refit the ordered logistic model, and compare the regression coefficients and cutpoints between the two analyses. If the single latent variable assumption is valid, the coefficients and cutpoints should match. This can be seen as a Hausman-style specification test. Estimation of the ordered logistic model parameters for survey data is by maximum pseudolikelihood. Neither estimator is fully efficient, and thus the assumptions for the classic Hausman test and for the `hausman` command are not satisfied. With `suest`, we can obtain an appropriate Hausman test for survey data.

To perform the Hausman test, we are already almost halfway there by following steps 1 and 2 for one of the models. We just need to store the current estimation results before moving on to the next model. Here we store the results with `estimates store` under the name H5, indicating that in this analysis, the dependent variable `health` has five categories.

```
. estimates store H5
```

We proceed by generating a new dependent variable `health3`, which maps values 1 and 2 into 2, 3 into 3, and 4 and 5 into 4. This transformation is conveniently accomplished with the `clip()` function. We then fit an `ologit` model with this new dependent variable and store the estimation results under the name H3.

```
. gen health3 = clip(health, 2, 4)
(2 missing values generated)
```

```
. svy: ologit health3 female black age c.age#c.age
(running ologit on estimation sample)
```

Survey: Ordered logistic regression

Number of strata	=	31	Number of obs	=	10335
Number of PSUs	=	62	Population size	=	116997257
			Design df	=	31
			F(4, 28)	=	197.08
			Prob > F	=	0.0000

health3	Coef.	Linearized Std. Err.	t	P>|t|	[95% Conf. Interval]
female	-.1551238	.0563809	-2.75	0.010	-.2701133 -.0401342
black	-1.046316	.0728274	-14.37	0.000	-1.194849 -.8977836
age	-.0365408	.0073653	-4.96	0.000	-.0515624 -.0215192
c.age#c.age	-.00009	.0000791	-1.14	0.264	-.0002512 .0000713
/cut1	-3.655498	.1610211	-22.70	0.000	-3.983903 -3.327093
/cut2	-2.109584	.1597057	-13.21	0.000	-2.435306 -1.783862

```
. estimates store H3
```

We can now obtain the combined estimation results of the two models stored under H5 and H3 with design-based standard errors.

(Continued on next page)

```
. suest H5 H3
```

Simultaneous survey results for H5, H3

Number of strata	=	31	Number of obs	=	10335
Number of PSUs	=	62	Population size	=	116997257
			Design df	=	31

	Coef.	Linearized Std. Err.	t	P>|t|	[95% Conf. Interval]
H5_health						
female	-.1615219	.0523678	-3.08	0.004	-.2683267	-.054717
black	-.986568	.0790277	-12.48	0.000	-1.147746	-.8253899
age	-.0119491	.0082974	-1.44	0.160	-.0288717	.0049736
c.age#c.age	-.0003234	.000091	-3.55	0.001	-.000509	-.0001377
H5_cut1						
_cons	-4.566229	.1632561	-27.97	0.000	-4.899192	-4.233266
H5_cut2						
_cons	-3.057415	.1699944	-17.99	0.000	-3.404121	-2.710709
H5_cut3						
_cons	-1.520596	.1714342	-8.87	0.000	-1.870239	-1.170954
H5_cut4						
_cons	-.242785	.1703965	-1.42	0.164	-.590311	.104741
H3_health3						
female	-.1551238	.0563809	-2.75	0.010	-.2701133	-.0401342
black	-1.046316	.0728274	-14.37	0.000	-1.194849	-.8977836
age	-.0365408	.0073653	-4.96	0.000	-.0515624	-.0215192
c.age#c.age	-.00009	.0000791	-1.14	0.264	-.0002512	.0000713
H3_cut1						
_cons	-3.655498	.1610211	-22.70	0.000	-3.983903	-3.327093
H3_cut2						
_cons	-2.109584	.1597057	-13.21	0.000	-2.435306	-1.783862

The coefficients of H3 and H5 look rather similar. We now use `test` to perform a formal Hausman-type test for the hypothesis that the regression coefficients are indeed the same, as we would expect if there is indeed a one-dimensional latent dimension for health. Thus we test that the coefficients in the equation H5_health are equal to those in H3_health3.

```
. test [H5_health=H3_health3]
Adjusted Wald test
 ( 1)  [H5_health]female - [H3_health3]female = 0
 ( 2)  [H5_health]black - [H3_health3]black = 0
 ( 3)  [H5_health]age - [H3_health3]age = 0
 ( 4)  [H5_health]c.age#c.age - [H3_health3]c.age#c.age = 0
       F( 4,    28) =   17.13
          Prob > F =    0.0000
```

We can reject the null hypothesis, which indicates that the ordered logistic regression model is indeed misspecified. Another specification test can be conducted with respect to the cutpoints. Variable `health3` was constructed from `health` by collapsing the two top categories into value 2 and the two bottom categories into value 4. This action effectively has removed two cutpoints, but if the model fits the data, it should not affect the other two cutpoints. The comparison is hampered by a difference in the names of the cutpoints between the models, as illustrated in the figure below:

		cut1	cut2	cut3	cut4	
H5	latent	——x——	—x——	—x——	—x——	
	observed	1	2	3	4	5

		cut1	cut2	
H3	latent	————————x——	—x——	
	observed	2	3	4

Cutpoint /cut2 of model H5 should be compared with cutpoint /cut1 of H3, and similarly, /cut3 of H5 with /cut2 of H3.

```
. test ([H5_cut2]_cons=[H3_cut1]_cons) ([H5_cut3]_cons=[H3_cut2]_cons)

Adjusted Wald test

 ( 1)  [H5_cut2]_cons - [H3_cut1]_cons = 0
 ( 2)  [H5_cut3]_cons - [H3_cut2]_cons = 0

      F(  2,     30) =    33.49
           Prob > F =     0.0000
```

We conclude that the invariance of the cutpoints under the collapse of categories is not supported by the data, again providing evidence against the reduced specification of the ordered logistic model in this case.

◁

▷ Example 7: Using suest with survey data, the svy option

Not all estimation commands support the svy prefix, but you can use the svy option with suest to get survey estimation results. If you can use suest after a command, you can use suest, svy. Here are the corresponding Stata commands to perform the analysis in the previous example, using the svy option instead of the svy prefix.

```
. use http://www.stata-press.com/data/r11/nhanes2f, clear
. svyset psuid [pw=finalwgt], strata(stratid)
. ologit health female black age c.age#c.age [iw=finalwgt]
. estimates store H5
. gen health3 = clip(health,2,4)
. ologit health3 female black age c.age#c.age [iw=finalwgt]
. estimates store H3
. suest H5 H3, svy
. test [H5_health=H3_health3]
. test ([H5_cut2]_cons=[H3_cut1]_cons) ([H5_cut3]_cons=[H3_cut2]_cons)
```

The calls to ologit now use iweights instead of the svy prefix, and the svy option was added to suest. No other changes are required.

◁

References

Eltinge, J. L., and W. M. Sribney. 1996. svy5: Estimates of linear combinations and hypothesis tests for survey data. *Stata Technical Bulletin* 31: 31–42. Reprinted in *Stata Technical Bulletin Reprints*, vol. 6, pp. 246–259. College Station, TX: Stata Press.

Graubard, B. I., and E. L. Korn. 2004. Predictive margins with survey data. *Biometrics* 55: 652–659.

Korn, E. L., and B. I. Graubard. 1990. Simultaneous testing of regression coefficients with complex survey data: Use of Bonferroni *t* statistics. *American Statistician* 44: 270–276.

McDowell, A., A. Engel, J. T. Massey, and K. Maurer. 1981. Plan and operation of the Second National Health and Nutrition Examination Survey, 1976–1980. *Vital and Health Statistics* 1(15): 1–144.

Also see

[SVY] **svy estimation** — Estimation commands for survey data

[SVY] **svy brr** — Balanced repeated replication for survey data

[SVY] **svy jackknife** — Jackknife estimation for survey data

[SVY] **estat** — Postestimation statistics for survey data

[U] **13.5 Accessing coefficients and standard errors**

[U] **20 Estimation and postestimation commands**

Title

svy: tabulate oneway — One-way tables for survey data

Syntax

Basic syntax

> svy: <u>tab</u>ulate *varname*

Full syntax

> svy $\big[$ *vcetype* $\big]$ $\big[$, *svy_options* $\big]$: <u>tab</u>ulate *varname* $\big[$ *if* $\big]$ $\big[$ *in* $\big]$
>
> $\big[$, *tabulate_options display_items display_options* $\big]$

Syntax to report results

> svy $\big[$, *display_items display_options* $\big]$

vcetype	description
SE	
<u>linea</u>rized	Taylor linearized variance estimation
brr	BRR variance estimation; see [SVY] **svy brr**
jackknife	jackknife variance estimation; see [SVY] **svy jackknife**

Specifying a *vcetype* overrides the default from svyset.

svy_options	description
if/in	
<u>sub</u>pop($\big[$ *varname* $\big]$ $\big[$ *if* $\big]$)	identify a subpopulation
SE	
brr_options	more options allowed with BRR variance estimation; see [SVY] ***brr_options***
jackknife_options	more options allowed with jackknife variance estimation; see [SVY] ***jackknife_options***

svy requires that the survey design variables be identified using svyset; see [SVY] **svyset**.

See [U] **20 Estimation and postestimation commands** for more capabilities of estimation commands.

Warning: Using if or in restrictions will often not produce correct variance estimates for subpopulations. To compute estimates for a subpopulation, use the subpop() option.

107

tabulate_options	description
Model	
stdize(*varname*)	variable identifying strata for standardization
stdweight(*varname*)	weight variable for standardization
tab(*varname*)	variable for which to compute cell totals/proportions
missing	treat missing values like other values

display_items	description
Table items	
cell	cell proportions
count	weighted cell counts
se	standard errors
ci	confidence intervals
deff	display the DEFF design effects
deft	display the DEFT design effects
srssubpop	report design effects assuming SRS within subpopulation
obs	cell observations

When any of se, ci, deff, deft, or srssubpop is specified, only one of cell or count can be specified. If none of se, ci, deff, deft, or srssubpop is specified, both cell and count can be specified.

display_options	description
Reporting	
level(#)	set confidence level; default is level(95)
†proportion	display proportions; the default
percent	display percentages instead of proportions
nomarginal	suppress column marginal
nolabel	suppress displaying value labels
cellwidth(#)	cell width
csepwidth(#)	column-separation width
stubwidth(#)	stub width
format(%*fmt*)	cell format; default is format(%6.0g)

†proportion is not shown in the dialog box.

Menu

Statistics > Survey data analysis > Tables > One-way tables

Description

svy: tabulate produces one-way tabulations for complex survey data. See [SVY] **svy: tabulate twoway** for two-way tabulations for complex survey data.

Options

svy_options; see [SVY] **svy**.

    ⌐ Model ⌐

stdize(*varname*) specifies that the point estimates be adjusted by direct standardization across the strata identified by *varname*. This option requires the stdweight() option.

stdweight(*varname*) specifies the weight variable associated with the strata identified in the stdize() option. The standardization weights must be constant within the standard strata.

tab(*varname*) specifies that counts be cell totals of this variable and that proportions (or percentages) be relative to (i.e., weighted by) this variable. For example, if this variable denotes income, then the cell "counts" are instead totals of income for each cell, and the cell proportions are proportions of income for each cell.

missing specifies that missing values in *varname* be treated as another row category rather than be omitted from the analysis (the default).

    ⌐ Table items ⌐

cell requests that cell proportions (or percentages) be displayed. This is the default if count is not specified.

count requests that weighted cell counts be displayed.

se requests that the standard errors of cell proportions (the default) or weighted counts be displayed. When se (or ci, deff, or deft) is specified, only one of cell or count can be selected. The standard error computed is the standard error of the one selected.

ci requests confidence intervals for cell proportions or weighted counts.

deff and deft request that the design-effect measures DEFF and DEFT be displayed for each cell proportion or weighted count. See [SVY] **estat** for details.

Options deff and deft are not allowed with estimation results that used direct standardization or poststratification.

srssubpop requests that DEFF and DEFT be computed using an estimate of SRS (simple random sampling) variance for sampling within a subpopulation. By default, DEFF and DEFT are computed using an estimate of the SRS variance for sampling from the entire population. Typically, srssubpop would be given when computing subpopulation estimates by strata or by groups of strata.

obs requests that the number of observations for each cell be displayed.

    ⌐ Reporting ⌐

level(*#*) specifies the confidence level, as a percentage, for confidence intervals. The default is level(95) or as set by set level; see [U] **20.7 Specifying the width of confidence intervals**.

proportion, the default, requests that proportions be displayed.

percent requests that percentages be displayed instead of proportions.

nomarginal requests that the column marginal not be displayed.

nolabel requests that variable labels and value labels be ignored.

cellwidth(*#*), csepwidth(*#*), and stubwidth(*#*) specify widths of table elements in the output; see [P] **tabdisp**. Acceptable values for the stubwidth() option range from 4 to 32.

format(%*fmt*) specifies a format for the items in the table. The default is format(%6.0g). See [U]
12.5 Formats: Controlling how data are displayed.

svy: tabulate uses the tabdisp command (see [P] **tabdisp**) to produce the table. Only five items
can be displayed in the table at one time. The ci option implies two items. If too many items are
selected, a warning will appear immediately. To view more items, redisplay the table while specifying
different options.

Remarks

Despite the long list of options for svy: tabulate, it is a simple command to use. Using the
svy: tabulate command is just like using tabulate to produce one-way tables for ordinary data.
The main difference is that svy: tabulate computes standard errors appropriate for complex survey
data.

Standard errors and confidence intervals can optionally be displayed for weighted counts or cell
proportions. The confidence intervals for proportions are constructed using a logit transform so that
their endpoints always lie between 0 and 1; see [SVY] **svy: tabulate twoway**. Associated design
effects (DEFF and DEFT) can be viewed for the variance estimates.

▷ Example 1

Here we use svy: tabulate to estimate the distribution of the race category variable from our
NHANES II dataset (McDowell et al. 1981). Before calling svy: tabulate, we use svyset to declare
the survey structure of the data.

```
. use http://www.stata-press.com/data/r11/nhanes2b

. svyset psuid [pweight=finalwgt], strata(stratid)
      pweight: finalwgt
          VCE: linearized
  Single unit: missing
     Strata 1: stratid
         SU 1: psuid
        FPC 1: <zero>

. svy: tabulate race
(running tabulate on estimation sample)
```

Number of strata	=	31		Number of obs	=	10351
Number of PSUs	=	62		Population size	=	117157513
				Design df	=	31

1=white, 2=black, 3=other	proportions
White	.8792
Black	.0955
Other	.0253
Total	1

Key: proportions = cell proportions

Here we display weighted counts for each category of race along with the 95% confidence bounds, as well as the design effects DEFF and DEFT. We also use the format() option to improve the look of the table.

```
. svy: tabulate race, format(%11.3g) count ci deff deft
(running tabulate on estimation sample)
Number of strata    =        31        Number of obs       =       10351
Number of PSUs      =        62        Population size     =   117157513
                                       Design df           =          31
```

1=white, 2=black, 3=other	count	lb	ub	deff	deft
White	102999549	97060400	108938698	60.2	7.76
Black	11189236	8213964	14164508	18.6	4.31
Other	2968728	414930	5522526	47.9	6.92
Total	117157513				

```
Key:   count   =   weighted counts
       lb      =   lower 95% confidence bounds for weighted counts
       ub      =   upper 95% confidence bounds for weighted counts
       deff    =   deff for variances of weighted counts
       deft    =   deft for variances of weighted counts
```

From the above results, we can conclude with 95% confidence that the number of people in the population that fall within the White category is between 97,060,400 and 108,938,698.

◁

Saved results

In addition to the results documented in [SVY] **svy**, svy: tabulate also saves the following in e():

Scalars

e(r)	number of rows		e(total)	weighted sum of tab() variable

Macros

e(cmd)	tabulate		e(rowvlab)	row variable label
e(tab)	tab() variable		e(rowvar)	*varname*, the row variable
e(rowlab)	label or empty		e(setype)	cell or count

Matrices

e(Prop)	matrix of cell proportions		e(V_row)	variance for row totals
e(Obs)	matrix of observation counts		e(V_srs_row)	V_{srs} for row totals
e(Deff)	DEFF vector for e(setype) items		e(Deff_row)	DEFF for row totals
e(Deft)	DEFT vector for e(setype) items		e(Deft_row)	DEFT for row totals
e(Row)	values for row variable			

Methods and formulas

svy: tabulate is implemented as an ado-file.

See *Methods and formulas* in [SVY] **svy: tabulate twoway** for a discussion of how table items and confidence intervals are computed. A one-way table is really just a two-way table that has one row or column.

Reference

McDowell, A., A. Engel, J. T. Massey, and K. Maurer. 1981. Plan and operation of the Second National Health and Nutrition Examination Survey, 1976–1980. *Vital and Health Statistics* 1(15): 1–144.

Also see

[SVY] **svy postestimation** — Postestimation tools for svy

[SVY] **svydescribe** — Describe survey data

[R] **tabulate oneway** — One-way tables of frequencies

[SVY] **svy: tabulate twoway** — Two-way tables for survey data

[U] **20 Estimation and postestimation commands**

[SVY] **direct standardization** — Direct standardization of means, proportions, and ratios

[SVY] **poststratification** — Poststratification for survey data

[SVY] **subpopulation estimation** — Subpopulation estimation for survey data

[SVY] **svy** — The survey prefix command

[SVY] **variance estimation** — Variance estimation for survey data

Title

svy: tabulate twoway — Two-way tables for survey data

Syntax

Basic syntax

svy: <u>tab</u>ulate *varname*$_1$ *varname*$_2$

Full syntax

svy $\big[$ *vcetype* $\big]$ $\big[$, *svy_options* $\big]$: <u>tab</u>ulate *varname*$_1$ *varname*$_2$ $\big[$ *if* $\big]$ $\big[$ *in* $\big]$

$\big[$, *tabulate_options display_items display_options statistic_options* $\big]$

Syntax to report results

svy $\big[$, *display_items display_options statistic_options* $\big]$

vcetype	description
SE	
<u>linear</u>ized	Taylor linearized variance estimation
brr	BRR variance estimation; see [SVY] **svy brr**
jackknife	jackknife variance estimation; see [SVY] **svy jackknife**

Specifying a *vcetype* overrides the default from svyset.

svy_options	description
if/in	
<u>sub</u>pop($\big[$ *varname* $\big]$ $\big[$ *if* $\big]$)	identify a subpopulation
SE	
brr_options	more options allowed with BRR variance estimation; see [SVY] ***brr_options***
jackknife_options	more options allowed with jackknife variance estimation; see [SVY] ***jackknife_options***

svy requires that the survey design variables be identified using svyset; see [SVY] **svyset**.

See [U] **20 Estimation and postestimation commands** for more capabilities of estimation commands.

Warning: Using if or in restrictions will often not produce correct variance estimates for subpopulations. To compute estimates for a subpopulation, use the subpop() option.

tabulate_options	description
Model	
<u>std</u>ize(*varname*)	variable identifying strata for standardization
<u>stdw</u>eight(*varname*)	weight variable for standardization
tab(*varname*)	variable for which to compute cell totals/proportions
<u>miss</u>ing	treat missing values like other values

display_items	description
Table items	
<u>cell</u>	cell proportions
<u>count</u>	weighted cell counts
<u>col</u>umn	within-column proportions
row	within-row proportions
se	standard errors
ci	confidence intervals
deff	display the DEFF design effects
deft	display the DEFT design effects
<u>srs</u>subpop	report design effects assuming SRS within subpopulation
obs	cell observations

When any of se, ci, deff, deft, or srssubpop is specified, only one of cell, count, column, or row can be specified. If none of se, ci, deff, deft, or srssubpop is specified, any or all of cell, count, column, and row can be specified.

display_options	description
Reporting	
<u>level</u>(#)	set confidence level; default is level(95)
†<u>prop</u>ortion	display proportions; the default
<u>per</u>cent	display percentages instead of proportions
<u>vert</u>ical	stack confidence interval endpoints vertically
<u>nom</u>arginals	suppress row and column marginals
<u>nol</u>abel	suppress displaying value labels
†<u>not</u>able	suppress displaying the table
<u>cellw</u>idth(#)	cell width
<u>csep</u>width(#)	column-separation width
<u>stubw</u>idth(#)	stub width
<u>f</u>ormat(%*fmt*)	cell format; default is format(%6.0g)

†proportion and notable are not shown in the dialog box.

statistic_options	description
Test statistics	
pearson	Pearson's chi-squared
lr	likelihood ratio
null	display null-based statistics
wald	adjusted Wald
llwald	adjusted log-linear Wald
noadjust	report unadjusted Wald statistics

Menu

Statistics > Survey data analysis > Tables > Two-way tables

Description

svy: tabulate produces two-way tabulations with tests of independence for complex survey data. See [SVY] **svy: tabulate oneway** for one-way tabulations for complex survey data.

Options

svy_options; see [SVY] **svy**.

Model

stdize(*varname*) specifies that the point estimates be adjusted by direct standardization across the strata identified by *varname*. This option requires the stdweight() option.

stdweight(*varname*) specifies the weight variable associated with the standard strata identified in the stdize() option. The standardization weights must be constant within the standard strata.

tab(*varname*) specifies that counts be cell totals of this variable and that proportions (or percentages) be relative to (i.e., weighted by) this variable. For example, if this variable denotes income, the cell "counts" are instead totals of income for each cell, and the cell proportions are proportions of income for each cell.

missing specifies that missing values in $varname_1$ and $varname_2$ be treated as another row or column category rather than be omitted from the analysis (the default).

Table items

cell requests that cell proportions (or percentages) be displayed. This is the default if none of count, row, or column is specified.

count requests that weighted cell counts be displayed.

column or row requests that column or row proportions (or percentages) be displayed.

se requests that the standard errors of cell proportions (the default), weighted counts, or row or column proportions be displayed. When se (or ci, deff, or deft) is specified, only one of cell, count, row, or column can be selected. The standard error computed is the standard error of the one selected.

ci requests confidence intervals for cell proportions, weighted counts, or row or column proportions. The confidence intervals are constructed using a logit transform so that their endpoints always lie between 0 and 1.

deff and deft request that the design-effect measures DEFF and DEFT be displayed for each cell proportion, count, or row or column proportion. See [SVY] **estat** for details. The mean generalized DEFF is also displayed when deff, deft, or subpop is requested; see *Methods and formulas* for an explanation.

The deff and deft options are not allowed with estimation results that used direct standardization or poststratification.

srssubpop requests that DEFF and DEFT be computed using an estimate of SRS (simple random sampling) variance for sampling within a subpopulation. By default, DEFF and DEFT are computed using an estimate of the SRS variance for sampling from the entire population. Typically, srssubpop would be given when computing subpopulation estimates by strata or by groups of strata.

obs requests that the number of observations for each cell be displayed.

___Reporting___

level(*#*) specifies the confidence level, as a percentage, for confidence intervals. The default is level(95) or as set by set level; see [U] **20.7 Specifying the width of confidence intervals**.

proportion, the default, requests that proportions be displayed.

percent requests that percentages be displayed instead of proportions.

vertical requests that the endpoints of confidence intervals be stacked vertically on display.

nomarginals requests that row and column marginals not be displayed.

nolabel requests that variable labels and value labels be ignored.

notable prevents the header and table from being displayed in the output. When specified, only the results of the requested test statistics are displayed. This option may not be specified with any other option in *display_options* except the level() option.

cellwidth(*#*), csepwidth(*#*), and stubwidth(*#*) specify widths of table elements in the output; see [P] **tabdisp**. Acceptable values for the stubwidth() option range from 4 to 32.

format(%*fmt*) specifies a format for the items in the table. The default is format(%6.0g). See [U] **12.5 Formats: Controlling how data are displayed**.

___Test statistics___

pearson requests that the Pearson χ^2 statistic be computed. By default, this is the test of independence that is displayed. The Pearson χ^2 statistic is corrected for the survey design with the second-order correction of Rao and Scott (1984) and is converted into an F statistic. One term in the correction formula can be calculated using either observed cell proportions or proportions under the null hypothesis (i.e., the product of the marginals). By default, observed cell proportions are used. If the null option is selected, then a statistic corrected using proportions under the null hypothesis is displayed as well. See the following discussion for details.

lr requests that the likelihood-ratio test statistic for proportions be computed. This statistic is not defined when there are one or more zero cells in the table. The statistic is corrected for the survey design by using the same correction procedure that is used with the pearson statistic. Again either observed cell proportions or proportions under the null hypothesis can be used in the correction formula. By default, the former is used; specifying the null option gives both the former and the latter. Neither variant of this statistic is recommended for sparse tables. For nonsparse tables, the lr statistics are similar to the corresponding pearson statistics.

null modifies the pearson and lr options only. If null is specified, two corrected statistics are displayed. The statistic labeled D–B (null) (D–B stands for design-based) uses proportions under the null hypothesis (i.e., the product of the marginals) in the Rao and Scott (1984) correction. The statistic labeled merely Design-based uses observed cell proportions. If null is not specified, only the correction that uses observed proportions is displayed. See the following discussion for details.

wald requests a Wald test of whether observed weighted counts equal the product of the marginals (Koch, Freeman Jr., and Freeman 1975). By default, an adjusted F statistic is produced; an unadjusted statistic can be produced by specifying noadjust. The unadjusted F statistic can yield extremely anticonservative p-values (i.e., p-values that are too small) when the degrees of freedom of the variance estimates (the number of sampled PSUs minus the number of strata) are small relative to the $(R-1)(C-1)$ degrees of freedom of the table (where R is the number of rows and C is the number of columns). Hence, the statistic produced by wald and noadjust should not be used for inference unless it is essentially identical to the adjusted statistic.

This option must be specified at run time in order to be used on subsequent calls to svy to report results.

llwald requests a Wald test of the log-linear model of independence (Koch, Freeman Jr., and Freeman 1975). The statistic is not defined when there are one or more zero cells in the table. The adjusted statistic (the default) can produce anticonservative p-values, especially for sparse tables, when the degrees of freedom of the variance estimates are small relative to the degrees of freedom of the table. Specifying noadjust yields a statistic with more severe problems. Neither the adjusted nor the unadjusted statistic is recommended for inference; the statistics are made available only for comparative and pedagogical purposes.

noadjust modifies the wald and llwald options only. It requests that an unadjusted F statistic be displayed in addition to the adjusted statistic.

svy: tabulate uses the tabdisp command (see [P] **tabdisp**) to produce the table. Only five items can be displayed in the table at one time. The ci option implies two items. If too many items are selected, a warning will appear immediately. To view more items, redisplay the table while specifying different options.

Remarks

Remarks are presented under the following headings:

> Introduction
> The Rao and Scott correction
> Wald statistics
> Properties of the statistics

Introduction

Despite the long list of options for svy: tabulate, it is a simple command to use. Using the svy: tabulate command is just like using tabulate to produce two-way tables for ordinary data. The main difference is that svy: tabulate computes a test of independence that is appropriate for complex survey data.

The test of independence that is displayed by default is based on the usual Pearson χ^2 statistic for two-way tables. To account for the survey design, the statistic is turned into an F statistic with noninteger degrees of freedom by using a second-order Rao and Scott (1981, 1984) correction. Although the theory behind the Rao and Scott correction is complicated, the p-value for the corrected F statistic can be interpreted in the same way as a p-value for the Pearson χ^2 statistic for "ordinary" data (i.e., data that are assumed independent and identically distributed [i.i.d.]).

svy: tabulate, in fact, computes four statistics for the test of independence with two variants of each, for a total of eight statistics. The option combination for each of the eight statistics are the following:

1. pearson (the default)

2. pearson null

3. lr

4. lr null

5. wald

6. wald noadjust

7. llwald

8. llwald noadjust

The wald and llwald options with noadjust yield the statistics developed by Koch, Freeman, and Freeman (1975), which have been implemented in the CROSSTAB procedure of the SUDAAN software (Research Triangle Institute 1997, release 7.5).

These eight statistics, along with other variants, have been evaluated in simulations (Sribney 1998). On the basis of these simulations, we advise researchers to use the default statistic (the pearson option) in all situations. We recommend that the other statistics be used only for comparative or pedagogical purposes. Sribney (1998) gives a detailed comparison of the statistics; a summary of his conclusions is provided later in this entry.

Other than the test-statistic options (*statistic_options*) and the survey design options (*svy_options*), most of the other options of svy: tabulate simply relate to different choices for what can be displayed in the body of the table. By default, cell proportions are displayed, but viewing either row or column proportions or weighted counts usually makes more sense.

Standard errors and confidence intervals can optionally be displayed for weighted counts or cell, row, or column proportions. The confidence intervals for proportions are constructed using a logit transform so that their endpoints always lie between 0 and 1. Associated design effects (DEFF and DEFT) can be viewed for the variance estimates. The mean generalized DEFF (Rao and Scott 1984) is also displayed when option deff, deft, or srssubpop is specified. The mean generalized DEFF is essentially a design effect for the asymptotic distribution of the test statistic; see the *Methods and formulas* section at the end of this entry.

▷ Example 1

Using data from the Second National Health and Nutrition Examination Survey (NHANES II) (McDowell et al. 1981), we identify the survey design characteristics with svyset and then produce a two-way table of cell proportions with svy: tabulate.

```
. use http://www.stata-press.com/data/r11/nhanes2b
. svyset psuid [pweight=finalwgt], strata(stratid)
      pweight: finalwgt
          VCE: linearized
  Single unit: missing
     Strata 1: stratid
         SU 1: psuid
        FPC 1: <zero>
```

```
. svy: tabulate race diabetes
(running tabulate on estimation sample)
Number of strata     =        31          Number of obs     =       10349
Number of PSUs       =        62          Population size   =   117131111
                                          Design df         =          31

1=white,
2=black,       diabetes, 1=yes, 0=no
3=other          0        1     Total

   White        .851    .0281    .8791
   Black       .0899    .0056    .0955
   Other       .0248  5.2e-04    .0253

   Total       .9658    .0342        1

Key:  cell proportions

Pearson:
   Uncorrected   chi2(2)           =    21.3483
   Design-based  F(1.52, 47.26)    =    15.0056      P = 0.0000
```

The default table displays only cell proportions, and this makes it difficult to compare the incidence of diabetes in white, black, and "other" racial groups. It would be better to look at row proportions. This can be done by redisplaying the results (i.e., reissuing the command without specifying any variables) with the row option.

```
. svy: tabulate, row
Number of strata     =        31          Number of obs     =       10349
Number of PSUs       =        62          Population size   =   117131111
                                          Design df         =          31

1=white,       diabetes, 1=yes,
2=black,            0=no
3=other          0        1    Total

   White        .968     .032        1
   Black        .941     .059        1
   Other       .9797    .0203        1

   Total       .9658    .0342        1

Key:  row proportions

Pearson:
   Uncorrected   chi2(2)           =    21.3483
   Design-based  F(1.52, 47.26)    =    15.0056      P = 0.0000
```

This table is much easier to interpret. A larger proportion of blacks have diabetes than do whites or persons in the "other" racial category. The test of independence for a two-way contingency table is equivalent to the test of homogeneity of row (or column) proportions. Hence, we can conclude that there is a highly significant difference between the incidence of diabetes among the three racial groups.

We may now wish to compute confidence intervals for the row proportions. If we try to redisplay, specifying ci along with row, we get the following result:

```
. svy: tabulate, row ci
confidence intervals are only available for cells to compute row confidence
intervals, rerun command with row and ci options
r(111);
```

There are limits to what svy: tabulate can redisplay. Basically, any of the options relating to variance estimation (i.e., se, ci, deff, and deft) must be specified at run time along with the single item (i.e., count, cell, row, or column) for which you want standard errors, confidence intervals, DEFF, or DEFT. So to get confidence intervals for row proportions, we must rerun the command. We do so below, requesting not only ci but also se.

```
. svy: tabulate race diabetes, row se ci format(%7.4f)
(running tabulate on estimation sample)
```

Number of strata	=	31	
Number of PSUs	=	62	

Number of obs	=	10349
Population size	=	117131111
Design df	=	31

1=white, 2=black, 3=other	diabetes, 1=yes, 0=no		
	0	1	Total
White	0.9680 (0.0020) [0.9638,0.9718]	0.0320 (0.0020) [0.0282,0.0362]	1.0000
Black	0.9410 (0.0061) [0.9271,0.9523]	0.0590 (0.0061) [0.0477,0.0729]	1.0000
Other	0.9797 (0.0076) [0.9566,0.9906]	0.0203 (0.0076) [0.0094,0.0434]	1.0000
Total	0.9658 (0.0018) [0.9619,0.9693]	0.0342 (0.0018) [0.0307,0.0381]	1.0000

```
  Key:  row proportions
        (linearized standard errors of row proportions)
        [95% confidence intervals for row proportions]

  Pearson:
    Uncorrected   chi2(2)          =    21.3483
    Design-based  F(1.52, 47.26)   =    15.0056     P = 0.0000
```

In the above table, we specified a %7.4f format rather than using the default %6.0g format. The single format applies to every item in the table. We can omit the marginal totals by specifying nomarginals. If the above style for displaying the confidence intervals is obtrusive—and it can be in a wider table—we can use the vertical option to stack the endpoints of the confidence interval, one over the other, and omit the brackets (the parentheses around the standard errors are also omitted when vertical is specified). To express results as percentages, as with the tabulate command (see [R] **tabulate twoway**), we can use the percent option. Or we can play around with these display options until we get a table that we are satisfied with, first making changes to the options on redisplay (i.e., omitting the cross-tabulated variables when we issue the command).

◁

❑ Technical note

The standard errors computed by svy: tabulate are the same as those produced by svy: mean, svy: proportion, and svy: ratio. Indeed, svy: tabulate uses these commands as subroutines to produce its table.

In the previous example, the estimate of the proportion of African Americans with diabetes (the second proportion in the second row of the preceding table) is simply a ratio estimate; hence, we can also obtain the same estimates by using svy: ratio:

```
. drop black
. gen black = (race==2) if !missing(race)
. gen diablk = diabetes*black
(2 missing values generated)
. svy: ratio diablk/black
(running ratio on estimation sample)
Survey: Ratio estimation
Number of strata =      31      Number of obs    =      10349
Number of PSUs   =      62      Population size  =  117131111
                                Design df        =         31

     _ratio_1: diablk/black
```

	Ratio	Linearized Std. Err.	[95% Conf. Interval]	
_ratio_1	.0590349	.0061443	.0465035	.0715662

Although the standard errors are the same, the confidence intervals are slightly different. The svy: tabulate command produced the confidence interval $[0.0477, 0.0729]$, and svy: ratio gave $[0.0465, 0.0716]$. The difference is because svy: tabulate uses a logit transform to produce confidence intervals whose endpoints are always between 0 and 1. This transformation also shifts the confidence intervals slightly toward 0.5, which is beneficial because the untransformed confidence intervals tend to be, on average, biased away from 0.5. See *Methods and formulas* for details.

❏

▷ Example 2: The tab() option

The tab() option allows us to compute proportions relative to a certain variable. Suppose that we wish to compare the proportion of total income among different racial groups in males with that of females. We do so below with fictitious data:

```
. use http://www.stata-press.com/data/r11/svy_tabopt, clear
. svy: tabulate gender race, tab(income) row
(running tabulate on estimation sample)
Number of strata   =      31        Number of obs     =      10351
Number of PSUs     =      62        Population size   =  117157513
                                    Design df         =         31
```

Gender	Race			Total
	White	Black	Other	
Male	.8857	.0875	.0268	1
Female	.884	.094	.022	1
Total	.8848	.0909	.0243	1

```
Tabulated variable:  income
Key:  row proportions
Pearson:
   Uncorrected    chi2(2)        =     3.6241
   Design-based   F(1.91, 59.12) =     0.8626    P = 0.4227
```

◁

The Rao and Scott correction

svy: tabulate can produce eight different statistics for the test of independence. By default, svy: tabulate displays the Pearson χ^2 statistic with the Rao and Scott (1981, 1984) second-order correction. On the basis of simulations Sribney (1998), we recommend that you use this statistic in all situations. The statistical literature, however, contains several alternatives, along with other possibilities for implementing the Rao and Scott correction. Hence, for comparative or pedagogical purposes, you may want to view some of the other statistics computed by svy: tabulate. This section briefly describes the differences among these statistics; for a more detailed discussion, see Sribney (1998).

Two statistics commonly used for i.i.d. data for the test of independence of $R \times C$ tables (R rows and C columns) are the Pearson χ^2 statistic

$$X_{\rm P}^2 = m \sum_{r=1}^{R} \sum_{c=1}^{C} (\widehat{p}_{rc} - \widehat{p}_{0rc})^2 / \widehat{p}_{0rc}$$

and the likelihood-ratio χ^2 statistic

$$X_{\rm LR}^2 = 2m \sum_{r=1}^{R} \sum_{c=1}^{C} \widehat{p}_{rc} \ln (\widehat{p}_{rc} / \widehat{p}_{0rc})$$

where m is the total number of sampled individuals, $\widehat{p}_{rc}$ is the estimated proportion for the cell in the rth row and cth column of the table, and $\widehat{p}_{0rc}$ is the estimated proportion under the null hypothesis of independence; i.e., $\widehat{p}_{0rc} = \widehat{p}_{r.}\widehat{p}_{.c}$, the product of the row and column marginals: $\widehat{p}_{r.} = \sum_{c=1}^{C} \widehat{p}_{rc}$ and $\widehat{p}_{.c} = \sum_{r=1}^{R} \widehat{p}_{rc}$.

For i.i.d. data, both these statistics are distributed asymptotically as $\chi^2_{(R-1)(C-1)}$. The likelihood-ratio statistic is not defined when one or more of the cells in the table are empty. The Pearson statistic, however, can be calculated when one or more cells in the table are empty—the statistic may not have good properties in this case, but the statistic still has a computable value.

For survey data, $X_{\rm P}^2$ and $X_{\rm LR}^2$ can be computed using weighted estimates of $\widehat{p}_{rc}$ and $\widehat{p}_{0rc}$. However, for a complex sampling design, one can no longer claim that they are distributed as $\chi^2_{(R-1)(C-1)}$, but you can estimate the variance of $\widehat{p}_{rc}$ under the sampling design. For instance, in Stata, this variance can be estimated via linearization methods by using svy: mean or svy: ratio.

Rao and Scott (1981, 1984) derived the asymptotic distribution of $X_{\rm P}^2$ and $X_{\rm LR}^2$ in terms of the variance of $\widehat{p}_{rc}$. Unfortunately, the result (see (1) in *Methods and formulas*) is not computationally feasible, but it can be approximated using correction formulas. svy: tabulate uses the second-order correction developed by Rao and Scott (1984). By default, or when the pearson option is specified, svy: tabulate displays the second-order correction of the Pearson statistic. The lr option gives the second-order correction of the likelihood-ratio statistic. Because it is the default of svy: tabulate, the correction computed with $\widehat{p}_{rc}$ is referred to as the default correction.

The Rao and Scott papers, however, left some details outstanding about the computation of the correction. One term in the correction formula can be computed using either $\widehat{p}_{rc}$ or $\widehat{p}_{0rc}$. Because under the null hypothesis both are asymptotically equivalent, theory offers no guidance about which is best. By default, svy: tabulate uses $\widehat{p}_{rc}$ for the corrections of the Pearson and likelihood-ratio statistics. If the null option is specified, the correction is computed using $\widehat{p}_{0rc}$. For nonsparse tables, these two correction methods yield almost identical results. However, in simulations of sparse tables, Sribney (1998) found that the null-corrected statistics were extremely anticonservative for 2×2 tables (i.e., under the null, "significance" was declared too often) and were too conservative for other tables. The default correction, however, had better properties. Hence, we do not recommend using null.

For the computational details of the Rao and Scott–corrected statistics, see *Methods and formulas*.

Wald statistics

Prior to the work by Rao and Scott (1981, 1984), Wald tests for the test of independence for two-way tables were developed by Koch, Freeman Jr., and Freeman (1975). Two Wald statistics have been proposed. The first, similar to the Pearson statistic, is based on

$$\widehat{Y}_{rc} = \widehat{N}_{rc} - \widehat{N}_{r\cdot}\widehat{N}_{\cdot c}/\widehat{N}_{\cdot\cdot}$$

where $\widehat{N}_{rc}$ is the estimated weighted count for the r, cth cell. The delta method can be used to approximate the variance of $\widehat{Y}_{rc}$, and a Wald statistic can be calculated as usual. A second Wald statistic can be constructed based on a log-linear model for the table. Like the likelihood-ratio statistic, this statistic is undefined when there is a zero proportion in the table.

These Wald statistics are initially χ^2 statistics, but they have better properties when converted into F statistics with denominator degrees of freedom that account for the degrees of freedom of the variance estimator. They can be converted to F statistics in two ways.

One method is the standard manner: divide by the χ^2 degrees of freedom $d_0 = (R-1)(C-1)$ to get an F statistic with d_0 numerator degrees of freedom and $\nu = n - L$ denominator degrees of freedom. This is the form of the F statistic suggested by Koch, Freeman, and Freeman (1975) and implemented in the CROSSTAB procedure of the SUDAAN software (Research Triangle Institute 1997, release 7.5), and it is the method used by svy: tabulate when the noadjust option is specified with wald or llwald.

Another technique is to adjust the F statistic by using

$$F_{\mathrm{adj}} = (\nu - d_0 + 1)W/(\nu d_0) \qquad \text{with} \qquad F_{\mathrm{adj}} \sim F(d_0, \nu - d_0 + 1)$$

This is the default adjustment for svy: tabulate. test and the other svy estimation commands produce adjusted F statistics by default, using the same adjustment procedure. See Korn and Graubard (1990) for a justification of the procedure.

The adjusted F statistic is identical to the unadjusted F statistic when $d_0 = 1$, that is, for 2×2 tables.

As Thomas and Rao (1987) point out (also see Korn and Graubard [1990]), the unadjusted F statistics can become extremely anticonservative as d_0 increases when ν is small or moderate; i.e., under the null, the statistics are "significant" far more often than they should be. Because the unadjusted statistics behave so poorly for larger tables when ν is not large, their use can be justified only for small tables or when ν is large. But when the table is small or when ν is large, the unadjusted statistic is essentially identical to the adjusted statistic. Hence, for statistical inference, looking at the unadjusted statistics has no point.

The adjusted "Pearson" Wald F statistic usually behaves reasonably under the null. However, even the adjusted F statistic for the log-linear Wald test tends to be moderately anticonservative when ν is not large (Thomas and Rao 1987; Sribney 1998).

▷ Example 3

With the NHANES II data, we tabulate, for the male subpopulation, high blood pressure (highbp) versus a variable (sizplace) that indicates the degree of urbanity/ruralness. We request that all eight statistics for the test of independence be displayed.

```
. use http://www.stata-press.com/data/r11/nhanes2b
. gen male = (sex==1) if !missing(sex)
```

```
. svy, subpop(male): tabulate highbp sizplace, col obs pearson lr null wald
> llwald noadj
(running tabulate on estimation sample)
```

Number of strata	=	31		Number of obs	=	10351
Number of PSUs	=	62		Population size	=	117157513
				Subpop. no. of obs	=	4915
				Subpop. size	=	56159480
				Design df	=	31

1 if BP > 140/90, 0 otherwise	1	2	3	1=urban,..., 8=rural 4	5	6	7	8	Total
0	.8489	.8929	.9213	.8509	.8413	.9242	.8707	.8674	.8764
	431	527	558	371	186	210	314	1619	4216
1	.1511	.1071	.0787	.1491	.1587	.0758	.1293	.1326	.1236
	95	80	64	74	36	20	57	273	699
Total	1	1	1	1	1	1	1	1	1
	526	607	622	445	222	230	371	1892	4915

```
Key:   column proportions
       number of observations

Pearson:
    Uncorrected    chi2(7)            =      64.4581
    D-B (null)     F(5.30, 164.45) =      2.2078       P = 0.0522
    Design-based   F(5.54, 171.87) =      2.6863       P = 0.0189

Likelihood ratio:
    Uncorrected    chi2(7)            =      68.2365
    D-B (null)     F(5.30, 164.45) =      2.3372       P = 0.0408
    Design-based   F(5.54, 171.87) =      2.8437       P = 0.0138

Wald (Pearson):
    Unadjusted     chi2(7)            =      21.2704
    Unadjusted     F(7, 31)           =      3.0386       P = 0.0149
    Adjusted       F(7, 25)           =      2.4505       P = 0.0465

Wald (log-linear):
    Unadjusted     chi2(7)            =      25.7644
    Unadjusted     F(7, 31)           =      3.6806       P = 0.0052
    Adjusted       F(7, 25)           =      2.9683       P = 0.0208
```

The p-values from the null-corrected Pearson and likelihood-ratio statistics (lines labeled "D-B (null)"; "D-B" stands for "design-based") are bigger than the corresponding default-corrected statistics (lines labeled "Design-based"). Simulations (Sribney 1998) show that the null-corrected statistics are overly conservative for many sparse tables (except 2×2 tables); this appears to be the case here, although this table is hardly sparse. The default-corrected Pearson statistic has good properties under the null for both sparse and nonsparse tables; hence, the smaller p-value for it should be considered reliable.

The default-corrected likelihood-ratio statistic is usually similar to the default-corrected Pearson statistic except for sparse tables, when it tends to be anticonservative. This example follows this pattern, with its p-value being slightly smaller than that of the default-corrected Pearson statistic.

For tables of these dimensions (2×8), the unadjusted "Pearson" Wald and log-linear Wald F statistics are extremely anticonservative under the null when the variance degrees of freedom is small. Here the variance degrees of freedom is only 31 (62 PSUs minus 31 strata), so we expect that the unadjusted Wald F statistics yield smaller p-values than the adjusted F statistics. Because of their poor behavior under the null for small variance degrees of freedom, they cannot be trusted here.

Simulations show that although the adjusted "Pearson" Wald F statistic has good properties under the null, it is often less powerful than the default Rao and Scott–corrected statistics. That is probably the explanation for the larger p-value for the adjusted "Pearson" Wald F statistic than that for the default-corrected Pearson and likelihood-ratio statistics.

The p-value for the adjusted log-linear Wald F statistic is about the same as that for the trustworthy default-corrected Pearson statistic. However, that is probably because of the anticonservatism of the log-linear Wald under the null balancing out its lower power under alternative hypotheses.

The "uncorrected" χ^2 Pearson and likelihood-ratio statistics displayed in the table are misspecified statistics; that is, they are based on an i.i.d. assumption, which is not valid for complex survey data. Hence, they are not correct, even asymptotically. The "unadjusted" Wald χ^2 statistics, on the other hand, are completely different. They are valid asymptotically as the variance degrees of freedom becomes large.

◁

Properties of the statistics

This section briefly summarizes the properties of the eight statistics computed by svy: tabulate. For details, see Sribney (1998), Rao and Thomas (1989), Thomas and Rao (1987), and Korn and Graubard (1990).

pearson is the Rao and Scott (1984) second-order corrected Pearson statistic, computed using $\widehat{p}_{rc}$ in the correction (default correction). It is displayed by default. Simulations show it to have good properties under the null for both sparse and nonsparse tables. Its power is similar to that of the lr statistic in most situations. It often appears to be more powerful than the adjusted "Pearson" Wald F statistic (wald option), especially for larger tables. We recommend using this statistic in all situations.

pearson null is the Rao and Scott second-order corrected Pearson statistic, computed using $\widehat{p}_{0rc}$ in the correction. It is numerically similar to the pearson statistic for nonsparse tables. For sparse tables, it can be erratic. Under the null, it can be anticonservative for sparse 2×2 tables but conservative for larger sparse tables.

lr is the Rao and Scott second-order corrected likelihood-ratio statistic, computed using $\widehat{p}_{rc}$ in the correction (default correction). The correction is identical to that for pearson. It is numerically similar to the pearson statistic for nonsparse tables. It can be anticonservative (p-values too small) in sparse tables. If there is a zero cell, it cannot be computed.

lr null is the Rao and Scott second-order corrected likelihood-ratio statistic, computed using $\widehat{p}_{0rc}$ in the correction. The correction is identical to that for pearson null. It is numerically similar to the lr statistic for nonsparse tables. For sparse tables, it can be overly conservative. If there is a zero cell, it cannot be computed.

wald statistic is the adjusted "Pearson" Wald F statistic. It has good properties under the null for nonsparse tables. It can be erratic for sparse 2×2 tables and some sparse large tables. The pearson statistic often appears to be more powerful.

wald noadjust is the unadjusted "Pearson" Wald F statistic. It can be extremely anticonservative under the null when the table degrees of freedom (number of rows minus one times the number of columns minus one) approaches the variance degrees of freedom (number of sampled PSUs minus the number of strata). It is the same as the adjusted wald statistic for 2×2 tables. It is similar to the adjusted wald statistic for small tables, large variance degrees of freedom, or both.

llwald statistic is the adjusted log-linear Wald F statistic. It can be anticonservative for both sparse and nonsparse tables. If there is a zero cell, it cannot be computed.

llwald noadjust statistic is the unadjusted log-linear Wald F statistic. Like wald noadjust, it can be extremely anticonservative under the null when the table degrees of freedom approaches the variance degrees of freedom. It also suffers from the same general anticonservatism of the llwald statistic. If there is a zero cell, it cannot be computed.

Saved results

In addition to the results documented in [SVY] **svy**, svy: tabulate saves the following in e():

Scalars

e(r)	number of rows	e(c)	number of columns
e(cvgdeff)	c.v. of generalized DEFF eigenvalues	e(mgdeff)	mean generalized DEFF
e(total)	weighted sum of tab() variable		
e(F_Pear)	default-corrected Pearson F	e(F_Penl)	null-corrected Pearson F
e(df1_Pear)	numerator d.f. for e(F_Pear)	e(df1_Penl)	numerator d.f. for e(F_Penl)
e(df2_Pear)	denominator d.f. for e(F_Pear)	e(df2_Penl)	denominator d.f. for e(F_Penl)
e(p_Pear)	p-value for e(F_Pear)	e(p_Penl)	p-value for e(F_Penl)
e(cun_Pear)	uncorrected Pearson χ^2	e(cun_Penl)	null variant uncorrected Pearson χ^2
e(F_LR)	default-corrected likelihood-ratio F	e(F_LRnl)	null-corrected likelihood-ratio F
e(df1_LR)	numerator d.f. for e(F_LR)	e(df1_LRnl)	numerator d.f. for e(F_LRnl)
e(df2_LR)	denominator d.f. for e(F_LR)	e(df2_LRnl)	denominator d.f. for e(F_LRnl)
e(p_LR)	p-value for e(F_LR)	e(p_LRnl)	p-value for e(F_LRnl)
e(cun_LR)	uncorrected likelihood-ratio χ^2	e(cun_LRln)	null variant uncorrected likelihood-ratio χ^2
e(F_Wald)	adjusted "Pearson" Wald F	e(F_LLW)	adjusted log-linear Wald F
e(p_Wald)	p-value for e(F_Wald)	e(p_LLW)	p-value for e(F_LLW)
e(Fun_Wald)	unadjusted "Pearson" Wald F	e(Fun_LLW)	unadjusted log-linear Wald F
e(pun_Wald)	p-value for e(Fun_Wald)	e(pun_LLW)	p-value for e(Fun_LLW)
e(cun_Wald)	unadjusted "Pearson" Wald χ^2	e(cun_LLW)	unadjusted log-linear Wald χ^2

Macros

e(cmd)	tabulate	e(colvlab)	column variable label
e(tab)	tab() variable	e(rowvar)	*varname$_1$*, the row variable
e(rowlab)	label or empty	e(colvar)	*varname$_2$*, the column variable
e(collab)	label or empty	e(setype)	cell, count, column, or row
e(rowvlab)	row variable label		

Matrices

e(Prop)	matrix of cell proportions	e(V_col)	variance for column totals
e(Obs)	matrix of observation counts	e(V_srs_row)	V_{srs} for row totals
e(Deff)	DEFF vector for e(setype) items	e(V_srs_col)	V_{srs} for column totals
e(Deft)	DEFT vector for e(setype) items	e(Deff_row)	DEFF for row totals
e(Row)	values for row variable	e(Deff_col)	DEFF for column totals
e(Col)	values for column variable	e(Deft_row)	DEFT for row totals
e(V_row)	variance for row totals	e(Deft_col)	DEFT for column totals

Methods and formulas

svy: tabulate is implemented as an ado-file.

Methods and formulas are presented under the following headings:

> *The table items*
> *Confidence intervals*
> *The test statistics*

The table items

For a table of R rows by C columns with cells indexed by r, c, let
$$y_{(rc)j} = \begin{cases} 1 & \text{if the } j\text{th observation of the data is in the } r, c\text{th cell} \\ 0 & \text{otherwise} \end{cases}$$
where $j = 1, \ldots, m$ indexes individuals in the sample. Weighted cell counts (count option) are
$$\widehat{N}_{rc} = \sum_{j=1}^{m} w_j \, y_{(rc)j}$$
where w_j is a sampling weight. If a variable, x_j, is specified with the tab() option, $\widehat{N}_{rc}$ becomes
$$\widehat{N}_{rc} = \sum_{j=1}^{m} w_j \, x_j \, y_{(rc)j}$$

Let
$$\widehat{N}_{r\cdot} = \sum_{c=1}^{C} \widehat{N}_{rc}, \qquad \widehat{N}_{\cdot c} = \sum_{r=1}^{R} \widehat{N}_{rc}, \qquad \text{and} \qquad \widehat{N}_{\cdot\cdot} = \sum_{r=1}^{R} \sum_{c=1}^{C} \widehat{N}_{rc}$$

Estimated cell proportions are $\widehat{p}_{rc} = \widehat{N}_{rc} / \widehat{N}_{\cdot\cdot}$; estimated row proportions (row option) are $\widehat{p}_{\text{row } rc} = \widehat{N}_{rc} / \widehat{N}_{r\cdot}$; estimated column proportions (column option) are $\widehat{p}_{\text{col} rc} = \widehat{N}_{rc} / \widehat{N}_{\cdot c}$; estimated row marginals are $\widehat{p}_{r\cdot} = \widehat{N}_{r\cdot} / \widehat{N}_{\cdot\cdot}$; and estimated column marginals are $\widehat{p}_{\cdot c} = \widehat{N}_{\cdot c} / \widehat{N}_{\cdot\cdot}$.

$\widehat{N}_{rc}$ is a total, the proportion estimators are ratios, and their variances can be estimated using linearization methods as outlined in [SVY] **variance estimation**. svy: tabulate computes the variance estimates by using svy: mean, svy: ratio, and svy: total.

Confidence intervals

Confidence intervals for proportions are calculated using a logit transform so that the endpoints lie between 0 and 1. Let $\widehat{p}$ be an estimated proportion and $\widehat{s}$ be an estimate of its standard error. Let
$$f(\widehat{p}) = \ln\left(\frac{\widehat{p}}{1 - \widehat{p}}\right)$$
be the logit transform of the proportion. In this metric, an estimate of the standard error is
$$\widehat{\text{SE}}\{f(\widehat{p})\} = f'(\widehat{p})\widehat{s} = \frac{\widehat{s}}{\widehat{p}(1 - \widehat{p})}$$
Thus a $100(1 - \alpha)\%$ confidence interval in this metric is
$$\ln\left(\frac{\widehat{p}}{1 - \widehat{p}}\right) \pm \frac{t_{1-\alpha/2,\nu}\,\widehat{s}}{\widehat{p}(1 - \widehat{p})}$$
where $t_{1-\alpha/2,\nu}$ is the $(1 - \alpha/2)$th quantile of Student's t distribution with ν degrees of freedom. The endpoints of this confidence interval are transformed back to the proportion metric by using the inverse of the logit transform
$$f^{-1}(y) = \frac{e^y}{1 + e^y}$$
Hence, the displayed confidence intervals for proportions are
$$f^{-1}\left\{\ln\left(\frac{\widehat{p}}{1 - \widehat{p}}\right) \pm \frac{t_{1-\alpha/2,\nu}\,\widehat{s}}{\widehat{p}(1 - \widehat{p})}\right\}$$
Confidence intervals for weighted counts are untransformed and are identical to the intervals produced by svy: total.

The test statistics

The uncorrected Pearson χ^2 statistic is

$$X_P^2 = m \sum_{r=1}^{R} \sum_{c=1}^{C} (\widehat{p}_{rc} - \widehat{p}_{0rc})^2 / \widehat{p}_{0rc}$$

and the uncorrected likelihood-ratio χ^2 statistic is

$$X_{LR}^2 = 2m \sum_{r=1}^{R} \sum_{c=1}^{C} \widehat{p}_{rc} \ln (\widehat{p}_{rc}/\widehat{p}_{0rc})$$

where m is the total number of sampled individuals, $\widehat{p}_{rc}$ is the estimated proportion for the cell in the rth row and cth column of the table as defined earlier, and $\widehat{p}_{0rc}$ is the estimated proportion under the null hypothesis of independence; i.e., $\widehat{p}_{0rc} = \widehat{p}_{r.}\widehat{p}_{.c}$, the product of the row and column marginals.

Rao and Scott (1981, 1984) show that, asymptotically, X_P^2 and X_{LR}^2 are distributed as

$$X^2 \sim \sum_{k=1}^{(R-1)(C-1)} \delta_k W_k \tag{1}$$

where the W_k are independent χ_1^2 variables and the δ_k are the eigenvalues of

$$\Delta = (\widetilde{\mathbf{X}}_2' \mathbf{V}_{srs} \widetilde{\mathbf{X}}_2)^{-1} (\widetilde{\mathbf{X}}_2' \mathbf{V} \widetilde{\mathbf{X}}_2) \tag{2}$$

where $\mathbf{V}$ is the variance of the $\widehat{p}_{rc}$ under the survey design and $\mathbf{V}_{srs}$ is the variance of the $\widehat{p}_{rc}$ that you would have if the design were simple random sampling; namely, $\mathbf{V}_{srs}$ has diagonal elements $p_{rc}(1 - p_{rc})/m$ and off-diagonal elements $-p_{rc}p_{st}/m$.

$\widetilde{\mathbf{X}}_2$ is calculated as follows. Rao and Scott do their development in a log-linear modeling context, so consider $[\mathbf{1} \mid \mathbf{X_1} \mid \mathbf{X_2}]$ as predictors for the cell counts of the $R \times C$ table in a log-linear model. The $\mathbf{X_1}$ matrix of dimension $RC \times (R + C - 2)$ contains the $R - 1$ "main effects" for the rows and the $C - 1$ "main effects" for the columns. The $\mathbf{X_2}$ matrix of dimension $RC \times (R - 1)(C - 1)$ contains the row and column "interactions". Hence, fitting $[\mathbf{1} \mid \mathbf{X_1} \mid \mathbf{X_2}]$ gives the fully saturated model (i.e., fits the observed values perfectly) and $[\mathbf{1} \mid \mathbf{X_1}]$ gives the independence model. The $\widetilde{\mathbf{X}}_2$ matrix is the projection of $\mathbf{X_2}$ onto the orthogonal complement of the space spanned by the columns of $\mathbf{X_1}$, where the orthogonality is defined with respect to $\mathbf{V}_{srs}$; i.e., $\widetilde{\mathbf{X}}_2' \mathbf{V}_{srs} \mathbf{X_1} = \mathbf{0}$.

See Rao and Scott (1984) for the proof justifying (1) and (2). However, even without a full understanding, you can get a feeling for Δ. It is like a ratio (although remember that it is a matrix) of two variances. The variance in the numerator involves the variance under the true survey design, and the variance in the denominator involves the variance assuming that the design was simple random sampling. The design effect DEFF for an estimated proportion (see [SVY] **estat**) is defined as

$$\text{DEFF} = \frac{\widehat{V}(\widehat{p}_{rc})}{\widetilde{V}_{srsor}(\widetilde{p}_{rc})}$$

Hence, Δ can be regarded as a design-effects matrix, and Rao and Scott call its eigenvalues, the δ_ks, the "generalized design effects".

Computing an estimate for Δ by using estimates for $\mathbf{V}$ and $\mathbf{V}_{\mathrm{srs}}$ is easy. Rao and Scott (1984) derive a simpler formula for $\widehat{\Delta}$:

$$\widehat{\Delta} = \left(\mathbf{C}'\mathbf{D}_{\widehat{\mathbf{p}}}^{-1}\widehat{V}_{\mathrm{srs}}\mathbf{D}_{\widehat{\mathbf{p}}}^{-1}\mathbf{C}\right)^{-1}\left(\mathbf{C}'\mathbf{D}_{\widehat{\mathbf{p}}}^{-1}\widehat{V}\mathbf{D}_{\widehat{\mathbf{p}}}^{-1}\mathbf{C}\right)$$

Here $\mathbf{C}$ is a contrast matrix that is any $RC \times (R-1)(C-1)$ full-rank matrix orthogonal to $[\mathbf{1}\,|\,\mathbf{X}_1]$; i.e., $\mathbf{C}'\mathbf{1} = \mathbf{0}$ and $\mathbf{C}'\mathbf{X}_1 = \mathbf{0}$. $\mathbf{D}_{\widehat{\mathbf{p}}}$ is a diagonal matrix with the estimated proportions $\widehat{p}_{rc}$ on the diagonal. When one of the $\widehat{p}_{rc}$ is zero, the corresponding variance estimate is also zero; hence, the corresponding element for $\mathbf{D}_{\widehat{\mathbf{p}}}^{-1}$ is immaterial for computing $\widehat{\Delta}$.

Unfortunately, (1) is not practical for computing a p-value. However, you can compute simple first-order and second-order corrections based on it. A first-order correction is based on downweighting the i.i.d. statistics by the average eigenvalue of $\widehat{\Delta}$; namely, you compute

$$X_{\mathrm{P}}^2(\widehat{\delta}.) = X_{\mathrm{P}}^2/\widehat{\delta}. \qquad \text{and} \qquad X_{\mathrm{LR}}^2(\widehat{\delta}.) = X_{\mathrm{LR}}^2/\widehat{\delta}.$$

where $\widehat{\delta}.$ is the mean-generalized DEFF

$$\widehat{\delta}. = \frac{1}{(R-1)(C-1)}\sum_{k=1}^{(R-1)(C-1)}\delta_k$$

These corrected statistics are asymptotically distributed as $\chi_{(R-1)(C-1)}^2$. Thus, to first-order, you can view the i.i.d. statistics X_{P}^2 and X_{LR}^2 as being "too big" by a factor of $\widehat{\delta}.$ for true survey design.

A better second-order correction can be obtained by using the Satterthwaite approximation to the distribution of a weighted sum of χ_1^2 variables. Here the Pearson statistic becomes

$$X_{\mathrm{P}}^2(\widehat{\delta}., \widehat{a}) = \frac{X_{\mathrm{P}}^2}{\widehat{\delta}.(\widehat{a}^2 + 1)} \tag{3}$$

where $\widehat{a}$ is the coefficient of variation of the eigenvalues:

$$\widehat{a}^2 = \frac{\sum\widehat{\delta}_k^2}{(R-1)(C-1)\widehat{\delta}.^2} - 1$$

Because $\sum\widehat{\delta}_k = \operatorname{tr}\widehat{\Delta}$ and $\sum\widehat{\delta}_k^2 = \operatorname{tr}\widehat{\Delta}^2$, (3) can be written in an easily computable form as

$$X_{\mathrm{P}}^2(\widehat{\delta}., \widehat{a}) = \frac{\operatorname{tr}\widehat{\Delta}}{\operatorname{tr}\widehat{\Delta}^2}\,X_{\mathrm{P}}^2$$

These corrected statistics are asymptotically distributed as χ_d^2, with

$$d = \frac{(R-1)(C-1)}{\widehat{a}^2 + 1} = \frac{(\operatorname{tr}\widehat{\Delta})^2}{\operatorname{tr}\widehat{\Delta}^2}$$

i.e., a χ^2 with, in general, noninteger degrees of freedom. The likelihood-ratio statistic X_{LR}^2 can also be given this second-order correction in an identical manner.

Two issues remain. First, there are two possible ways to compute the variance estimate $\widehat{V}_{\text{srs}}$, which is used to compute $\widehat{\Delta}$. $\mathbf{V}_{\text{srs}}$ has diagonal elements $p_{rc}(1 - p_{rc})/m$ and off-diagonal elements $-p_{rc}p_{st}/m$, but here p_{rc} is the true, not estimated, proportion. Hence, the question is what to use to estimate p_{rc}: the observed proportions, $\widehat{p}_{rc}$, or the proportions estimated under the null hypothesis of independence, $\widehat{p}_{0rc} = \widehat{p}_r.\widehat{p}._c$? Rao and Scott (1984, 53) leave this as an open question.

Because of the question of using $\widehat{p}_{rc}$ or $\widehat{p}_{0rc}$ to compute $\widehat{V}_{\text{srs}}$, svy: tabulate can compute both corrections. By default, when the null option is not specified, only the correction based on $\widehat{p}_{rc}$ is displayed. If null is specified, two corrected statistics and corresponding p-values are displayed, one computed using $\widehat{p}_{rc}$ and the other using $\widehat{p}_{0rc}$.

The second outstanding issue concerns the degrees of freedom resulting from the variance estimate, $\widehat{V}$, of the cell proportions under the survey design. The customary degrees of freedom for t statistics resulting from this variance estimate is $\nu = n - L$, where n is the number of PSUs in the sample and L is the number of strata.

Rao and Thomas (1989) suggest turning the corrected χ^2 statistic into an F statistic by dividing it by its degrees of freedom, $d_0 = (R - 1)(C - 1)$. The F statistic is then taken to have numerator degrees of freedom equal to d_0 and denominator degrees of freedom equal to νd_0. Hence, the corrected Pearson F statistic is

$$F_{\text{P}} = \frac{X_{\text{P}}^2}{\text{tr}\,\widehat{\Delta}} \quad \text{with} \quad F_{\text{P}} \sim F(d, \nu d) \quad \text{where} \quad d = \frac{(\text{tr}\,\widehat{\Delta})^2}{\text{tr}\,\widehat{\Delta}^2} \quad \text{and} \quad \nu = n - L \qquad (4)$$

This is the corrected statistic that svy: tabulate displays by default or when the pearson option is specified. When the lr option is specified, an identical correction is produced for the likelihood-ratio statistic X_{LR}^2. When null is specified, (4) is also used. For the statistic labeled "D-B (null)", $\widehat{\Delta}$ is computed using $\widehat{p}_{0rc}$. For the statistic labeled "Design-based", $\widehat{\Delta}$ is computed using $\widehat{p}_{rc}$.

The Wald statistics computed by svy: tabulate with the wald and llwald options were developed by Koch, Freeman, and Freeman (1975). The statistic given by the wald option is similar to the Pearson statistic because it is based on

$$\widehat{Y}_{rc} = \widehat{N}_{rc} - \widehat{N}_r.\widehat{N}._c/\widehat{N}..$$

where $r = 1, \ldots, R - 1$ and $c = 1, \ldots, C - 1$. The delta method can be used to estimate the variance of $\widehat{\mathbf{Y}}$ (which is $\widehat{Y}_{rc}$ stacked into a vector), and a Wald statistic can be constructed in the usual manner:

$$W = \widehat{\mathbf{Y}}' \big\{ \mathbf{J}_{\mathbf{N}} \widehat{V}(\widehat{\mathbf{N}}) \mathbf{J}_{\mathbf{N}}' \big\}^{-1} \widehat{\mathbf{Y}} \quad \text{where} \quad \mathbf{J}_{\mathbf{N}} = \partial\widehat{\mathbf{Y}}/\partial\widehat{\mathbf{N}}'$$

The statistic given by the llwald option is based on the log-linear model with predictors $[\mathbf{1}|\mathbf{X}_1|\mathbf{X}_2]$ that was mentioned earlier. This Wald statistic is

$$W_{\text{LL}} = \big(\mathbf{X}_2' \ln\widehat{\mathbf{p}}\big)' \big\{ \mathbf{X}_2' \mathbf{J}_{\mathbf{p}} \widehat{V}(\widehat{\mathbf{p}}) \mathbf{J}_{\mathbf{p}}' \mathbf{X}_2 \big\}^{-1} \big(\mathbf{X}_2' \ln\widehat{\mathbf{p}}\big)$$

where $\mathbf{J}_{\mathbf{p}}$ is the matrix of first derivatives of $\ln\widehat{\mathbf{p}}$ with respect to $\widehat{\mathbf{p}}$, which is, of course, just a matrix with $\widehat{p}_{rc}^{-1}$ on the diagonal and zero elsewhere. This log-linear Wald statistic is undefined when there is a zero cell in the table.

Unadjusted F statistics (noadjust option) are produced using

$$F_{\text{unadj}} = W/d_0 \quad \text{with} \quad F_{\text{unadj}} \sim F(d_0, \nu)$$

Adjusted F statistics are produced using

$$F_{\text{adj}} = (\nu - d_0 + 1)W/(\nu d_0) \qquad \text{with} \qquad F_{\text{adj}} \sim F(d_0, \nu - d_0 + 1)$$

The other svy estimators also use this adjustment procedure for F statistics. See Korn and Graubard (1990) for a justification of the procedure.

References

Fuller, W. A., W. J. Kennedy Jr., D. Schnell, G. Sullivan, and H. J. Park. 1986. *PC CARP*. Software package. Ames, IA: Statistical Laboratory, Iowa State University.

Jann, B. 2008. Multinomial goodness-of-fit: Large-sample tests with survey design correction and exact tests for small samples. *Stata Journal* 8: 147–169.

Koch, G. G., D. H. Freeman Jr., and J. L. Freeman. 1975. Strategies in the multivariate analysis of data from complex surveys. *International Statistical Review* 43: 59–78.

Korn, E. L., and B. I. Graubard. 1990. Simultaneous testing of regression coefficients with complex survey data: Use of Bonferroni t statistics. *American Statistician* 44: 270–276.

McDowell, A., A. Engel, J. T. Massey, and K. Maurer. 1981. Plan and operation of the Second National Health and Nutrition Examination Survey, 1976–1980. *Vital and Health Statistics* 1(15): 1–144.

Rao, J. N. K., and A. J. Scott. 1981. The analysis of categorical data from complex sample surveys: Chi-squared tests for goodness of fit and independence in two-way tables. *Journal of the American Statistical Association* 76: 221–230.

———. 1984. On chi-squared tests for multiway contingency tables with cell proportions estimated from survey data. *Annals of Statistics* 12: 46–60.

Rao, J. N. K., and D. R. Thomas. 1989. Chi-squared tests for contingency tables. In *Analysis of Complex Surveys*, ed. C. J. Skinner, D. Holt, and T. M. F. Smith, 89–114. New York: Wiley.

Research Triangle Institute. 1997. *SUDAAN User's Manual, Release 7.5*. Research Triangle Park, NC: Research Triangle Institute.

Sribney, W. M. 1998. svy7: Two-way contingency tables for survey or clustered data. *Stata Technical Bulletin* 45: 33–49. Reprinted in *Stata Technical Bulletin Reprints*, vol. 8, pp. 297–322. College Station, TX: Stata Press.

Thomas, D. R., and J. N. K. Rao. 1987. Small-sample comparisons of level and power for simple goodness-of-fit statistics under cluster sampling. *Journal of the American Statistical Association* 82: 630–636.

Also see

Title

svydescribe — Describe survey data

Syntax

svydescribe [*varlist*] [*if*] [*in*] [, *options*]

options	description
Main	
stage(*#*)	sampling stage to describe; default is stage(1)
finalstage	display information per sampling unit in the final stage
single	display only the strata with one sampling unit
generate(*newvar*)	generate a variable identifying strata with one sampling unit

svydescribe requires that the survey design variables be identified using svyset; see [SVY] **svyset**.

Menu

Statistics > Survey data analysis > Setup and utilities > Describe survey data

Description

svydescribe displays a table that describes the strata and the sampling units for a given sampling stage in a survey dataset.

Options

> ⌐ Main ⌐

stage(*#*) specifies the sampling stage to describe. The default is stage(1).

finalstage specifies that results be displayed for each sampling unit in the final sampling stage; that is, a separate line of output is produced for every sampling unit in the final sampling stage. This option is not allowed with stage(), single, or generate().

single specifies that only the strata containing one sampling unit be displayed in the table.

generate(*newvar*) stores a variable that identifies strata containing one sampling unit for a given sampling stage.

Remarks

Survey datasets are typically the result of a stratified survey design with cluster sampling in one or more stages. Within a stratum for a given sampling stage, there are sampling units, which may be either clusters of observations or individual observations.

svydescribe displays a table that describes the strata and sampling units for a given sampling stage. One row of the table is produced for each stratum. Each row contains the number of sampling units, the range and mean of the number of observations per sampling unit, and the total number of observations. If the finalstage option is specified, one row of the table is produced for each sampling unit of the final stage. Here each row contains the number of observations for the respective sampling unit.

If a varlist is specified, svydescribe reports the number of sampling units that contain at least one observation with complete data (i.e., no missing values) for all variables in *varlist*. These are the sampling units that would be used to compute point estimates by using the variables in *varlist* with a given svy estimation command.

▷ Example 1: Strata with one sampling unit

We use data from the Second National Health and Nutrition Examination Survey (NHANES II) (McDowell et al. 1981) as our example. First, we set the PSU, pweight, and strata variables.

```
. use http://www.stata-press.com/data/r11/nhanes2b
. svyset psuid [pweight=finalwgt], strata(stratid)
      pweight: finalwgt
          VCE: linearized
  Single unit: missing
     Strata 1: stratid
        SU 1: psuid
       FPC 1: <zero>
```

svydescribe will display the strata and PSU arrangement of the dataset.

```
. svydescribe
Survey: Describing stage 1 sampling units
      pweight: finalwgt
          VCE: linearized
  Single unit: missing
     Strata 1: stratid
        SU 1: psuid
       FPC 1: <zero>
```

| | | | #Obs per Unit | | |
Stratum	#Units	#Obs	min	mean	max
1	2	380	165	190.0	215
2	2	185	67	92.5	118
3	2	348	149	174.0	199
(output omitted)					
17	2	393	180	196.5	213
18	2	359	144	179.5	215
20	2	285	125	142.5	160
21	2	214	102	107.0	112
(output omitted)					
31	2	308	143	154.0	165
32	2	450	211	225.0	239
31	62	10351	67	167.0	288

Our NHANES II dataset has 31 strata (stratum 19 is missing) and two PSUs per stratum.

The hdresult variable contains serum levels of high-density lipoprotein (HDL). If we try to estimate the mean of hdresult, we get a missing value for the standard-error estimate and a note explaining why.

```
. svy: mean hdresult
(running mean on estimation sample)

Survey: Mean estimation

Number of strata =      31      Number of obs    =      8720
Number of PSUs   =      60      Population size  = 98725345
                                Design df        =        29
```

	Mean	Linearized Std. Err.	[95% Conf. Interval]	
hdresult	49.67141	.	.	.

```
Note: missing standard error because of stratum with single
      sampling unit.
```

Running svydescribe with hdresult and the single option will show which strata have only one PSU.

```
. svydescribe hdresult, single
Survey: Describing strata with a single sampling unit in stage 1
        pweight: finalwgt
            VCE: linearized
    Single unit: missing
        Strata 1: stratid
           SU 1: psuid
          FPC 1: <zero>
```

			#Obs with	#Obs with	#Obs per included Unit		
Stratum	#Units included	#Units omitted	complete data	missing data	min	mean	max
1	1*	1	114	266	114	114.0	114
2	1*	1	98	87	98	98.0	98
	2						

Both stratid = 1 and stratid = 2 have only one PSU with nonmissing values of hdresult. Because this dataset has only 62 PSUs, the finalstage option produces a manageable amount of output:

```
. svydescribe hdresult, finalstage

Survey: Describing final stage sampling units

      pweight: finalwgt
          VCE: linearized
  Single unit: missing
     Strata 1: stratid
         SU 1: psuid
        FPC 1: <zero>
```

| | | #Obs with complete | #Obs with missing |
Stratum	Unit	data	data
1	1	0	215
1	2	114	51
2	1	98	20
2	2	0	67
(output omitted)			
32	2	203	8
31	62	8720	1631

```
                           10351
```

It is rather striking that there are two PSUs with no values for `hdresult`. All other PSUs have only a moderate number of missing values. Obviously, here a data analyst should first try to ascertain why these data are missing. The answer here (C. L. Johnson, 1995, pers. comm.) is that HDL measurements could not be collected until the third survey location. Thus there are no `hdresult` data for the first two locations: `stratid = 1`, `psuid = 1` and `stratid = 2`, `psuid = 2`.

Assuming that we wish to go ahead and analyze the `hdresult` data, we must collapse strata—that is, merge them—so that every stratum has at least two PSUs with some nonmissing values. We can accomplish this by collapsing `stratid = 1` into `stratid = 2`. To perform the stratum collapse, we create a new strata identifier, `newstr`, and a new PSU identifier, `newpsu`.

```
. gen newstr = stratid

. gen newpsu = psuid

. replace newpsu = psuid + 2 if stratid == 1
(380 real changes made)

. replace newstr = 2 if stratid == 1
(380 real changes made)
```

svyset the new PSU and strata variables.

```
. svyset newpsu [pweight=finalwgt], strata(newstr)

      pweight: finalwgt
          VCE: linearized
  Single unit: missing
     Strata 1: newstr
         SU 1: newpsu
        FPC 1: <zero>
```

Then use `svydescribe` to check what we have done.

```
. svydescribe hdresult, finalstage
Survey: Describing final stage sampling units
        pweight: finalwgt
            VCE: linearized
    Single unit: missing
       Strata 1: newstr
          SU 1: newpsu
         FPC 1: <zero>
```

		#Obs with complete data	#Obs with missing data
Stratum	Unit		
2	1	98	20
2	2	0	67
2	3	0	215
2	4	114	51
3	1	161	38
3	2	116	33
(output omitted)			
32	1	180	59
32	2	203	8
30	62	8720	1631

```
                        10351
```

The new stratum, `newstr` = 2, has four PSUs, two of which contain some nonmissing values of `hdresult`. This is sufficient to allow us to estimate the mean of `hdresult` and get a nonmissing standard-error estimate.

```
. svy: mean hdresult
(running mean on estimation sample)

Survey: Mean estimation

Number of strata =      30       Number of obs    =      8720
Number of PSUs   =      60       Population size  =  98725345
                                 Design df        =        30
```

	Mean	Linearized Std. Err.	[95% Conf. Interval]	
hdresult	49.67141	.3830147	48.88919	50.45364

◁

▷ Example 2: Using e(sample) to find strata with one sampling unit

Some estimation commands drop observations from the estimation sample when they encounter collinear predictors or perfect predictors. Ascertaining which strata contain one sampling unit is therefore difficult. We can then use if e(sample) instead of *varlist* when faced with the problem of strata with one sampling unit. We revisit the previous analysis to illustrate.

```
. use http://www.stata-press.com/data/r11/nhanes2b, clear

. svy: mean hdresult
(running mean on estimation sample)

Survey: Mean estimation

Number of strata =      31        Number of obs    =      8720
Number of PSUs   =      60        Population size   = 98725345
                                  Design df        =        29
```

	Mean	Linearized Std. Err.	[95% Conf. Interval]
hdresult	49.67141	.	. .

```
Note: missing standard error because of stratum with single
      sampling unit.

. svydescribe if e(sample), single

Survey: Describing strata with a single sampling unit in stage 1

      pweight: finalwgt
          VCE: linearized
  Single unit: missing
     Strata 1: stratid
         SU 1: psu
        FPC 1: <zero>
```

			#Obs per Unit		
Stratum	#Units	#Obs	min	mean	max
1	1*	114	114	114.0	114
2	1*	98	98	98.0	98
	2				

◁

Methods and formulas

svydescribe is implemented as an ado-file. See Eltinge and Sribney (1996) for an earlier implementation of svydescribe.

References

Eltinge, J. L., and W. M. Sribney. 1996. svy3: Describing survey data: Sampling design and missing data. *Stata Technical Bulletin* 31: 23–26. Reprinted in *Stata Technical Bulletin Reprints*, vol. 6, pp. 235–239. College Station, TX: Stata Press.

McDowell, A., A. Engel, J. T. Massey, and K. Maurer. 1981. Plan and operation of the Second National Health and Nutrition Examination Survey, 1976–1980. *Vital and Health Statistics* 1(15): 1–144.

Also see

[SVY] **svy** — The survey prefix command

[SVY] **svyset** — Declare survey design for dataset

[SVY] **survey** — Introduction to survey commands

[SVY] **variance estimation** — Variance estimation for survey data

Title

> **svymarkout** — Mark observations for exclusion on the basis of survey characteristics

Syntax

svymarkout [*markvar*]

Description

svymarkout is a programmer's command that resets the values of *markvar* to contain 0 wherever any of the survey-characteristic variables (previously set by svyset) contain missing values.

svymarkout assumes that *markvar* was created by marksample or mark; see [P] **mark**. This command is most helpful for developing estimation commands that use ml to fit models using maximum pseudolikelihood directly, instead of relying on the svy prefix; see [P] **program properties** for a discussion of how to write programs to be used with the svy prefix.

> ## Example 1

```
program mysvyprogram, ...
    ...
    syntax ...
    marksample touse
    svymarkout 'touse'
    ...
end
```

◁

Saved results

svymarkout saves the following in s():

Macros
  s(weight)   weight variable set by svyset

Methods and formulas

svymarkout is implemented as an ado-file.

Also see

[P] **mark** — Mark observations for inclusion

[P] **program properties** — Properties of user-defined programs

Title

> **svyset** — Declare survey design for dataset

Syntax

Single-stage design

> svyset $\left[\,psu\,\right]$ $\left[\,weight\,\right]$ $\left[\,,\ design\_options\ options\,\right]$

Multiple-stage design

> svyset psu $\left[\,weight\,\right]$ $\left[\,,\ design\_options\,\right]$ $\left[\,|\,|\ ssu,\ design\_options\,\right]$ ... $\left[\,options\,\right]$

Clear the current settings

> svyset, clear

Report the current settings

> svyset

design_options	description
Main	
<u>strata</u>(*varname*)	variable identifying strata
fpc(*varname*)	finite population correction

options	description
Weights	
<u>brrweight</u>(*varlist*)	balanced repeated replicate (BRR) weights
fay(*#*)	Fay's adjustment
<u>jkrweight</u>(*varlist*, ...)	jackknife replicate weights
SE	
vce(<u>linear</u>ized)	Taylor linearized variance estimation
vce(brr)	BRR variance estimation
vce(<u>jack</u>knife)	jackknife variance estimation
mse	use the MSE formula with vce(brr) or vce(jackknife)
<u>single</u>unit(*method*)	strata with one sampling unit; *method* may be <u>miss</u>ing, <u>cert</u>ainty, <u>sca</u>led, or <u>cen</u>tered
Poststratification	
<u>post</u>strata(*varname*)	variable identifying poststrata
<u>postw</u>eight(*varname*)	poststratum population sizes

†clear	clear all settings from the data
†noclear	change some of the settings without clearing the others
†clear(*opnames*)	clear specified settings without clearing all others; *opnames* may be one or more of <u>w</u>eight, vce, mse, <u>brr</u>weight, <u>jkr</u>weight, or <u>post</u>strata

†clear, noclear, and clear() are not shown in the dialog box.

pweights and iweights are allowed; see [U] **11.1.6 weight**.

The full specification for jkrweight() is

<u>jkr</u>weight(*varlist* [, <u>str</u>atum(# [# ...]) fpc(# [# ...]) <u>mult</u>iplier(# [# ...]) reset])

Menu

Statistics > Survey data analysis > Setup and utilities > Declare survey design for dataset

Description

svyset declares the data to be complex survey data, designates variables that contain information about the survey design, and specifies the default method for variance estimation. You must svyset your data before using any svy command; see [SVY] **svy estimation**.

psu is _n or the name of a variable (numeric or string) that contains identifiers for the primary sampling units (clusters). Use _n to indicate that individuals (instead of clusters) were randomly sampled if the design does not involve clustered sampling. In the single-stage syntax, *psu* is optional and defaults to _n.

ssu is _n or the name of a variable (numeric or string) that contains identifiers for sampling units (clusters) in subsequent stages of the survey design. Use _n to indicate that individuals were randomly sampled within the last sampling stage.

Settings made by svyset are saved with a dataset. So, if a dataset is saved after it has been svyset, it does not have to be set again.

The current settings are reported when svyset is called without arguments:

. svyset

Use the clear option to remove the current settings:

. svyset, clear

See [SVY] **poststratification** for a discussion with examples using the poststrata() and postweight() options.

Options

> Main

strata(*varname*) specifies the name of a variable (numeric or string) that contains stratum identifiers.

fpc(*varname*) requests a finite population correction for the variance estimates. If *varname* has values less than or equal to 1, it is interpreted as a stratum sampling rate $f_h = n_h/N_h$, where n_h = number of units sampled from stratum h and N_h = total number of units in the population belonging to stratum h. If *varname* has values greater than or equal to n_h, it is interpreted as containing N_h. It is an error for *varname* to have values between 1 and n_h or to have a mixture of sampling rates and stratum sizes.

<hr>

⌐ Weights ⌐

brrweight(*varlist*) specifies the replicate-weight variables to be used with vce(brr).

fay(*#*) specifies Fay's adjustment. The value specified in fay(*#*) is used to adjust the BRR weights and is present in the BRR variance formulas.

The sampling weight of the selected PSUs for a given replicate is multiplied by $2-\#$, where the sampling weight for the unselected PSUs is multiplied by $\#$. When brrweight(*varlist*) is specified, the replicate-weight variables in *varlist* are assumed to be adjusted using $\#$.

fay(0) is the default and is equivalent to the original BRR method. fay(1) is not allowed because this results in unadjusted weights.

jkrweight(*varlist*, ...) specifies the replicate-weight variables to be used with vce(jackknife).

The following options set characteristics on the jackknife replicate-weight variables. If one value is specified, all the specified jackknife replicate-weight variables will be supplied with the same characteristic. If multiple values are specified, each replicate-weight variable will be supplied with the corresponding value according to the order specified. These options are not shown in the dialog box.

stratum(# [# ...]) specifies an identifier for the stratum in which the sampling weights have been adjusted.

fpc(# [# ...]) specifies the FPC value to be added as a characteristic of the jackknife replicate-weight variables. The values set by this suboption have the same interpretation as the fpc(*varname*) option.

multiplier(# [# ...]) specifies the value of a jackknife multiplier to be added as a characteristic of the jackknife replicate-weight variables.

reset indicates that the characteristics for the replicate-weight variables may be overwritten or reset to the default, if they exist.

<hr>

⌐ SE ⌐

vce(*vcetype*) specifies the default method for variance estimation; see [SVY] **variance estimation**.

vce(linearized) sets the default to Taylor linearization.

vce(brr) sets the default to BRR; also see [SVY] **svy brr**.

vce(jackknife) sets the default to the jackknife; also see [SVY] **svy jackknife**.

mse specifies that the MSE formula be used when vce(brr) or vce(jackknife) is specified. This option requires vce(brr) or vce(jackknife).

singleunit(*method*) specifies how to handle strata with one sampling unit.

singleunit(missing) results in missing values for the standard errors and is the default.

singleunit(certainty) causes strata with single sampling units to be treated as certainty units. Certainty units contribute nothing to the standard error.

singleunit(scaled) results in a scaled version of singleunit(certainty). The scaling factor comes from using the average of the variances from the strata with multiple sampling units for each stratum with one sampling unit.

singleunit(centered) specifies that strata with one sampling unit are centered at the grand mean instead of the stratum mean.

⌐ Poststratification ⌐

poststrata(*varname*) specifies the name of the variable (numeric or string) that contains poststratum identifiers.

postweight(*varname*) specifies the name of the numeric variable that contains poststratum population totals (or sizes), i.e., the number of elementary sampling units in the population within each poststratum.

The following options are available with svyset but are not shown in the dialog box:

clear clears all the settings from the data. Typing

```
. svyset, clear
```

clears the survey design characteristics from the data in memory. Although this option may be specified with some of the other svyset options, it is redundant because svyset automatically clears the previous settings before setting new survey design characteristics.

noclear allows some of the options in *options* to be changed without clearing all the other settings. This option is not allowed with *psu*, *ssu*, *design_options*, or clear.

clear(*opnames*) allows some of the options in *options* to be cleared without clearing all the other settings. *opnames* refers to an option name and may be one or more of the following:

```
weight   vce   mse   brrweight   jkrweight   poststrata
```

This option implies the noclear option.

Remarks

Remarks are presented under the following headings:

> *Introduction to survey design characteristics*
> *Finite population correction (FPC)*
> *Multiple-stage designs and with-replacement sampling*
> *Replication-weight variables*
> *Combining datasets from multiple surveys*

Introduction to survey design characteristics

Stata's suite of commands for survey data analysis relies on properly identified survey design characteristics for point estimation, model fitting, and variance estimation. In fact, the svy prefix will report an error if no survey design characteristics have been identified using svyset. Typical survey design characteristics include sampling weights, one or more stages of clustered sampling, and stratification. O'Donnell et al. (2008, 26–27) show four survey sample designs with the corresponding svyset specification. Use svyset to declare your dataset to be complex survey data by specifying the survey design variables. We will use the following contrived dataset for the examples in this section.

```
. use http://www.stata-press.com/data/r11/stage5a
```

▷ Example 1: Simple random sampling with replacement

Use _n for *psu* to specify that the primary sampling units (PSUs) are the sampled individuals.

```
. svyset _n
      pweight: <none>
          VCE: linearized
  Single unit: missing
     Strata 1: <one>
         SU 1: <observations>
        FPC 1: <zero>
```

The output from svyset states that there are no sampling weights (each observation is given a sampling weight of 1), there is only one stratum (which is the same as no stratification), and the PSUs are the observed individuals.

◁

▷ Example 2: One-stage clustered design with stratification

The most commonly specified design, one-stage clustered design with stratification, can be used to approximate multiple-stage designs when only the first-stage information is available. In this design, the population is partitioned into strata and the PSUs are sampled independently within each stratum. A dataset from this design will have a variable that identifies the strata, another variable that identifies the PSUs, and a variable containing the sampling weights. Let's assume that these variables are, respectively, strata, su1, and pw.

```
. svyset su1 [pweight=pw], strata(strata)
      pweight: pw
          VCE: linearized
  Single unit: missing
     Strata 1: strata
         SU 1: su1
        FPC 1: <zero>
```

◁

▷ Example 3: Two-stage designs

In two-stage designs, the PSUs are sampled without replacement and then collections of individuals are sampled within the selected PSUs. svyset uses || (double "or" bars) to separate the stage-specific design specifications. The first-stage information is specified before ||, and the second-stage information is specified afterward. We will assume that the variables containing the finite population correction (FPC) information for the two stages are named fpc1 and fpc2; see the next section for a discussion about the FPC.

Use _n for *ssu* to specify that the second-stage sampling units are the sampled individuals.

```
. svyset su1 [pweight=pw], fpc(fpc1) || _n, fpc(fpc2)
      pweight: pw
          VCE: linearized
  Single unit: missing
     Strata 1: <one>
         SU 1: su1
        FPC 1: fpc1
     Strata 2: <one>
         SU 2: <observations>
        FPC 2: fpc2
```

Suppose that su2 identifies the clusters of individuals sampled in the second stage.

```
. svyset su1 [pweight=pw], fpc(fpc1) || su2, fpc(fpc2)

      pweight: pw
          VCE: linearized
  Single unit: missing
     Strata 1: <one>
        SU 1: su1
       FPC 1: fpc1
     Strata 2: <one>
        SU 2: su2
       FPC 2: fpc2
```

Stratification can take place in one or both of the sampling stages. Suppose that strata identifies the second-stage strata and the first stage was not stratified.

```
. svyset su1 [pweight=pw], fpc(fpc1) || su2, fpc(fpc2) strata(strata)

      pweight: pw
          VCE: linearized
  Single unit: missing
     Strata 1: <one>
        SU 1: su1
       FPC 1: fpc1
     Strata 2: strata
        SU 2: su2
       FPC 2: fpc2
```

◁

▷ Example 4: Multiple-stage designs

Specifying designs with three or more stages is not much more difficult than specifying two-stage designs. Each stage will have its own variables for identifying strata, sampling units, and the FPC. Not all stages will be stratified and some will be sampled with replacement; thus some stages may not have a variable for identifying strata or the FPC.

Suppose that we have a three-stage design with variables su# and fpc# for the sampling unit and FPC information in stage #. Also assume that the design called for stratification in the first stage only.

```
. svyset su1 [pweight=pw], fpc(fpc1) strata(strata)
>            || su2, fpc(fpc2)
>            || su3, fpc(fpc3)

      pweight: pw
          VCE: linearized
  Single unit: missing
     Strata 1: strata
        SU 1: su1
       FPC 1: fpc1
     Strata 2: <one>
        SU 2: su2
       FPC 2: fpc2
     Strata 3: <one>
        SU 3: su3
       FPC 3: fpc3
```

Use _n for *ssu* in the last stage if the individuals are sampled within the third stage of clustered sampling.

```
. svyset su1 [pweight=pw], fpc(fpc1) strata(strata)
>              || su2, fpc(fpc2)
>              || su3, fpc(fpc3)
>              || _n
      pweight: pw
          VCE: linearized
  Single unit: missing
     Strata 1: strata
         SU 1: su1
        FPC 1: fpc1
     Strata 2: <one>
         SU 2: su2
        FPC 2: fpc2
     Strata 3: <one>
         SU 3: su3
        FPC 3: fpc3
     Strata 4: <one>
         SU 4: <observations>
        FPC 4: <zero>
```

◁

Finite population correction (FPC)

An FPC accounts for the reduction in variance that occurs when sampling *without* replacement from a finite population compared to sampling *with* replacement from the same population. Specifying an FPC variable for stage i indicates that the sampling units in that stage were sampled without replacement. See Cochran (1977) for an introduction to variance estimation and sampling without replacement.

▷ Example 5

Consider the following dataset:

```
. use http://www.stata-press.com/data/r11/fpc
. list
```

	stratid	psuid	weight	nh	Nh	x
1.	1	1	3	5	15	2.8
2.	1	2	3	5	15	4.1
3.	1	3	3	5	15	6.8
4.	1	4	3	5	15	6.8
5.	1	5	3	5	15	9.2
6.	2	1	4	3	12	3.7
7.	2	2	4	3	12	6.6
8.	2	3	4	3	12	4.2

Here the variable nh is the number of PSUs per stratum that were sampled, Nh is the total number of PSUs per stratum in the sampling frame (i.e., the population), and x is our survey item of interest.

If we wish to use a finite population correction in our computations, we must svyset an FPC variable when we specify the variables for sampling weights, PSUs, and strata. The FPC variable typically contains the number of sampling units per stratum in the population; Nh is our FPC variable. Here we estimate the population mean of x assuming sampling without replacement.

```
. svyset psuid [pweight=weight], strata(stratid) fpc(Nh)

       pweight: weight
           VCE: linearized
   Single unit: missing
      Strata 1: stratid
          SU 1: psuid
         FPC 1: Nh

. svy: mean x
(running mean on estimation sample)

Survey: Mean estimation

Number of strata =        2      Number of obs    =        8
Number of PSUs   =        8      Population size  =       27
                                 Design df        =        6
```

		Linearized		
	Mean	Std. Err.	[95% Conf. Interval]	
x	5.448148	.6160407	3.940751	6.955545

We must respecify the survey design before estimating the population mean of x assuming sampling with replacement.

```
. svyset psuid [pweight=weight], strata(stratid)

       pweight: weight
           VCE: linearized
   Single unit: missing
      Strata 1: stratid
          SU 1: psuid
         FPC 1: <zero>

. svy: mean x
(running mean on estimation sample)

Survey: Mean estimation

Number of strata =        2      Number of obs    =        8
Number of PSUs   =        8      Population size  =       27
                                 Design df        =        6
```

		Linearized		
	Mean	Std. Err.	[95% Conf. Interval]	
x	5.448148	.7412683	3.63433	7.261966

Including an FPC always reduces the variance estimate. However, the reduction in the variance estimates will be small when the N_h are large relative to the n_h.

Rather than having a variable that represents the total number of PSUs per stratum in the sampling frame, we sometimes have a variable that represents a sampling rate $f_h = n_h/N_h$. The syntax for svyset is the same whether the FPC variable contains N_h or f_h. The survey variance-estimation routines in Stata are smart enough to identify what type of FPC information has been specified. If the FPC variable is less than or equal to 1, it is interpreted as a sampling rate; if it is greater than or equal to n_h, it is interpreted as containing N_h. It is an error for the FPC variable to have values between 1 and n_h or to have a mixture of sampling rates and stratum sizes.

◁

Multiple-stage designs and with-replacement sampling

Although survey data are seldom collected using with-replacement sampling, dropping the FPC information when the sampling fractions are small is common. In either case, svyset ignores the design variables specified in later sampling stages because this information is not necessary for variance estimation. In the following, we describe why this is true.

▷ Example 6

Consider the two-stage design where PSUs are sampled with replacement and individuals are sampled without replacement within the selected PSUs. Sampling the individuals with replacement would change some of the details in the following discussion, but the result would be the same.

Our population contains 100 PSUs, with five individuals in each, so our population size is 500. We will sample 10 PSUs with replacement and then sample two individuals without replacement from within each selected PSU. This results in a dataset with 10 PSUs, each with 2 observations, for a total of 20 observations. If our dataset contained the PSU information in variable su1 and the second-stage FPC information in variable fpc2, our svyset command would be as follows.

```
. use http://www.stata-press.com/data/r11/svyset_wr
. svyset su1 || _n, fpc(fpc2)
Note: stage 1 is sampled with replacement; all further stages will be ignored
      pweight: <none>
          VCE: linearized
  Single unit: missing
     Strata 1: <one>
         SU 1: su1
        FPC 1: <zero>
```

As expected, svyset tells us that it is ignoring the second-stage information because the first-stage units were sampled with replacement. Because we do not have an FPC variable for the first stage, we can regard the sampling of PSUs as a series of independently and identically distributed draws. The second-sampled PSU is drawn independently from the first and has the same sampling distribution because the first-sampled PSU is eligible to be sampled again.

Consider the following alternative scenario. Because there are 10 ways to pick two people of five, let's expand the 100 PSUs to form $100 \times 10 = 1,000$ "new PSUs" (NPSUs), each of size 2, representing all possible two-person groups that can be sampled from the original 100 groups of five people. We now have a population of $1,000 \times 2 = 2,000$ "new people"; each original person was replicated four times. We can select 10 NPSUs with replacement to end up with a dataset consisting of 10 groups of two to form samples of 20 people. If our "new" dataset contained the PSU information in variable nsu1, our svyset command would be as follows:

```
. svyset nsu1
      pweight: <none>
          VCE: linearized
  Single unit: missing
     Strata 1: <one>
         SU 1: nsu1
        FPC 1: <zero>
```

There is nothing from a sampling standpoint to distinguish between our two scenarios. The information contained in the variables su1 and nsu1 is equivalent; thus svyset can behave as if our dataset came from the second scenario.

The following questions may spring to mind after reading the above:

- The population in the first scenario has 500 people; the second has 2,000. Does that not invalidate the comparison between the two scenarios?

  Although the populations are different, the sampling schemes described for each scenario result in the same sampling space. By construction, each possible sample from the first scenario is also a possible sample from the second scenario. For the first scenario, the number of possible samples of 10 of 100 PSUs sampled with replacement, where two of five individuals are sampled without replacement, is

$$100^{10} \times \binom{5}{2}^{10} = 10^{30}$$

  For the second scenario, the number of possible samples of 10 of 1,000 NPSUs sampled with replacement, where each NPSU is sampled as a whole, is

$$1,000^{10} = 10^{30}$$

- Does the probability of being in the sample not depend on what happens in the first sampling stage?

  Not when the first stage is sampled with replacement. Sampling with replacement means that all PSUs have the same chance of being selected even after one of the PSUs has been selected. Thus each of the two-person groups that can possibly be sampled has the same chance of being sampled even after a specific two-person group has been selected.

- Is it valid to have replicated people in the population like the one in the second scenario?

  Yes, because each person in the population can be sampled more than once. Sampling with replacement allows us to construct the replicated people.

  ◁

Replication-weight variables

Many groups that collect survey data for public use have taken steps to protect the privacy of the survey participants. This may result in datasets that have replicate-weight variables instead of variables that identify the strata and sampling units from the sampling stages. These datasets require replication methods for variance estimation.

The brrweight() and jkrweight() options allow svyset to identify the set of replication weights for use with BRR and jackknife variance estimation (svy brr and svy jackknife), respectively. In addition to the weight variables, svyset also allows you to change the default variance estimation method from linearization to BRR or the jackknife.

▷ Example 7

Here are two simple examples using jackknife replication weights.

1. Data containing only sampling weights and jackknife replication weights, and we set the default variance estimator to the jackknife:

```
. use http://www.stata-press.com/data/r11/stage5a_jkw
. svyset [pweight=pw], jkrweight(jkw_*) vce(jackknife)
      pweight: pw
          VCE: jackknife
          MSE: off
    jkrweight: jkw_1 jkw_2 jkw_3 jkw_4 jkw_5 jkw_6 jkw_7 jkw_8 jkw_9
  Single unit: missing
     Strata 1: <one>
         SU 1: <observations>
        FPC 1: <zero>
```

2. Data containing only sampling weights and jackknife replication weights, and we set the default variance estimator to the jackknife by using the MSE formula:

```
. svyset [pweight=pw], jkrweight(jkw_*) vce(jackknife) mse
      pweight: pw
          VCE: jackknife
          MSE: on
    jkrweight: jkw_1 jkw_2 jkw_3 jkw_4 jkw_5 jkw_6 jkw_7 jkw_8 jkw_9
  Single unit: missing
     Strata 1: <one>
         SU 1: <observations>
        FPC 1: <zero>
```

◁

▷ Example 8: Characteristics for jackknife replicate-weight variables

The jkrweight() option has suboptions that allow you to identify certain characteristics of the jackknife replicate-weight variables. These characteristics include the following:

- An identifier for the stratum in which the sampling weights have been adjusted because one of its PSUs was dropped. We use the stratum() suboption to set these values. The default is one stratum for all the replicate-weight variables.

- The FPC value. We use the fpc() suboption to set these values. The default value is zero.

  This characteristic is ignored when the mse option is supplied to svy jackknife.

- A jackknife multiplier used in the formula for variance estimation. The multiplier for the standard leave-one-out jackknife method is

$$\frac{n_h - 1}{n_h}$$

where n_h is the number of PSUs sampled from stratum h. We use the multiplier() suboption to set these values. The default is derived from the above formula, assuming that n_h is equal to the number of replicate-weight variables for stratum h.

Because of privacy concerns, public survey datasets may not contain stratum-specific information. However, the population size and an overall jackknife multiplier will probably be provided. You must then supply this information to svyset for the jackknife replicate-weight variables. We will use the 1999–2000 NHANES data to illustrate how to set these characteristics.

The NHANES datasets for years 1999–2000 are available for download from the Centers for Disease Control and Prevention (CDC) web site, http://www.cdc.gov. This particular release of the NHANES data contains jackknife replication weights in addition to the usual PSU and stratum information. These variables are contained in the demographic dataset. In Stata, we copied the demographic data from the CDC web site by typing

```
. copy http://www.cdc.gov/nchs/about/major/nhanes/frequency/demo.xpt demo.xpt
```

The 1999–2000 NHANES datasets are distributed in SAS Transport format, so we use Stata's fdause command to read the data into memory. Because of the nature of the survey design, the demographic dataset demo.xpt has two sampling-weight variables. wtint2yr contains the sampling weights appropriate for the interview data, and wtmec2yr contains the sampling weights appropriate for the Mobile Examination Center (MEC) exam data. Consequently, there are two sets of jackknife replicate-weight variables. The jackknife replicate-weight variables for the interview data are named wtirep01, wtirep02, ..., wtirep52. The jackknife replicate-weight variables for the MEC exam data are named wtmrep01, wtmrep02, ..., wtmrep52. The documentation published with the NHANES data gives guidance on which weight variables to use.

```
. fdause demo.xpt

. describe wtint2yr wtmec2yr wtirep01 wtmrep01

              storage  display   value
variable name  type    format    label   variable label

wtint2yr      double  %10.0g              Full Sample 2 Year Interview
                                          Weight
wtmec2yr      double  %10.0g              Full Sample 2 Year Mec Exam
                                          Weight
wtirep01      double  %10.0g              Interview Weight Jack Knife
                                          Replicate 01
wtmrep01      double  %10.0g              Mec Exam Weight Jack Knife
                                          Replicate 01
```

The number of PSUs in the NHANES population is not apparent, so we will not set an FPC value, but we can set the standard jackknife multiplier for the 52 replicate-weight variables and save the results as a Stata dataset for future use. Also the NHANES datasets all contain a variable called seqn. This variable has a respondent sequence number that allows the dataset users to merge the demographic dataset with other 1999–2000 NHANES datasets, so we sort on seqn before saving demo99_00.dta.

```
. local mult = 51/52

. svyset, jkrweight(wtmrep*, multiplier('mult'))
  (output omitted )

. svyset, jkrweight(wtirep*, multiplier('mult'))
  (output omitted )

. svyset, clear

. sort seqn

. save demo99_00
file demo99_00.dta saved
```

To complete this example, we will perform a simple analysis using the blood pressure data; however, before we can perform any analysis, we have to merge the blood pressure dataset, bpx.xpt, with our demographic dataset, demo99_00.dta. In Stata, we copied the blood pressure dataset from the CDC web site by typing

```
. copy http://www.cdc.gov/nchs/data/nhanes/frequency/bpx.xpt bpx.xpt
```

We can then use fdause to read in the blood pressure data, sort on seqn, and save the resulting dataset to bpx99_00.dta. We read in our copy of the demographic data, drop the irrelevant weight variables, and merge in the blood pressure data from bpx99_00.dta. A quick call to tabulate on the _merge variable generated by merge indicates that 683 observations in the demographic data are not present in the blood pressure data. We do not drop these observations; otherwise, the estimate of the population size will be incorrect. Finally, we set the appropriate sampling and replicate-weight variables with svyset before replacing bpx99_00.dta with a more complete copy of the blood pressure data.

```
. fdause bpx.xpt

. sort seqn

. save bpx99_00
file bpx99_00.dta saved

. use demo99_00

. drop wtint?yr wtirep*

. merge 1:1 seqn using bpx99_00

    Result                          # of obs.

    not matched                          683
        from master                      683   (_merge==1)
        from using                         0   (_merge==2)

    matched                            9,282   (_merge==3)


. drop _merge

. svyset [pw=wtmec2yr], jkrweight(wtmrep*) vce(jackknife)
  (output omitted )

. save bpx99_00, replace
file bpx99_00.dta saved
```

Having saved our merged dataset (with svysettings), we estimate the mean systolic blood pressure for the population, using the MEC exam replication weights for jackknife variance estimation.

```
. svy: mean bpxsar
(running mean on estimation sample)

Jackknife replications (52)
─────┼── 1 ──┼── 2 ──┼── 3 ──┼── 4 ──┼── 5
.................................................   50
..

Survey: Mean estimation

Number of strata =        1      Number of obs    =        7215
                                 Population size   =   231756417
                                 Replications      =          52
                                 Design df         =          51

                            Jackknife
                  Mean      Std. Err.      [95% Conf. Interval]

      bpxsar   119.7056    .5109122        118.6799    120.7313
```

◁

Combining datasets from multiple surveys

The 2001–2002 NHANES datasets are also available from the CDC web site, http://www.cdc.gov. The guidelines that are published with these datasets recommend that the 1999–2000 and 2001–2002 NHANES datasets be combined to increase the accuracy of results. Combining datasets from multiple surveys is a complicated process, and Stata has no specific tools for this task. However, the distributors of the NHANES datasets provide sampling-weight variables for the 1999–2002 combined data in the respective demographic datasets. They also provide some simple instructions on how to combine the datasets from these two surveys.

In the previous example, we worked with the 1999–2000 NHANES data. The 2001–2002 NHANES demographics data are contained in demo_b.xpt, and the blood pressure data are contained in bpx_b.xpt. We follow the same steps as in the previous example to merge the blood pressure data with the demographic data for 2001–2002.

```
. copy http://www.cdc.gov/nchs/about/major/nhanes/nhanes2001-2002/bpx_b.xpt bpx_b.xpt
. copy http://www.cdc.gov/nchs/about/major/nhanes/nhanes2001-2002/demo_b.xpt demo_b.xpt
. fdause bpx_b.xpt
. sort seqn
. save bpx01_02
file bpx01_02.dta saved
. fdause demo_b.xpt
. drop wtint?yr
. sort seqn
. merge 1:1 seqn using bpx01_02

    Result                       # of obs.

    not matched                        562
        from master                    562  (_merge==1)
        from using                       0  (_merge==2)

    matched                         10,477  (_merge==3)

. drop _merge
. svyset sdmvpsu [pw=wtmec2yr], strata(sdmvstra)

      pweight: wtmec2yr
          VCE: linearized
  Single unit: missing
     Strata 1: sdmvstra
         SU 1: sdmvpsu
        FPC 1: <zero>

. save bpx01_02, replace
file bpx01_02.dta saved
```

The demographic dataset for 2001–2002 does not contain replicate-weight variables, but there are variables that provide information on PSUs and strata for variance estimation. The PSU information is contained in sdmvpsu, and the stratum information is in sdmvstra. See the documentation that comes with the NHANES datasets for the details regarding these variables.

This new blood pressure dataset (bpx01_02.dta) is all we need if we are interested in analyzing blood pressure data only for 2001–2002. However, we want to use the 1999–2002 combined data, so we will follow the advice in the guidelines and just combine the datasets from the two surveys.

For those concerned about overlapping stratum identifiers between the two survey datasets, it is a simple exercise to check that sdmvstra ranges from 1 to 13 for 1999–2000 but ranges from 14 to 28 for 2001–2002. Thus the stratum identifiers do not overlap, so we can simply append the data.

The 2001–2002 NHANES demographic dataset has no jackknife replicate-weight variables, so we drop the replicate-weight variables from the 1999–2000 dataset. The sampling-weight variable wtmec2yr is no longer appropriate for use with the combined data because its values are based on the survey designs individually, so we drop it from the combined dataset. Finally, we use svyset to identify the design variables for the combined surveys. wtmec4yr is the sampling-weight variable for the MEC exam data developed by the data producers for the combined 1999–2002 NHANES data.

```
. use bpx99_00

. drop wt?rep*

. append using bpx01_02

. drop wtmec2yr

. svyset sdmvpsu [pw=wtmec4yr], strata(sdmvstra)
      pweight: wtmec4yr
          VCE: linearized
  Single unit: missing
     Strata 1: sdmvstra
        SU 1: sdmvpsu
       FPC 1: <zero>

. save bpx99_02
file bpx99_02.dta saved
```

Now we can estimate the mean systolic blood pressure for our population by using the combined surveys and jackknife variance estimation.

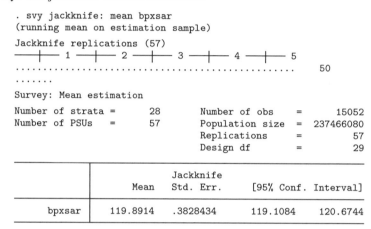

```
. svy jackknife: mean bpxsar
(running mean on estimation sample)
Jackknife replications (57)
──┼── 1 ──┼── 2 ──┼── 3 ──┼── 4 ──┼── 5
..................................................   50
.......

Survey: Mean estimation

Number of strata =      28      Number of obs    =       15052
Number of PSUs   =      57      Population size  =   237466080
                                Replications     =          57
                                Design df        =          29
```

	Mean	Jackknife Std. Err.	[95% Conf. Interval]	
bpxsar	119.8914	.3828434	119.1084	120.6744

(Continued on next page)

Saved results

svyset saves the following in r():

Scalars
    r(stages)   number of sampling stages

Macros
    r(wtype)   weight type
    r(wexp)   weight expression
    r(wvar)   weight variable name
    r(su#)   variable identifying sampling units for stage #
    r(strata#)   variable identifying strata for stage #
    r(fpc#)   FPC for stage #
    r(brrweight)   brrweight() variable list
    r(fay)   Fay's adjustment
    r(jkrweight)   jkrweight() variable list
    r(vce)   *vcetype* specified in vce()
    r(mse)   mse, if specified
    r(poststrata)   poststrata() variable
    r(postweight)   postweight() variable
    r(settings)   svyset arguments to reproduce the current settings
    r(singleunit)   singleunit() setting

Methods and formulas

svyset is implemented as an ado-file.

References

Cochran, W. G. 1977. *Sampling Techniques*. 3rd ed. New York: Wiley.

O'Donnell, O., E. van Doorslaer, A. Wagstaff, and M. Lindelow. 2008. *Analyzing Health Equity Using Household Survey Data: A Guide to Techniques and Their Implementation*. Washington, DC: The World Bank.

Also see

[SVY] **svy** — The survey prefix command

[SVY] **svydescribe** — Describe survey data

[SVY] **survey** — Introduction to survey commands

[SVY] **poststratification** — Poststratification for survey data

[SVY] **subpopulation estimation** — Subpopulation estimation for survey data

[SVY] **variance estimation** — Variance estimation for survey data

Title

> **variance estimation** — Variance estimation for survey data

Description

Stata's suite of estimation commands for survey data use the three most commonly used variance estimation techniques: BRR, jackknife, and linearization. This entry discusses the details of these variance estimation techniques.

Also see Cochran (1977), Wolter (2007), and Shao and Tu (1995) for some background on these variance estimators.

Remarks

Remarks are presented under the following headings:

> *Variance of the total*
>> *Stratified single-stage design*
>> *Stratified two-stage design*
> *Variance for census data*
> *Certainty sampling units*
> *Strata with one sampling unit*
> *Ratios and other functions of survey data*
>> *Revisiting the total estimator*
>> *The ratio estimator*
>> *A note about score variables*
> *Linearized/robust variance estimation*
> *BRR*
> *The jackknife*
>> *The delete-one jackknife*
>> *The delete-k jackknife*
> *Confidence intervals*

Variance of the total

This section describes the methods and formulas for svy: total. The variance estimators not using replication methods use the variance of a total as an important ingredient; this section therefore also introduces variance estimation for survey data.

We will discuss the variance estimators for two complex survey designs:

1. The stratified single-stage design is the simplest design that has the elements present in most complex survey designs.

2. Adding a second stage of clustering to the previous design results in a variance estimator for designs with multiple stages of clustered sampling.

Stratified single-stage design

The population is partitioned into groups called *strata*. Clusters of observations are randomly sampled—with or without replacement—from within each stratum. These clusters are called *primary sampling units* (PSUs). In single-stage designs, data are collected from every member of the sampled PSUs. When the observed data are analyzed, sampling weights are used to account for the survey design. If the PSUs were sampled without replacement, a finite population correction (FPC) is applied to the variance estimator.

The svyset syntax to specify this design is

svyset *psu* [pweight=*weight*], strata(*strata*) fpc(*fpc*)

The stratum identifiers are contained in the variable named *strata*, PSU identifiers are contained in variable *psu*, the sampling weights are contained in variable *weight*, and the values for the FPC are contained in variable *fpc*.

Let $h = 1, \ldots, L$ count the strata and (h, i) denote the ith PSU in stratum h, where $i = 1, \ldots, N_h$ and N_h is the number of PSUs in stratum h. Let (h, i, j) denote the jth individual from PSU (h, i) and M_{hi} be the number of individuals in PSU (h, i); then

$$M = \sum_{h=1}^{L} \sum_{i=1}^{N_h} M_{hi}$$

is the number of individuals in the population. Let Y_{hij} be a survey item for individual (h, i, j); for example, Y_{hij} might be income for adult j living in block i of county h. The associated population total is

$$Y = \sum_{h=1}^{L} \sum_{i=1}^{N_h} \sum_{j=1}^{M_{hi}} Y_{hij}$$

Let y_{hij} denote the items for individuals who are members of the sampled PSUs; here $h = 1, \ldots, L$; $i = 1, \ldots, n_h$; and $j = 1, \ldots, m_{hi}$. The number of individuals in the sample (number of observations) is

$$m = \sum_{h=1}^{L} \sum_{i=1}^{n_h} m_{hi}$$

The estimator for Y is

$$\widehat{Y} = \sum_{h=1}^{L} \sum_{i=1}^{n_h} \sum_{j=1}^{m_{hi}} w_{hij} y_{hij}$$

where w_{hij} is a sampling weight, and its unadjusted value for this design is $w_{hij} = N_h / n_h$. The estimator for the number of individuals in the population (population size) is

$$\widehat{M} = \sum_{h=1}^{L} \sum_{i=1}^{n_h} \sum_{j=1}^{m_{hi}} w_{hij}$$

The estimator for the variance of $\widehat{Y}$ is

$$\widehat{V}(\widehat{Y}) = \sum_{h=1}^{L} (1 - f_h) \frac{n_h}{n_h - 1} \sum_{i=1}^{n_h} (y_{hi} - \overline{y}_h)^2 \tag{1}$$

where y_{hi} is the weighted total for PSU (h, i),

$$y_{hi} = \sum_{j=1}^{m_{hi}} w_{hij} y_{hij}$$

and $\overline{y}_h$ is the mean of the PSU totals for stratum h:

$$\overline{y}_h = \frac{1}{n_h} \sum_{i=1}^{n_h} y_{hi}$$

The factor $(1 - f_h)$ is the FPC for stratum h, and f_h is the sampling rate for stratum h. The sampling rate f_h is derived from the variable specified in the fpc() option of svyset. If an FPC variable is not svyset, then $f_h = 0$. If an FPC variable is set and its values are greater than or equal to n_h, then the variable is assumed to contain the values of N_h, and f_h is given by $f_h = n_h/N_h$. If its values are less than or equal to 1, then the variable is assumed to contain the sampling rates f_h.

If multiple variables are supplied to svy: total, covariances are also computed. The estimator for the covariance between $\widehat{Y}$ and $\widehat{X}$ (notation for X is defined similarly to that of Y) is

$$\widehat{\mathrm{Cov}}(\widehat{Y}, \widehat{X}) = \sum_{h=1}^{L} (1 - f_h) \frac{n_h}{n_h - 1} \sum_{i=1}^{n_h} (y_{hi} - \overline{y}_h)(x_{hi} - \overline{x}_h)$$

Stratified two-stage design

The population is partitioned into strata. PSUs are randomly sampled without replacement from within each stratum. Clusters of observations are then randomly sampled—with or without replacement—from within the sampled PSUs. These clusters are called *secondary sampling units* (SSUs). Data are then collected from every member of the sampled SSUs. When the observed data are analyzed, sampling weights are used to account for the survey design. Each sampling stage provides a component to the variance estimator and has its own FPC.

The svyset syntax to specify this design is

svyset *psu* [pweight=*weight*], strata(*strata*) fpc(*fpc₁*) || *ssu*, fpc(*fpc₂*)

The stratum identifiers are contained in the variable named *strata*, PSU identifiers are contained in variable *psu*, the sampling weights are contained in variable *weight*, the values for the FPC for the first sampling stage are contained in variable *fpc₁*, SSU identifiers are contained in variable *ssu*, and the values for the FPC for the second sampling stage are contained in variable *fpc₂*.

The notation for this design is based on the previous notation. There still are L strata, and (h, i) identifies the ith PSU in stratum h. Let M_{hi} be the number of SSUs in PSU (h, i), M_{hij} be the number of individuals in SSU (h, i, j), and

$$M = \sum_{h=1}^{L} \sum_{i=1}^{N_h} \sum_{j=1}^{M_{hi}} M_{hij}$$

be the population size. Let Y_{hijk} be a survey item for individual (h, i, j, k); for example, Y_{hijk} might be income for adult k living in block j of county i of state h. The associated population total is

$$Y = \sum_{h=1}^{L} \sum_{i=1}^{N_h} \sum_{j=1}^{M_{hi}} \sum_{k=1}^{M_{hij}} Y_{hijk}$$

Let y_{hijk} denote the items for individuals who are members of the sampled SSUs; here $h = 1$, $\ldots$, L; $i = 1, \ldots, n_h$; $j = 1, \ldots, m_{hi}$; and $k = 1, \ldots, m_{hij}$. The number of observations is

$$m = \sum_{h=1}^{L} \sum_{i=1}^{n_h} \sum_{j=1}^{m_{hi}} m_{hij}$$

The estimator for Y is

$$\widehat{Y} = \sum_{h=1}^{L} \sum_{i=1}^{n_h} \sum_{j=1}^{m_{hi}} \sum_{k=1}^{m_{hij}} w_{hijk} y_{hijk}$$

where w_{hijk} is a sampling weight, and its unadjusted value for this design is

$$w_{hijk} = \left(\frac{N_h}{n_h} \right) \left(\frac{M_{hi}}{m_{hi}} \right)$$

The estimator for the population size is

$$\widehat{M} = \sum_{h=1}^{L} \sum_{i=1}^{n_h} \sum_{j=1}^{m_{hi}} \sum_{k=1}^{m_{hij}} w_{hijk}$$

The estimator for the variance of $\widehat{Y}$ is

$$\widehat{V}(\widehat{Y}) = \sum_{h=1}^{L} (1 - f_h) \frac{n_h}{n_h - 1} \sum_{i=1}^{n_h} (y_{hi} - \overline{y}_h)^2$$

$$+ \sum_{h=1}^{L} f_h \sum_{i=1}^{n_h} (1 - f_{hi}) \frac{m_{hi}}{m_{hi} - 1} \sum_{j=1}^{m_{hi}} (y_{hij} - \overline{y}_{hi})^2 \tag{2}$$

where y_{hi} is the weighted total for PSU (h, i); $\overline{y}_h$ is the mean of the PSU totals for stratum h; y_{hij} is the weighted total for SSU (h, i, j),

$$y_{hij} = \sum_{k=1}^{m_{hij}} w_{hijk} y_{hijk}$$

and $\overline{y}_{hi}$ is the mean of the SSU totals for PSU (h, i),

$$\overline{y}_{hi} = \frac{1}{m_{hi}} \sum_{j=1}^{m_{hi}} y_{hij}$$

Equation (2) is equivalent to (1) with an added term representing the increase in variability because of the second stage of sampling. The factor $(1 - f_h)$ is the FPC, and f_h is the sampling rate for the first stage of sampling. The factor $(1 - f_{hi})$ is the FPC, and f_{hi} is the sampling rate for PSU (h, i). The sampling rate f_{hi} is derived in the same manner as f_h.

If multiple variables are supplied to `svy: total`, covariances are also computed. For estimated totals $\widehat{Y}$ and $\widehat{X}$ (notation for X is defined similarly to that of Y), the covariance estimator is

$$\widehat{\text{Cov}}(\widehat{Y}, \widehat{X}) = \sum_{h=1}^{L} (1 - f_h) \frac{n_h}{n_h - 1} \sum_{i=1}^{n_h} (y_{hi} - \overline{y}_h)(x_{hi} - \overline{x}_h)$$

$$+ \sum_{h=1}^{L} f_h \sum_{i=1}^{n_h} (1 - f_{hi}) \frac{m_{hi}}{m_{hi} - 1} \sum_{j=1}^{m_{hi}} (y_{hij} - \overline{y}_{hi})(x_{hij} - \overline{x}_{hi})$$

On the basis of the formulas (1) and (2), writing down the variance estimator for a survey design with three or more stages is a matter of deriving the variance component for each sampling stage. The sampling units from a given stage pose as strata for the next sampling stage.

All but the last stage must be sampled without replacement to get nonzero variance components from each stage of clustered sampling. For example, if $f_h = 0$ in (2), the second stage contributes nothing to the variance estimator.

Variance for census data

The point estimates that result from the analysis of census data, in which the entire population was sampled without replacement, are the population's parameters instead of random variables. As such, there is no sample-to-sample variation if we consider the population fixed. Here the sampling fraction is one; thus, if the FPC variable you `svyset` for the first sampling stage is one, Stata will report a standard error of zero.

Certainty sampling units

Stata's svy commands identify strata with an FPC equal to one as units sampling with certainty. To properly determine the design degrees of freedom, certainty sampling units should be contained within their own strata, one for each certainty unit, in each sampling stage. Although the observations contained in certainty units have a role in parameter estimation, they contribute nothing to the variance.

Strata with one sampling unit

By default, Stata's svy commands report missing standard errors when they encounter a stratum with one sampling unit. Although the best way to solve this problem is to reassign the sampling unit to another appropriately chosen stratum, there are three automatic alternatives that you can choose from, in the `singleunit()` option, when you `svyset` your data.

`singleunit(certainty)` treats the strata with single sampling units as certainty units.

`singleunit(scaled)` treats the strata with single sampling units as certainty units but multiplies the variance components from each stage by a scaling factor. For a given sampling stage, suppose that L is the total number of strata, L_c is the number of certainty strata, and L_s is the number of strata with one sampling unit, and then the scaling factor is $(L - L_c)/(L - L_c - L_s)$. Using this scaling factor is the same as using the average of the variances from the strata with multiple sampling units for each stratum with one sampling unit.

`singleunit(centered)` specifies that strata with one sampling unit are centered at the population mean instead of the stratum mean. The quotient $n_h/(n_h - 1)$ in the variance formula is also taken to be 1 if $n_h = 1$.

Ratios and other functions of survey data

Shah (2004) points out a simple procedure for deriving the linearized variance for functions of survey data that are continuous functions of the sampling weights. Let θ be a (possibly vector-valued) function of the population data and $\widehat{\theta}$ be its associated estimator based on survey data.

1. Define the jth observation of the score variable by

$$z_j = \frac{\partial \widehat{\theta}}{\partial w_j}$$

If $\widehat{\theta}$ is implicitly defined through estimating equations, z_j can be computed by taking the partial derivative of the estimating equations with respect to w_j.

2. Define the weighted total of the score variable by

$$\widehat{Z} = \sum_{j=1}^{m} w_j z_j$$

3. Estimate the variance $V(\widehat{Z})$ by using the design-based variance estimator for the total $\widehat{Z}$. This variance estimator is an approximation of $V(\widehat{\theta})$.

Revisiting the total estimator

As a first example, we derive the variance of the total from a stratified single-stage design. Here you have $\widehat{\theta} = \widehat{Y}$, and deriving the score variable for $\widehat{Y}$ results in the original values of the variable of interest.

$$z_j(\widehat{\theta}) = z_j(\widehat{Y}) = \frac{\partial \widehat{Y}}{\partial w_j} = y_j$$

Thus you trivially recover the variance of the total given in (1) and (2).

The ratio estimator

The estimator for the population ratio is

$$\widehat{R} = \frac{\widehat{Y}}{\widehat{X}}$$

and its score variable is

$$z_j(\widehat{R}) = \frac{\partial \widehat{R}}{\partial w_j} = \frac{y_j - \widehat{R}\, x_j}{\widehat{X}}$$

Plugging this into (1) or (2) results in a variance estimator that is algebraically equivalent to the variance estimator derived from directly applying the delta method (a first-order Taylor expansion with respect to y and x)

$$\widehat{V}(\widehat{R}) = \frac{1}{\widehat{X}^2}\{\widehat{V}(\widehat{Y}) - 2\widehat{R}\,\widehat{\mathrm{Cov}}(\widehat{Y}, \widehat{X}) + \widehat{R}^2\,\widehat{V}(\widehat{X})\}$$

A note about score variables

The functional form of the score variable for each estimation command is detailed in the *Methods and formulas* section of its manual entry; see [R] **total**, [R] **ratio**, and [R] **mean**.

Although Deville (1999) and Demnati and Rao (2004) refer to z_j as the *linearized variable*, here it is referred to as the *score variable* to tie it more closely to the model-based estimators discussed in the following section.

Linearized/robust variance estimation

The regression models for survey data that allow the vce(linearized) option use *linearization*-based variance estimators that are natural extensions of the variance estimator for totals. For general background on regression and generalized linear model analysis of complex survey data, see Binder (1983); Cochran (1977); Fuller (1975); Godambe (1991); Kish and Frankel (1974); Särndal, Swensson, and Wretman (1992); and Skinner (1989).

Suppose that you observed $(Y_j, \mathbf{x}_j)$ for the entire population and are interested in modeling the relationship between Y_j and $\mathbf{x}_j$ by the vector of parameters β that solve the following estimating equations:

$$G(\beta) = \sum_{j=1}^{M} S(\beta; Y_j, \mathbf{x}_j) = 0$$

For ordinary least squares, $G(\beta)$ is the normal equations

$$G(\beta) = X'Y - X'X\beta = 0$$

where Y is the vector of outcomes for the full population and X is the matrix of explanatory variables for the full population. For a pseudolikelihood model—such as logistic regression—$G(\beta)$ is the first derivative of the log-pseudolikelihood function with respect to β. Estimate β by solving for $\widehat{\beta}$ from the weighted sample estimating equations

$$\widehat{G}(\beta) = \sum_{j=1}^{m} w_j S(\beta; y_j, \mathbf{x}_j) = 0 \tag{3}$$

The associated estimation command with iweights will produce point estimates $\widehat{\beta}$ equal to the solution of (3).

A first-order matrix Taylor-series expansion yields

$$\widehat{\beta} - \beta \approx - \left\{ \frac{\partial \widehat{G}(\beta)}{\partial \beta} \right\}^{-1} \widehat{G}(\beta)$$

with the following variance estimator for $\widehat{\beta}$:

$$\widehat{V}(\widehat{\beta}) = \left[\left\{ \frac{\partial \widehat{G}(\beta)}{\partial \beta} \right\}^{-1} \widehat{V}\{\widehat{G}(\beta)\} \left\{ \frac{\partial \widehat{G}(\beta)}{\partial \beta} \right\}^{-T} \right] \Bigg|_{\beta=\widehat{\beta}} = D\widehat{V}\{\widehat{G}(\beta)\} \Bigg|_{\beta=\widehat{\beta}} D'$$

where D is $(X'_s W X_s)^{-1}$ for linear regression (where W is a diagonal matrix of the sampling weights and X_s is the matrix of sampled explanatory variables) or the inverse of the negative Hessian matrix from the pseudolikelihood model. Write $\widehat{G}(\beta)$ as

$$\widehat{G}(\beta) = \sum_{j=1}^{m} w_j \mathbf{d}_j$$

where $\mathbf{d}_j = s_j \mathbf{x}_j$ and s_j is a residual for linear regression or an equation-level score from the pseudolikelihood model. The term *equation-level score* means the derivative of the log pseudolikelihood with respect to $\mathbf{x}_j \beta$. In either case, $\widehat{G}(\widehat{\beta})$ is an estimator for the total $G(\beta)$, and the variance estimator $\widehat{V}\{\widehat{G}(\beta)\}|_{\beta=\widehat{\beta}}$ is computed using the design-based variance estimator for a total.

The above result is easily extended to models with ancillary parameters, multiple regression equations, or both.

BRR

BRR was first introduced by McCarthy (1966, 1969a, and 1969b) as a method of variance estimation for designs with two PSUs in every stratum. The BRR variance estimator tends to give more reasonable variance estimates for this design than the linearized variance estimator, which can result in large values and undesirably wide confidence intervals.

The model is fit multiple times, once for each of a balanced set of combinations where one PSU is dropped (or downweighted) from each stratum. The variance is estimated using the resulting replicated point estimates (replicates). Although the BRR method has since been generalized to include other designs, Stata's implementation of BRR requires two PSUs per stratum.

Let $\widehat{\theta}$ be the vector of point estimates computed using the sampling weights for a given stratified survey design (e.g., $\widehat{\theta}$ could be a vector of means, ratios, or regression coefficients). Each BRR replicate is produced by dropping (or downweighting) a PSU from every stratum. This could result in as many as 2^L replicates for a dataset with L strata; however, the BRR method uses Hadamard matrices to identify a balanced subset of the combinations from which to produce the replicates.

A Hadamard matrix is a square matrix, H_r (with r rows and columns), such that $H'_r H_r = rI$, where I is the identity matrix. The elements of H_r are $+1$ and -1; -1 causes the first PSU to be downweighted and $+1$ causes the second PSU to be downweighted. Thus r must be greater than or equal to the number of strata.

Suppose that we are about to generate the adjusted-weight variable for the ith replication and w_j is the sampling weight attached to the jth observation, which happens to be in the first PSU of stratum h. The adjusted weight is

$$w_j^* = \begin{cases} f w_j, & \text{if } H_r[i,h] = -1 \\ (2-f)w_j, & \text{if } H_r[i,h] = +1 \end{cases}$$

where f is Fay's adjustment (Judkins 1990). By default, $f = 0$.

Each replicate is produced using an adjusted-weight variable with the estimation command that computed $\widehat{\theta}$. The adjusted-weight variables can be generated by Stata or supplied to svyset with the brrweight() option. We call the variables supplied to the brrweight() option "BRR replicate-weight variables".

Let $\widehat{\boldsymbol{\theta}}_{(i)}$ be the vector of point estimates from the ith replication. When the `mse` option is specified, the variance estimator is

$$\widehat{V}(\boldsymbol{\theta}) = \frac{1}{r(1-f)^2} \sum_{i=1}^{r} \{\widehat{\boldsymbol{\theta}}_{(i)} - \widehat{\boldsymbol{\theta}}\}\{\widehat{\boldsymbol{\theta}}_{(i)} - \widehat{\boldsymbol{\theta}}\}'$$

Otherwise, the variance estimator is

$$\widehat{V}(\boldsymbol{\theta}) = \frac{1}{r(1-f)^2} \sum_{i=1}^{r} \{\widehat{\boldsymbol{\theta}}_{(i)} - \overline{\boldsymbol{\theta}}_{(.)}\}\{\widehat{\boldsymbol{\theta}}_{(i)} - \overline{\boldsymbol{\theta}}_{(.)}\}'$$

where $\overline{\boldsymbol{\theta}}_{(.)}$ is the BRR mean,

$$\overline{\boldsymbol{\theta}}_{(.)} = \frac{1}{r} \sum_{i=1}^{r} \widehat{\boldsymbol{\theta}}_{(i)}$$

The jackknife

The jackknife method for variance estimation is appropriate for many models and survey designs. The model is fit multiple times, and each time one or more PSUs are dropped from the estimation sample. The variance is estimated using the resulting replicates (replicated point estimates).

Let $\widehat{\boldsymbol{\theta}}$ be the vector of point estimates computed using the sampling weights for a given survey design (e.g., $\widehat{\boldsymbol{\theta}}$ could be a vector of means, ratios, or regression coefficients). The dataset is resampled by dropping one or more PSUs from one stratum and adjusting the sampling weights before recomputing a replicate for $\widehat{\boldsymbol{\theta}}$.

Let w_{hij} be the sampling weight for the jth individual from PSU i in stratum h. Suppose that you are about to generate the adjusted weights for the replicate resulting from dropping k PSUs from stratum h. The adjusted weight is

$$w_{abj}^{*} = \begin{cases} 0, & \text{if } a = h \text{ and } b \text{ is dropped} \\ \dfrac{n_h}{n_h - k} w_{abj}, & \text{if } a = h \text{ and } b \text{ is not dropped} \\ w_{abj}, & \text{otherwise} \end{cases}$$

Each replicate is produced by using the adjusted-weight variable with the estimation command that produced $\widehat{\boldsymbol{\theta}}$. For the delete-one jackknife (where one PSU is dropped for each replicate), adjusted weights can be generated by Stata or supplied to `svyset` with the `jkrweight()` option. For the delete-k jackknife (where $k > 1$ PSUs are dropped for each replicate), the adjusted-weight variables must be supplied to `svyset` using the `jkrweight()` option. The variables supplied to the `jkrweight()` option are called *jackknife replicate-weight variables*.

The delete-one jackknife

Let $\widehat{\boldsymbol{\theta}}_{(h,i)}$ be the point estimates (replicate) from leaving out the ith PSU from stratum h. The pseudovalue for replicate (h, i) is

$$\widehat{\boldsymbol{\theta}}_{h,i}^{*} = \widehat{\boldsymbol{\theta}}_{(h,i)} + n_h\{\widehat{\boldsymbol{\theta}} - \widehat{\boldsymbol{\theta}}_{(h,i)}\}$$

When the `mse` option is specified, the variance estimator is

$$\widehat{V}(\boldsymbol{\theta}) = \sum_{h=1}^{L}(1 - f_h)\, m_h \sum_{i=1}^{n_h}\{\widehat{\boldsymbol{\theta}}_{(h,i)} - \widehat{\boldsymbol{\theta}}\}\{\widehat{\boldsymbol{\theta}}_{(h,i)} - \widehat{\boldsymbol{\theta}}\}'$$

and the jackknife mean is

$$\overline{\boldsymbol{\theta}}_{(.)} = \frac{1}{n}\sum_{h=1}^{L}\sum_{i=1}^{n_h}\widehat{\boldsymbol{\theta}}_{(h,i)}$$

where f_h is the sampling rate and m_h is the jackknife multiplier associated with stratum h. Otherwise, the variance estimator is

$$\widehat{V}(\boldsymbol{\theta}) = \sum_{h=1}^{L}(1 - f_h)\, m_h \sum_{i=1}^{n_h}\{\widehat{\boldsymbol{\theta}}_{(h,i)} - \overline{\boldsymbol{\theta}}_h\}\{\widehat{\boldsymbol{\theta}}_{(h,i)} - \overline{\boldsymbol{\theta}}_h\}', \qquad \overline{\boldsymbol{\theta}}_h = \frac{1}{n_h}\sum_{i=1}^{n_h}\widehat{\boldsymbol{\theta}}_{(h,i)}$$

and the jackknife mean is

$$\overline{\boldsymbol{\theta}}^* = \frac{1}{n}\sum_{h=1}^{L}\sum_{i=1}^{n_h}\widehat{\boldsymbol{\theta}}^*_{h,i}$$

The multiplier for the delete-one jackknife is

$$m_h = \frac{n_h - 1}{n_h}$$

The delete-k jackknife

Let $\widetilde{\boldsymbol{\theta}}_{(h,d)}$ be one of the point estimates that resulted from leaving out k PSUs from stratum h. Let c_h be the number of such combinations that were used to generate a replicate for stratum h; then $d = 1, \ldots, c_h$. If all combinations were used, then

$$c_h = \frac{n_h!}{(n_h - k)!\,k!}$$

The pseudovalue for replicate (h, d) is

$$\widetilde{\boldsymbol{\theta}}^*_{h,d} = \widetilde{\boldsymbol{\theta}}_{(h,d)} + c_h\{\widehat{\boldsymbol{\theta}} - \widetilde{\boldsymbol{\theta}}_{(h,d)}\}$$

When the `mse` option is specified, the variance estimator is

$$\widehat{V}(\boldsymbol{\theta}) = \sum_{h=1}^{L}(1 - f_h)\, m_h \sum_{d=1}^{c_h}\{\widetilde{\boldsymbol{\theta}}_{(h,d)} - \widehat{\boldsymbol{\theta}}\}\{\widetilde{\boldsymbol{\theta}}_{(h,d)} - \widehat{\boldsymbol{\theta}}\}'$$

and the jackknife mean is

$$\overline{\boldsymbol{\theta}}_{(.)} = \frac{1}{C}\sum_{h=1}^{L}\sum_{d=1}^{c_h}\widetilde{\boldsymbol{\theta}}_{(h,d)}, \quad C = \sum_{h=1}^{L}c_h$$

Otherwise, the variance estimator is

$$\widehat{V}(\boldsymbol{\theta}) = \sum_{h=1}^{L}(1 - f_h)\, m_h \sum_{d=1}^{c_h}\{\widetilde{\boldsymbol{\theta}}_{(h,d)} - \overline{\boldsymbol{\theta}}_h\}\{\widetilde{\boldsymbol{\theta}}_{(h,d)} - \overline{\boldsymbol{\theta}}_h\}', \qquad \overline{\boldsymbol{\theta}}_h = \frac{1}{c_h}\sum_{d=1}^{c_h}\widetilde{\boldsymbol{\theta}}_{(h,d)}$$

and the jackknife mean is

$$\overline{\boldsymbol{\theta}}^* = \frac{1}{C}\sum_{h=1}^{L}\sum_{d=1}^{c_h}\widetilde{\boldsymbol{\theta}}_{h,d}^*$$

The multiplier for the delete-k jackknife is

$$m_h = \frac{n_h - k}{c_h k}$$

Variables containing the values for the stratum identifier h, the sampling rate f_h, and the jackknife multiplier m_h can be svyset using the respective suboptions of the jkrweight() option: stratum(), fpc(), and multiplier().

Confidence intervals

In survey data analysis, the customary number of degrees of freedom attributed to a test statistic is $d = n - L$, where n is the number of PSUs and L is the number of strata. Under regularity conditions, an approximate $100(1 - \alpha)\%$ confidence interval for a parameter θ (e.g., θ could be a total, ratio, or regression coefficient) is

$$\widehat{\theta} \pm t_{1-\alpha/2,d}\,\{\widehat{V}(\widehat{\theta})\}^{1/2}$$

Cochran (1977, sec. 2.8) and Korn and Graubard (1990) give some theoretical justification for using $d = n - L$ to compute univariate confidence intervals and p-values. However, for some cases, inferences based on the customary $n - L$ degrees-of-freedom calculation may be excessively liberal; the resulting confidence intervals may have coverage rates substantially less than the nominal $1 - \alpha$. This problem generally is of the greatest practical concern when the population of interest has a skewed or heavy-tailed distribution or is concentrated in a few PSUs. In some of these cases, the user may want to consider constructing confidence intervals based on alternative degrees-of-freedom terms, based on the Satterthwaite (1941, 1946) approximation and modifications thereof; see, for example, Cochran (1977, sec. 5.4) and Eltinge and Jang (1996).

Sometimes there is no information on n or L for datasets that contain replicate-weight variables but no PSU or strata variables. Here the number of degrees of freedom for svy brr: and svy jackknife: is $d = r - 1$, where r is the number of replications.

References

Binder, D. A. 1983. On the variances of asymptotically normal estimators from complex surveys. *International Statistical Review* 51: 279–292.

Cochran, W. G. 1977. *Sampling Techniques*. 3rd ed. New York: Wiley.

Demnati, A., and J. N. K. Rao. 2004. Linearization variance estimators for survey data. *Survey Methodology* 30: 17–26.

Deville, J.-C. 1999. Variance estimation for complex statistics and estimators: Linearization and residual techniques. *Survey Methodology* 25: 193–203.

Eltinge, J. L., and D. S. Jang. 1996. Stability measures for variance component estimators under a stratified multistage design. *Survey Methodology* 22: 157–165.

Fuller, W. A. 1975. Regression analysis for sample survey. *Sankhyā, Series C* 37: 117–132.

Godambe, V. P., ed. 1991. *Estimating Functions.* Oxford: Oxford University Press.

Judkins, D. R. 1990. Fay's method for variance estimation. *Journal of Official Statistics* 6: 223–239.

Kish, L., and M. R. Frankel. 1974. Inference from complex samples. *Journal of the Royal Statistical Society, Series B* 36: 1–37.

Korn, E. L., and B. I. Graubard. 1990. Simultaneous testing of regression coefficients with complex survey data: Use of Bonferroni *t* statistics. *American Statistician* 44: 270–276.

McCarthy, P. J. 1966. Replication: An approach to the analysis of data from complex surveys. In *Vital and Health Statistics*, series 2. Hyattsville, MD: National Center for Health Statistics.

——. 1969a. Pseudoreplication: Further evaluation and application of the balanced half-sample technique. In *Vital and Health Statistics*, series 2. Hyattsville, MD: National Center for Health Statistics.

——. 1969b. Pseudo-replication: Half-samples. *Revue de l'Institut International de Statistique* 37: 239–264.

Särndal, C.-E., B. Swensson, and J. Wretman. 1992. *Model Assisted Survey Sampling.* New York: Springer.

Satterthwaite, F. E. 1941. Synthesis of variance. *Psychometrika* 6: 309–316.

——. 1946. An approximate distribution of estimates of variance components. *Biometrics Bulletin* 2: 110–114.

Shah, B. V. 2004. Comment [on Demnati and Rao (2004)]. *Survey Methodology* 30: 29.

Shao, J., and D. Tu. 1995. *The Jackknife and Bootstrap.* New York: Springer.

Skinner, C. J. 1989. Introduction to part A. In *Analysis of Complex Surveys*, ed. C. J. Skinner, D. Holt, and T. M. F. Smith, 23–58. New York: Wiley.

Wolter, K. M. 2007. *Introduction to Variance Estimation.* 2nd ed. New York: Springer.

Also see

[SVY] **svy** — The survey prefix command

[SVY] **svyset** — Declare survey design for dataset

[SVY] **survey** — Introduction to survey commands

[P] **_robust** — Robust variance estimates

Glossary

100% sample. See *census*.

balanced repeated replication. See *BRR*.

BRR. BRR stands for *balanced repeated replication*. BRR is a method of variance estimation for designs with two PSUs in every stratum. The BRR variance estimator tends to give more reasonable variance estimates for this design than does the linearized variance estimator, which can result in large values and undesirably wide confidence intervals. The BRR variance estimator is described in [SVY] **variance estimation**.

census. When a census of the population is conducted, every individual in the population participates in the survey. Because of the time, cost, and other constraints, the data collected in a census are typically limited to items that can be quickly and easily determined, usually through a questionnaire.

cluster. A cluster is a collection of individuals that are sampled as a group. Although the cost in time and money can be greatly decreased, cluster sampling usually results in larger variance estimates when compared with designs in which individuals are sampled independently.

DEFF and **DEFT**. DEFF and DEFT are design effects. Design effects compare the sample-to-sample variability from a given survey dataset with a hypothetical SRS design with the same number of individuals sampled from the population.

DEFF is the ratio of two variance estimates. The design-based variance is in the numerator; the hypothetical SRS variance is in the denominator.

DEFT is the ratio of two standard-error estimates. The design-based standard error is in the numerator; the hypothetical SRS with-replacement standard error is in the denominator. If the given survey design is sampled with replacement, DEFT is the square root of DEFF.

design effects. See *DEFF* and *DEFT*.

direct standardization. Direct standardization is an estimation method that allows comparing rates that come from different frequency distributions.

Estimated rates (means, proportions, and ratios) are adjusted according to the frequency distribution from a standard population. The standard population is partitioned into categories called standard strata. The stratum frequencies for the standard population are called standard weights. The standardizing frequency distribution typically comes from census data, and the standard strata are most commonly identified by demographic information such as age, sex, and ethnicity.

finite population correction. See *FPC*.

FPC. FPC stands for finite population correction. An FPC is an adjustment applied to the variance of a point estimator because of sampling without replacement, resulting in variance estimates that are smaller than the variance estimates from comparable with-replacement sampling designs.

Hadamard matrix. A Hadamard matrix is a square matrix with r rows and columns that has the property

$$H'_r H_r = r I_r$$

where I_r is the identity matrix of order r. Generating a Hadamard matrix with order $r = 2^p$ is easily accomplished. Start with a Hadamard matrix of order 2 (H_2), and build your H_r by repeatedly applying Kronecker products with H_2.

jackknife. The jackknife is a data-dependent way to estimate the variance of a statistic, such as a mean, ratio, or regression coefficient. Unlike BRR, the jackknife can be applied to practically any survey design. The jackknife variance estimator is described in [SVY] **variance estimation**.

linearization. Linearization is short for Taylor linearization. Also known as the delta method or the Huber/White/robust sandwich variance estimator, linearization is a method for deriving an approximation to the variance of a point estimator, such as a ratio or regression coefficient. The linearized variance estimator is described in [SVY] **variance estimation**.

MEFF and **MEFT**. MEFF and MEFT are misspecification effects. Misspecification effects compare the variance estimate from a given survey dataset with the variance from a misspecified model. In Stata, the misspecified model is fit without weighting, clustering, or stratification.

MEFF is the ratio of two variance estimates. The design-based variance is in the numerator; the misspecified variance is in the denominator.

MEFT is the ratio of two standard-error estimates. The design-based standard error is in the numerator; the misspecified standard error is in the denominator. MEFT is the square root of MEFF.

misspecification effects. See *MEFF* and *MEFT*.

point estimate. A point estimate is another name for a statistic, such as a mean or regression coefficient.

poststratification. Poststratification is a method for adjusting sampling weights, usually to account for underrepresented groups in the population. This usually results in decreased bias because of nonresponse and underrepresented groups in the population. Poststratification also tends to result in smaller variance estimates.

The population is partitioned into categories, called poststrata. The sampling weights are adjusted so that the sum of the weights within each poststratum is equal to the respective poststratum size. The poststratum size is the number of individuals in the population that are in the poststratum. The frequency distribution of the poststrata typically comes from census data, and the poststrata are most commonly identified by demographic information such as age, sex, and ethnicity.

predictive margins. Predictive margins provide a way of exploring the response surface of a fitted model in any response metric of interest—means, linear predictions, probabilities, marginal effects, risk differences, and so on. Predictive margins are estimates of responses (or outcomes) for the groups represented by the levels of a factor variable, controlling for the differing covariate distributions across the groups. They are the survey-data and nonlinear response analogue to what are often called estimated marginal means or least-squares means for linear models.

Because these margins are population-weighted averages over the estimation sample or subsamples, and because they take account of the sampling distribution of the covariates, they can be used to make inferences about treatment effects for the population.

primary sampling unit. See *PSU*.

probability weight. Probability weight is another term for sampling weight.

pseudolikelihood. A pseudolikelihood is a weighted likelihood that is used for point estimation. Pseudolikelihoods are not true likelihoods because they do not represent the distribution function for the sample data from a survey. The sampling distribution is instead determined by the survey design.

PSU. PSU stands for primary sampling unit. A PSU is a cluster that was sampled in the first sampling stage; see *cluster*.

replicate-weight variable. A replicate-weight variable contains sampling weight values that were adjusted for resampling the data; see [SVY] **variance estimation** for more details.

resampling. Resampling refers to the process of sampling from the dataset. In the delete-one jackknife, the dataset is resampled by dropping one PSU and producing a replicate of the point estimates. In the BRR method, the dataset is resampled by dropping combinations of one PSU from each stratum. The resulting replicates of the point estimates are used to estimate their variances and covariances.

sample. A sample is the collection of individuals in the population that were chosen as part of the survey. Sample is also used to refer to the data, typically in the form of answered questions, collected from the sampled individuals.

sampling stage. Complex survey data are typically collected using multiple stages of clustered sampling. In the first stage, the PSUs are independently selected within each stratum. In the second stage, smaller sampling units are selected within the PSUs. In later stages, smaller and smaller sampling units are selected within the clusters from the previous stage.

sampling unit. A sampling unit is an individual or collection of individuals from the population that can be selected in a specific stage of a given survey design. Examples of sampling units include city blocks, high schools, hospitals, and houses.

sampling weight. Given a survey design, the sampling weight for an individual is the reciprocal of the probability of being sampled. The probability for being sampled is derived from stratification and clustering in the survey design. A sampling weight is typically considered to be the number of individuals in the population represented by the sampled individual.

sampling with and without replacement. Sampling units may be chosen more than once in designs that use sampling with replacement. Sampling units may be chosen at most once in designs that use sampling without replacement. Variance estimates from with-replacement designs tend to be larger than those from corresponding without-replacement designs.

secondary sampling unit. See *SSU*.

simple random sample. See *SRS*.

SRS. SRS stands for simple random sample. In a simple random sample, individuals are independently sampled—each with the same probability of being chosen.

SSU. SSU stands for secondary sampling unit. An SSU is a cluster that was sampled from within a PSU in the second sampling stage. SSU is also used as a generic term unit to indicate any sampling unit that is not from the first sampling stage.

standard strata. See *direct standardization*.

standard weights. See *direct standardization*.

stratification. The population is partitioned into well-defined groups of individuals, called strata. In the first sampling stage, PSUs are independently sampled from within each stratum. In later sampling stages, SSUs are independently sampled from within each stratum for that stage.

Survey designs that use stratification typically result in smaller variance estimates than do similar designs that do not use stratification. Stratification is most effective in decreasing variability when sampling units are more similar within the strata than between them.

subpopulation estimation. Subpopulation estimation focuses on computing point and variance estimates for part of the population. The variance estimates measure the sample-to-sample variability, assuming that the same survey design is used to select individuals for observation from the population. This approach results in a different variance than measuring the sample-to-sample variability by restricting the samples to individuals within the subpopulation; see [SVY] **subpopulation estimation**.

survey data. Survey data consist of information about individuals that were sampled from a population according to a survey design. Survey data distinguishes itself from other forms of data by the complex nature under which individuals are selected from the population.

In survey data analysis, the sample is used to draw inferences about the population. Furthermore, the variance estimates measure the sample-to-sample variability that results from the survey design applied to the fixed population. This approach differs from standard statistical analysis, in which the sample is used to draw inferences about a physical process and the variance measures the sample-to-sample variability that results from independently collecting the same number of observations from the same process.

survey design. A survey design describes how to sample individuals from the population. Survey designs typically include stratification and cluster sampling at one or more stages.

variance estimation. Variance estimation refers to the collection of methods used to measure the amount of sample-to-sample variation of point estimates; see [SVY] **variance estimation**.

Subject and author index

This is the subject and author index for the *Survey Data Reference Manual*. Readers interested in topics other than survey data should see the combined subject index (and the combined author index) in the *Quick Reference and Index*. The combined index indexes the *Getting Started* manuals, the *User's Guide*, and all the reference manuals except the *Mata Reference Manual*.

Semicolons set off the most important entries from the rest. Sometimes no entry will be set off with semicolons, meaning that all entries are equally important.